Building for the Arts

Building for the Arts

THE STRATEGIC DESIGN
of CULTURAL FACILITIES

Peter Frumkin & Ana Kolendo

THE UNIVERSITY OF CHICAGO PRESS | CHICAGO AND LONDON

Peter Frumkin is professor of social policy and faculty director of the Center for High Impact Philanthropy at the University of Pennsylvania. He is the author of *Strategic Giving* and *The Essence of Strategic Giving*, both also published by the University of Chicago Press. **Ana Kolendo** is a research fellow at the Center for High Impact Philanthropy at the University of Pennsylvania.

The University of Chicago Press, Chicago 60637
The University of Chicago Press, Ltd., London
© 2014 by The University of Chicago
All rights reserved. Published 2014.
Printed in the United States of America

23 22 21 20 19 18 17 16 15 14   1 2 3 4 5

ISBN-13: 978-0-226-09961-3 (cloth)
ISBN-13: 978-0-226-09975-0 (e-book)
DOI: 10.7208/chicago/9780226099750.001.0001

Library of Congress Cataloging-in-Publication Data

Frumkin, Peter, author.
    Building for the arts : the strategic design of cultural facilities / Peter Frumkin and Ana Kolendo.
        pages ; cm
    Includes bibliographical references and index.
    ISBN 978-0-226-09961-3 (cloth : alk. paper) — ISBN 978-0-226-09975-0 (e-book)
    1. Arts facilities—Planning. 2. Arts facilities—Design and construction. 3. Arts facilities—United States—Design and construction. 4. Strategic planning. I. Kolendo, Ana, author. II. Title.
    NX798.F78 2014
    727'.7—dc23

                                        2013025707

⊚ This paper meets the requirements of ANSI/NISO Z39.48–1992 (Permanence of Paper).

Contents

Acknowledgments

In writing this book, we have accumulated many debts to scholars and practitioners who care about the cultural sector. Their comments, concerns, interjections, objections, and contributions have substantially improved the book you now hold.

The idea for this book on cultural infrastructure originated in a meeting where Carroll Joynes of the University of Chicago asked the provocative question: Is the cultural infrastructure in America overbuilt? For three years following the posing of that initial question, the University of Chicago's Cultural Policy Center assembled researchers and practitioners interested in the future of the arts to examine the scope of cultural building, the process used by arts leaders to guide these projects to completion, and the effects of cultural building efforts on the local arts community.

The Chicago team set about assembling a large array of data, conducting field work around the country, and then synthesizing the information. We are grateful to the entire Chicago team for the camaraderie, the willingness to take risks, and the propensity to always ask tough questions as we carried out the fieldwork component of the larger project. Norman Bradburn provided a steady and experienced hand on the wheel. Carroll Joynes raised critical funds for the project and helped shape the overall direction, while Bruce Seaman and Rob Gertner contributed to the project's many different components. At the Cultural Policy Center, Betsy

Farrell, Will Anderson, and Michael Kuby provided critical support and help at various stages of the project's development. Finally, we want to thank Joanna Woronkowicz for her tireless work designing surveys, managing data, writing reports, and doing what needed to be done to ensure this project reached a successful conclusion.

Throughout the project, we had the benefit of talking to arts leaders across the country who were or had been on the front lines of the cultural building process. We are grateful for the time they spent with us sharing their stories and recollections. Sometimes they were brimming with pride, other times they were cringing at the memories they recollected. No matter. Without their cooperation and insights, we would not have been able to complete this book. Both space and confidentiality concerns prevent us from thanking them all by name, but our sources' hospitality and help remain immensely appreciated.

Outside the project group, several other organizations helped us to advance our thinking and refine our arguments. At National Arts Strategies, we owe special thanks to Russell Willis Taylor, Gail Crider, and Jim Rosenberg for their input and support at various stages. All the members of Culture Lab weighed in astutely and helpfully at various points on the overall direction of the broader project, including especially Adrian Ellis and Duncan Webb. The staff at the RGK Center for Philanthropy and Community Service at the University of Texas at Austin played a critical role in providing a supportive institutional home for our work during the project. We thank the Mellon, MacArthur and Kresge Foundations for their support of the broader project. Finally, we thank John Tryneski at the University of Chicago Press for helping us shape and prepare the book for publication.

One more acknowledgment is due. The authors both wish to thank their families for putting up with frequent absences due to travel related to the research project, but more importantly for being there for us when it mattered most.

1 | *The Idea of Strategic Design*

"It's not surprising that there's no art in it. Art couldn't compete," wrote *Boston Globe* architecture critic Robert Campbell in his 2002 review of the then-new Quadracci Pavilion of the Milwaukee Art Museum.[1] This $130 million building had a massive hydraulically powered sunshade that slowly undulated, like the wings of a swan. The new building's 142,050 square feet mostly contained public spaces, all making a grand architectural statement and catapulting the Milwaukee museum to the status of an architectural landmark. Visitors and tourism increased, yet many came to see the building rather than the collection inside. By moving public spaces to the addition, the main museum building was able to increase its gallery space. The building's initial plans had called for a budget of $35 million. Eventually, Santiaga Calatrava's bold architectural concept convinced the board to raise this budget to $100 million. Cost overruns during construction added another $30 million to the price tag, resulting in a facility that cost $130 million—and contained little additional space for the display of art from the Milwaukee Art Museum's collection.

Milwaukee's approach posed a fundamental question about what purpose an art museum building is supposed to serve. To some extent, the Quadracci Pavilion was a metaphor. Its absence of galleries embodied the cultural sector's worst fears: that buildings now existed just for buildings' sake, that resources were increasingly dedicated to facilities and attention-drawing marquee architecture over collections, and that art in the collections was being symbolically and literally displaced by other concerns.[2]

1.1 Milwaukee Art Museum's Quadracci Pavilion. Photo by Steven Andrew Miller.

The outcome also provided a chilling insight into the question about the harm that a single building project could do. The Quadracci Pavilion left the Milwaukee Art Museum with over $30 million in unanticipated debt. Annual interest payments reached over $1 million. With a new expensive building to maintain, operating costs increased dramatically. Whereas before the expansion, the endowment covered 25 percent of operating costs, after expansion the same endowment covered only 8 percent. Years of massive budget deficits—$3.3 million in fiscal year 2003 and $2 million in 2004—followed. The Milwaukee Art Museum was eventually able to right itself, raising money to pay off the debt through a herculean effort that commandeered all the organization's energies. The museum's time on the brink called attention to the havoc some new buildings wreak on the arts organizations they are intended to benefit. See figure 1.1.

In the early 2000s, stories like the Milwaukee Art Museum's—narratives about building projects followed by cost overruns, scheduling delays, mounting deficits, staff layoffs, cuts in opening hours, decreases in the number of artistic productions—became increasingly common in the news. Problems related to ambitious building programs surfaced in places ranging from Miami, Florida, to Madison, Wisconsin. Of course, stories of triumphs, like the Guggenheim Museum in Bilbao, Spain, appeared as well, fueling the dream of institutions to build their way to relevance and transformation. Some arts institutions with new buildings were plunged into crises, while others flourished after completing their constructions.

In this book, we suggest that these differences in outcomes can be understood by examining the strategy and tactics deployed in capital projects. But what do we know about effective strategy for cultural facility construction? Our answer begins with understanding the quality of the match between the local community needs and the available arts offerings, then considers the four most critical dimensions of the strategic planning process.

To Build or Not to Build

One of the first strategic questions that must be answered is whether a building project should be undertaken at all. Any answer to this question must begin with a consideration of the relationship between the arts organization and its community, which in the ideal scenario is mutually beneficial. For arts organizations, their host communities can be a source of philanthropic and public funds, skilled volunteers, and loan or bond guarantees. The host community is also an arts organization's source for both creative and operational partnerships, from small groups with whom they can collaborate to larger museums, performing arts centers, and universities, who may offer space, operational subsidies, and technical assistance. Last but not least, arts organizations look to their communities for opportunities to connect, serve, and have an impact.

In exchange, communities benefit primarily from the availability of artistic experiences. Cultural offerings enhance the community's quality of life. At their best, the arts can unify people through a shared experience. In addition, some arts organizations provide educational programs in the schools, pioneer community revitalization efforts, as well as spur economic development.[3] Though generally seen as desirable by the communities, this development can occasionally—when linked to gentrification—have the negative effect of displacing lower income families when the cost of living and value of real estate increase. The arts also contribute to a community's reputation by building cultural cachet and prestige. Both new buildings and the renovation of old buildings into arts facilities serve as monuments to civic pride and community commitment.

Yet these relationships do not always benefit each partner equally, and in some cases, community or artistic leaders look to a new facility to fix deeply rooted problems. Projects can and do become projection screens for dreams. An opera may hope for larger turnouts and greater revenues at a different location. A museum might hope that a larger, better space will help it convince collectors to make significant bequests. A city may hope that its local groups, if given a better equipped facility, will meet its citizenry's expectation for skill and artistic vision. The proponents of construction projects claim that the quality, quantity, and diversity of artistic experiences available to the public will increase, that access will be made easier with features like prominent facades and greater space to accommodate school groups, and that a better, larger space and upgraded amenities will boost operating income and the financial sustainability of the arts. A cultural edifice is also sold as an aid to a neighborhood's economic development, a spur to tourism, and a contribution to a city's quality of life. In short, new cultural facilities can benefit both the community and its artists. At least in theory, that is.

The opportunity to realize these benefits is predicated on the existence of a strong and balanced relationship between the arts and their community. If the interests of the community and the local arts organization are not well matched, a new building and the attendant shared responsibilities and conflicting expectations have the potential to stress rather than strengthen an imperfect marriage between these partners. Take for example the Kimmel Center for the Performing Arts, a $325 million facility that in 2011 found itself in the middle of the news story about the bankruptcy of one of its tenants, the Philadelphia Orchestra. The orchestra had sought bankruptcy protection in order to renegotiate its lease, citing among other reasons an increased financial burden when the occupancy costs at the Kimmel were compared with its old facility. Just a year before, the Kimmel had laid off its own programming and educational staff in order to cut its resident companies' costs. Its own series of presented programs, which was meant to serve a larger audience than that of the classical companies, was crippled as a result. Even nine years after opening, the financial obligations incurred by building a new venue still managed to force a choice between the artistic missions of individual companies and a performing arts center's mission to serve a diverse set of constituents. Moreover, the conflict of interests between various stakeholders landed the Kimmel in the center of a controversy, exposing a strained relationship. Before any building project in the arts is undertaken, a serious and objective examination of the match between the host community and the programs that will be presented in the new space needs to be undertaken.

The quality, quantity, and variety of artistic experiences made available to the community may each give rise to a mismatch between the level of community support available to the arts and the level of artistic assets available to the community. The question here is not just about taste, though in some communities taste is a factor. Performances of Racine and Wagner and exhibitions of European religious paintings, no matter how canonical and no matter how skillfully presented, may not flourish in cities with young populations with countercultural norms. Conversely, a staging of a Shakespeare play that includes frontal nudity and hip-hop references may cost a theater its community support regardless of the skill and sophistication of the production if its audience is conservative in its tastes. An extremely diverse community may, however, accommodate and demand many types of programming. Yet the question of the match between the host community and its art also involves questions of volume and quality. Sometimes, a community may have an excellent, popular local theater or a museum that is incapable of producing enough performances or exhibits to fully satisfy its community's demands. At other times, an arts group's struggle to connect to its community may be rooted in the issue of quality—the fact that its programs may have suitable ambitions and availability, but fail on the level of execution. Thus, when considering whether a community and the artistic experiences made available there are well matched, leaders must weigh not only the quality of the available programming, but also its philosophy, variety, and quantity.

Similarly, a community's needs and assets must be matched to the capacity of an arts organization if a new facility is to work. If attendance is already a problem, an expansion of programs is unlikely to succeed. Enough funding must be available for current operations before a capital project and greater operating costs can be considered. Creative and operational partnerships must be fruitful and strong before multiple groups begin to jointly provide the programming and financial support for operations of a new venue. Board members and other volunteers must have the skill set to effectively oversee and advocate for an artistic institution before they undertake a capital campaign and a project that tests the strength of their commitment and their financial prudence. Broad and deep community support for current artistic programs is needed before a new facility is undertaken.

This assessment of the quality of the match between the community and the arts that are produced is likely to be difficult and require objective, skilled observers with local expertise. Descriptive data, such as audience size and whether its composition is representative of the community at large, may be a rough starting point for establishing the quality of this match, but these data will never provide the full picture.[4] Not surprisingly, few if any professional consultants who specialize in guiding communities and artistic institutions through capital projects are willing to offer evaluations of artistic merit or audience sophistication. In the interests of being cordial and avoiding offending someone, few arts leaders like to discuss these topics. Still, the issue of a quality match is real. The key is to have an open examination of these issues and to work on identifying and fixing obvious mismatches before embarking on a major capital project.

The appropriate response for an arts organization contemplating a building project depends on the match between the artistic value offered with the level of community support present. The interaction of these two dimensions can be summed up with a matrix with four cells (see table 1.1). In scenario 1, the artistic offerings and community needs are well matched, and the artists and the community can readily consider the expansion of cultural facilities. In the other scenarios, the needs of an arts organization are not aligned with the community assets, or the needs of the community are not well matched with what the organization can offer. In almost all cases, a good match needs to be achieved before beginning any attempt to build. Otherwise, the cultural vitality of the community and the arts organizations' ability to execute their missions may be imperiled. Too many organizations build with the hope that the match will be enhanced, only to find that the opposite happens. When the project is framed and pursued during a period when the artistic value produced is aligned with community demand, the entire building process becomes far less contentious.

In scenario 2, the arts organization considering a building project finds the community satisfied with the type, quality, and quantity of its programming and yet the level of community support is insufficient. This group's primary tasks should be marketing and fundraising.[5] Its tactics could include diversifying and expanding its funding sources and locating sources of funding external to the community, like state and federal governments and foundations. The group may undertake an awareness-building campaign meant to expand a culture of giving in its community. It may embark on an audience educational campaign to foster an appreciation of its art form among a greater portion of the community, thereby increasing its ticket revenues. If the problem is the size of the audience, the group may also seek funding for a reduced-price ticket program to make its programming more affordable for a larger portion of its community. The group may seek partners like existing groups, mu-

Table 1.1. Value and Support

		Artistic Value Produced (Quality, quantity, and diversity of programming)	
		Low	High
Local Support for the Arts (Funding, audiences, volunteers, partners)	Low	Work on Positioning and Planning 4	Focus on Marketing and Fundraising 2
	High	Enhance Programming 3	Build 1

seums, theaters, and universities to share or underwrite operating expenses. All these initiatives could help form a better match between the community and the arts by either reducing the need of arts organizations for community assets or by increasing the availability of these resources. Ideally, these initiatives ought to be undertaken first, before a building project begins.

In scenario 3, an arts organization struggles to connect with the abundant audiences, donors, volunteers, and partners in its host community. Many times, a group in this position will attempt to prove its worth to its community by expanding its mission to include universally acclaimed goals like education, environmental sustainability, or community outreach programs and events unrelated to its art form. In the end, however, an artistic institution will live or die by its programming. Thus, the first focus of a group in this kind of position should be on enhancing the quality and quantity of its programming. A theater group can develop its artistic talent pool through training and recruitment. A museum can focus on the development of its collection and curatorial staff. Creative collaborations with others may prove fruitful. The group may also need to examine its programming philosophy and assumptions and evaluate whether they fit with their host community's expectations and culture. If not, the group needs to either educate and convince its prospective audience or move to a more hospitable environment. In the end, the development of the group's programming is the path most likely to result in a mutually beneficial, supportive, long-lasting relationship with its community.

In scenario 4, a group finds itself struggling to produce quality programs in a community that lacks the resources to support them. A museum or a new theater may fail to take hold in a rural community with few other existing institutions and little money for support. Its leadership needs a strategic plan for how to both develop artistic capabilities and ensure financial sustainability. Many of the tactics listed above may still work, though for this group the journey toward a quality match will prove long and arduous. Fixing one side of this equation is challenging. Fixing both sides is daunting. As a consequence, big questions will arise about whether to soldier on or start over somewhere else.

Realistically assessing the quality of the match between an organization's art and the local community is therefore fundamental to making a rational decision to engage in planning, marketing and fundraising, programming, or building. However tempting and desirable it might appear on the drawing board, a new facility is unlikely to prove to be a shortcut to success for any arts organization that finds itself badly matched with its community. Strategies for building a quality match must be pursued first, before any building project can be sensibly contemplated.

Strategic Design and the Four Cornerstones of Cultural Building Projects

If the decision to build is made, there are four main forces that animate cultural building projects that must be taken into account while answering the next question—namely, how to build. First, there is the desire to elevate artistic quality and enhance mission achievement. For museums, expansions are a way to show more art and to enhance an organization's ability to acquire or borrow through gifts and institutional loans. After all, few collectors want to bequeath objects only so they can languish in storage. For performing arts organizations, new buildings can also mean an increase in the quantity and quality of programs through benefits like an increase in the availability of leasable dates and the ability to attract better performers. To some extent, such issues can be solved by increases in budgets rather than changes in physical facilities. Others—like leaking pipes and bad lighting in galleries, sight line obstructions and dead acoustics in performance venues—can be resolved only through either a move or a renovation. Thus, facility shortcomings can affect program quality, and this sometimes serves as the impetus to consider building.

Second, projects can and do spring from desire to improve operational capacity. A new building can signal a change of status for an organization, the kind of change that attracts more and better performers, donors, staff, and trustees. Or at least many arts leaders believe this is the case. A better building will excite the people who create programs by giving them a wider range of tools. An organization that transitions from being a renter to being an owner acquires a perception of permanence, of being more established, of becoming an institution. Many fledgling arts organizations spend years taking on and training enthusiastic but inexperienced staff and trustees, then losing them or the grants that fund their positions. An enhancement of the organization's profile enabled by a new building is one way to stanch these losses. In this way, a facility can have an effect on its inhabitants' human capacity. Of course, the inverse is also true. Human capacity—or the capabilities and skills of staff, volunteers, consultants, and trustees—in turn has a profound effect on the ambition and success of any building project.

A third such reciprocal relationship exists between a building and its tenants' funding. Many capital projects start as decisions about an organization's financial plan when leaders try to deal with either financial deficits or abundance. A supporter may approach the organization with an offer of a large gift for a new facility (especially one bearing the family name). Alternatively, a struggling organization may become convinced a larger building would be a panacea for its budget woes. Part of the logic of "If we build it, they will come" stems from the assumption that increased capacity will generate more artistic consumption and with it increased revenues. Far from scaring off arts leaders, low revenues may actually provoke a conversation about what the financial picture might look like with a better facility. Economic analysis performed at the outset of project planning may suggest that a new venue will substantially increase income, and these forecasts are often potent triggers to the building ambition that is possessed by almost all organizations. A larger building can serve more people, justify higher entry fees, and mobilize donors. However, experience has shown that though a few major building projects become triumphant turning points for arts organizations' finances, they can also become tragic Waterloos.

Fourth and finally, some projects are the product of intense civic pride and a community desire to improve itself. An impressive building can bring the spotlight to a city and make it appear "world class," especially if the project architect falls into the small group of recognized superstars.

For civic boosters, new buildings also offer the promise of opening up arts organizations to the community around them, and in the process these projects can contribute to local community development. Rather than worrying about the underlying financial realities or the present level of community interest, leaders will projects to reality in hopes that culture will become a focal tool in the community evolution.

In this book, we explore the ways in which the design and execution of a building initiative leads an organization to either thrive or stumble. Guiding this analysis is a strategic framework for understanding how major cultural building projects can best be planned and executed. The framework's descriptive and diagnostic value is in allowing a project to be dissected for diagnosis of what worked and what did not. The framework also has normative content, since it points toward best practices and defines what needs to happen for the design process to be truly strategic.

The strategic design of arts facilities entails juggling, balancing, and trading off among four managerial challenges: managing the demands of mission, building the operational capacity of the organization, garnering broad-based community support, and securing the necessary funding.[6] These challenges are, of course, interrelated, but success with any one is almost never enough to drive a project from the drawing board to actuality. We define *strategic design* here as the moment when an arts organization brings into alignment, fit, and coherence its mission, capacity, funding, and community to realize a building project.[7] Strategic design implies that an organization stays in alignment during all stages of its capital project, from the beginning of planning through design and construction, and long after a new building's opening. To be sure, there may well be gaps at the start, such as a community group that opposes the project or a funder who is not fully committed. And there may be a moment during the process when artistic or acoustic excellence has to be compromised. But at the end of the day, the arts organization emerges stronger by virtue of the capital campaign and physical facility enhancements.

Few projects start off in perfect alignment and even fewer end there. Still, if strategic design is to be understood as the process of imagining and then realizing a cultural infrastructure project, it is useful to define the four cornerstones that together can alternatively support or bring down any building project (mission, capacity, funding, and community) and the four critical connectors that link these cornerstones (feasibility, sustainability, viability, and credibility). These cornerstones and connectors are represented in figure 1.2.

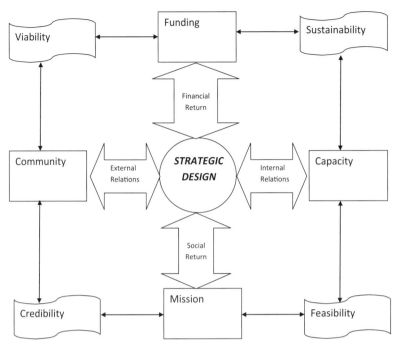

1.2 Framework for Strategic Design

Mission

Building projects are often the product of arts organizations asking "What if?" as part of their search for either greater artistic excellence or mission impact. While the goals are not mutually exclusive, they are different. Sometimes the projects reflect a desire first and foremost to increase artistic quality and to take the organization to a higher level in terms of the plays that are produced, the art that is viewed by the public, or the musical experience that concertgoers enjoy. Constructing a new building is seen as a critical first step toward being "a world-class organization." In the search for excellence, many factors may come into play including civic pride and artistic ego. However, there comes a point for any arts organization when it must ask and answer a simple question honestly: What can we do to improve the artistic quality and impact of the work that we do? When this question is posed earnestly and in the context of a broader planning process, the answer may involve some element of facility design or redesign.

In some cases, arts organizations are blocked from achieving the artistic goals to which they aspire by their facility. For a theater, the absence of a fly space may limit the number and quality of set changes. For an orchestra, a second-rate building may produce muffled and uninspiring acoustics that compromise the listening experience and diminish patrons' enjoyment. In the case of museums, the absence of a high-quality exhibition space may make it impossible to show critical elements of a permanent collection or preclude the museum from hosting a traveling show that would advance the museum's mission. In these cases, the design process may begin from a perceived deficit and evolve by virtue of the creative imagination of the organization's leadership. A poor facility may impinge not just on artistic quality, but on the broader notion of impact. Without adequate facilities, many arts organizations are unable to reach and serve their audiences. In this sense, questions about the design of a new facility or renovation of an existing facility may focus not just on the quantity but also on the quality of the art that is presented.

Not all visions of mission advancement are equal, however. In some cases, performing arts buildings and museums may construct elaborate visions of greater artistic quality and impact that are not grounded in fact or reality. New facilities can and do become talismans for solving all of an organization's problems. Instead of looking at the root causes of program mediocrity, it is often far easier to point to the building and blame it for the organization's inability to achieve its artistic ambitions. For example, in Austin, Texas, in the 1970s, two organizations were engaged in an attempt to create two museums of art. The leadership of the Austin Museum of Art decided to first build a permanent home and then a collection, while the university's Blanton Museum focused its first efforts and spent its funds on amassing a collection through donations and acquisitions, believing that the programming must precede a building. Now the Blanton has both a permanent home of its own—the largest university-affiliated museum in the country—and a collection renowned for depth in a few key areas. By contrast, the Austin Museum of Art has recently cancelled its third capital campaign. Thus, when thinking about the relationship between mission success and cultural facilities, arts leaders need to be sure that they have correctly established a real causal linkage between their building ambitions and their mission.

One way to establish plausible causality between mission advancement and facility design is to define an organization's intended impact in very specific terms and then to ask: What would enable us to achieve our ultimate artistic and programmatic vision? In some cases, the facility will indeed be the only possible answer, but not always. Sometimes, the largest obstacle to delivery of mission is the vagueness of vision. Other times, it may be a breakdown in the internal operating systems, a shortage of funding, or just plain community apathy. Looking outward for solutions to these difficult problems that have worked elsewhere, organizations may find convincing stories of buildings that had a tremendous positive impact in the areas that are the sources of pain. Yet buildings rarely fix problems—though they do sometimes serve as levers that raise the impact of an organization's preexisting capacity for excellence, thus creating the myth that a building may be a panacea. For example, the Denver Art Museum began its journey toward an expansion in the late 1990s. One of the stated goals of the expansion was enhancing the museum's ability to book and accommodate traveling exhibits, which were at the time believed to be the magic bullet for increasing operating income. Yet after the $110 million expansion opened in 2006, the attendance did not live up to expectations and the museum quickly found itself in financial trouble. The museum was forced to lay off staff and curtail the expenditures on traveling exhibitions that had served as the justification for the expansion. Rather than improving the museum's earned income, the building was harmful to both its finances and capacity to execute its mission. In this way, managing mission may come down to managing a project that turns out to have unexpected operational, financial, or political dimensions.

A new facility can be a moment of triumph and hope when anything and everything appears possible. This is a moment that can be filled with a deep clarity about purpose, value, and mission, or it can be a moment full of profound obfuscation and massive denial. It can be the moment when the organization's deepest needs are identified and addressed. Or it can be a time when blame is shifted and deep-rooted problems avoided. When the design process begins, organizations will start to envision what they will look like once the project is complete. New standards of artistic excellence will seem reachable, which will in turn drive improved performance across all areas. The key challenge of course is to be sure that these critical causal linkages are real.

In thinking about the connection between mission and the design of cultural building projects, it is important to remember that there should be a tight link between mission and an organization's operational capacity. Not only must an arts organization have the talent and expertise to carry out its mission, but that mission and artistic vision must also be compelling and clear enough to attract talented and committed people to the organization. When mission and capacity are aligned, a theater, dance company, orchestra, or museum will find itself with both a clear conception of value and the ability to deliver on the vision. In this sense, capacity and mission together ensure feasibility. It is not always the case that artistic dreams are feasible. In the world of the arts and in the broader nonprofit sector, there are many organizations that have grand visions and lofty missions, but little or no capacity to deliver on these dreams. These organizations fail the test of feasibility and are likely to find themselves at a profound disadvantage when it comes to designing and completing a building project. Flexible and responsive internal and external capacity is needed to turn mission into reality.

Capacity

Arts organizations of all sizes and shapes depend on committed people and effective administrative systems. The professional staff of museums, operas, symphonies, theaters, and dance companies often operate behind the scenes. And when artists get a moment in the limelight, it is often the presence of a few core elements of capacity that made success possible. As one considers the managerial challenges in arts organizations, and the translation of mission into reality, the issue of operational capacity arises almost immediately. By *operational capacity*, we mean the board, staff, and volunteers who constitute the core of the organization as well as the administrative apparatus (including the information technology, development, and human resources systems) that makes the mission of the organization more than just words. Capacity exists both inside and outside an organization. While it is tempting to "build capacity" by creating internal hierarchies designed to accomplish narrow tasks, it is often possible to reach out to partner organizations around the focal organization, and to tap their resources and expertise. By using resources that can be borrowed from outside the formal boundaries of the organization, capacity can be extended, often with less cost and risk. For this reason, many arts organizations grow their capacity by engaging volunteers, sharing back office services with other organizations, and generally looking for opportunities to tap existing resources in the community around them.

Not surprisingly, many successful arts groups have a single person or a small group of people who take the initiative for everything from small things, like finding a donated copier, all the way to driving a major building project to completion. These key entrepreneurs often do not wait for operational capacity to come to the organization in terms of partnerships or volunteers or even new staff. Instead, the entrepreneur, in a literal translation of the word itself, "takes within the hand" the challenge that lies before the organization. Absent such initiative and drive, organizations can struggle and wallow in mediocrity for long periods of time.

An active and engaged board involved in decisions beyond fiduciary oversight can make a huge difference in securing support and hiring talented staff leaders. Boards can thus be critical components of capacity and can drive building projects from idea to reality. While it is tempting to relegate accounting, legal, and fundraising tasks to boards, their highest use lies elsewhere. Generative work that asks fundamental questions about mission achievement and purpose is more important to properly conceptualizing a new building than narrow technical work. When it comes to putting together a plan for a capital campaign, boards play a central role in defining and authorizing the scope and focus of the project. They do this work by asking audacious questions about what an arts organization might look like with a new and better home.

As large building projects unfold, they can stress the existing capacity of arts organizations. Box office staff, actors, marketing staff, curators, and registrars can be drawn into the journey. This can put stress on ongoing administrative and program functions. At the same time, it can be challenging to bring on additional workers and administrative capacity at the outset of a capital campaign or building project. Resources may simply be stretched too thin to allow for an organization to staff up to meet the demands of these kinds of projects. Well-managed projects find a way to build capacity during the building process so that once the new facility is complete, there are people on staff ready to operate and sustain it.

When a project actually strengthens and builds capacity, it almost always succeeds in mobilizing resources that can allow the organization to operate at a high level once all the brick-and-mortar work is complete. A capital campaign and the building of a new concert hall or set of galleries must generate reliable and appropriate operating income streams. Buildings cost money to operate and staff, and a well-executed project will find a way to sustain and nourish the organization well after opening night. This entails doing everything from generating endowment income that will support operations and internal capacity to providing for increased earned income from ticket sales that will cover the new costs associated with managing and staffing a larger building. When this work is done well, the project meets the test of sustainability.

Funding

To get a big project onto and then off the drawing board, funding is needed. In some cases, a lot of funding is needed. For this reason, it is difficult to think about strategic design without taking into consideration the very concrete issue of money. A project cannot be completed without resources, no matter the power of the vision, the magnificence of the design, or the passion of its supporters. Funding can come in many different forms. In some cases, it comes from one magnificent gift, but in most cases it is cobbled together through a long process of conversation and pleading with supporters, lenders, and directors.

Grants from individuals are an obvious starting point when casting about for ways to fund a project. Many large arts building projects originate in the boardrooms of organizations when a key trustee makes a major personal pledge to get the fundraising started. Sometimes persons wanting to get their names attached to a major project who have little prior connection to the organization or even the art form may step forward and make a gift, especially if their name will go on the finished building. The process of cultivating donors can be long and painstaking, or it can be stunningly quick and easy. Many of the largest cultural projects feature individual philanthropy at their origin, in one form or another. The first large gift, often from a trustee, can kick off fundraising and give the campaign a sense of inevitability, especially if it covers a substantial part of the campaign goal. Matching grants also may help leverage additional philanthropic support. There is no set practice when it comes to timing the announcement of a capital campaign, and some projects operate in the "quiet phase" because a core or anchor donor has yet to be secured.

An arts entrepreneur must pursue or at least investigate many other sources of funding when starting down the long road of financing a building project. Foundations and corporations do give to the arts and can be a source of support.[8] A few institutional donors actually focus on financing capital construction and they are on the list of most arts leaders working to erect a new building. Local governments, through cultural affairs offices or community development departments, may be in a position to support the funding of these projects, though with the tightening of budgets and the growing fiscal strain of states and cities, this is becoming harder by the year. A city's manager of cultural affairs may be in a position to do more than just provide a check, however. A critical political introduction may open the door for a bond issue or set the stage for broad community involvement.

When cash is not readily available or when only a part of the funds needed for construction is raised, some arts organizations take on debt. This can take the form of a bond issue approved by the local authorities or simple bank loans that have to be paid off over time. The one challenge with taking on debt to build a new performing arts facility or museum wing is that service on the debt can put substantial pressure on the operating budget of the organization for years after completion. Sometimes, the impact of the debt is even immediate, as was the case with the Fresno Metropolitan Museum in California. In 2008, the museum reopened after a three-year, $28 million renovation that had gone over budget. Even after the city of Fresno stepped in to take over a $15 million construction loan on which the museum defaulted, the museum struggled to pay $5 million in remaining obligations to local businesses for services during renovations and reopening. In 2010, the museum closed and its assets were auctioned. One way to rationalize the assumption of debt to build a new facility is that revenue from tickets and philanthropy may increase once the organization reaches a higher level of artistic excellence and has increased capacity to serve patrons. However, the relationship between operating income and capital expenditure may not prove to be positive and linear. At some point, capital fundraising can interfere with and undermine annual operating funding. Good project managers are sensitive to this reality and plan for this dangerous contingency. Few things are sadder than seeing a major addition to the cultural infrastructure of America open its doors only to put the occupant or tenants in fiscal trouble.

The challenge for arts leaders is to develop a funding strategy to support construction projects that allows the organization to move forward without exposing the organization to excessive risk on one hand or causing demoralizing delays on the other. Beyond worrying about the mix of philanthropy and borrowing, arts leaders must also think very carefully about the effects of undertaking a major capital campaign on the ability of the organization to operate and maintain its community support during a period when a building is being built or when the current facility undergoes substantial renovations.[9] For projects to be viable, they must have community acceptance or better still, enthusiasm. Viability comes from the achievement of a fit between the organization's financial needs at the time of project launch, the stakeholders' emotions inspired by the project, and the willingness they display to contribute constructively to the effort.

Community

To erect a new building is to make an overture to the community to see an arts organization in a new light and to claim the project as part of its civic identity. Projects are driven by an earnest desire to find ways to make the institution more open and accessible to the community, and in the process meet the needs of the patrons. There is also a sense that a city or region's identity is formed by these projects.[10] Whether it is a lesser version of the Bilbao effect or simply an addition to a city's existing stock of cultural capital, an arts building is a public way to project how a city sees itself and how it welcomes guests. Tied up in the whole process is a mix of civic pride and opportunism.

Large arts projects can inject substantial amounts of resources into communities that have been neglected for decades or more.[11] This only raises the stakes and deepens community interest, because in addition to serving as palaces for the visual and performing arts, these projects hold out the promise of driving up local property values and fueling business development in the surrounding neighborhood.

When contemplating a new building, an arts organization will inevitably ask: "What does the community want?" The strength of commitment to answering this question will of course vary, but all organizations understand that they are embedded in often complex external relationships with audience members, local artists, other arts organizations in the city, policy makers, civic leaders, donors, and nearby residents. It is impossible to manage successfully without looking outside the formal boundaries of an organization to see what is happening in the broader authorizing environment within which an arts organization finds itself operating. Arts organizations are not closed. In fact, they are deeply exposed to the community around them and their success or failure depends heavily on this external environment. This is due to the fact that the community includes individuals and institutions that control funding and resources.

Stakeholders in the community, including self-appointed activists, abutters, artists, audience members, policy makers, and the media, all play a role in shaping the development of these projects. While they may not be in the room with the donors and architects, stakeholders can and do exercise power by making demands, threatening legal action to delay groundbreaking, or just shaping public opinion for or against the endeavor. Rather than treating these external groups' potential to derail the project as a nuisance, effective leaders know how to harness these groups' ability to provide needed intelligence about potential risks and community sentiment. By engaging with select stakeholders, these leaders are able to adjust the course of their projects. Failure to take community views into consideration can lead to conflict and wasted time and money. In Madison, Wisconsin, a private $100 million gift was made by a local philanthropist, Jerome Frautchi, to create the Overture Center for the Arts. Soon, however, community activists began to demand a greater degree of community control over the ambitious plans, leading to a public debate and acrimony. In this sense, managing a building project is a very political process that demands people skills and the capacity to listen and react to the views of people outside the project. Having a store of good-will and support is crucial since projects rarely unfold exactly as planned. There is a moment when improvisation becomes critical and the ability of the project leader to adjust may be heavily dependent on the way relationships within the surrounding community have been managed.

One challenge of community engagement is that an agreement about what kind of a building is needed or wanted may be absent. In this way, starting a project with a series of community town halls or open houses may backfire. Not only is it uncertain that a clear direction will emerge from the process, it is also possible that a wrong direction might be dictated. In the end, not all community groups are created equal. Some have a more legitimate claim to make demands than others, and prioritizing the competing claims according to stakeholder saliency is a central task of community engagement. The task of strategically designing an arts building involves a delicate calibration of both external and internal demands, one that involves listening and responding to the pull of demand coming from outside the organization as well as to the powerful vision inside the organization.

Managing community relations is thus one of the main elements of successfully executing a construction project. Support from the community lends real legitimacy to a project. It justifies the time and effort that is needed to make artistic expression possible. At the same time, it makes the mission of the organization credible. Art must have an audience and when the audience is enthusiastic and supportive, the claim of artistic relevance can be made. The nexus between community support and mission ultimately must be managed actively with a sensitivity for building and holding on to institutional credibility.

The Importance of Strategy

The central framework presented here draws our attention to four cornerstones of the strategic design of cultural facilities. In thinking about what makes projects succeed and what causes them to struggle, the level of coherence and fit among mission, capacity, funding, and community turns out to be critical. Failure on one or more dimensions, be it lack of funding or weak community support or inadequate governance and management capacity or an artistic vision that simply is not compelling, is enough to cause a project to go very wrong. It is tempting to try to establish a hierarchy among these four elements, but this would be a mistake. Across many cases studied, projects have floundered for a diverse set of reasons.

Four significant connectors emerge from the interaction of these four cornerstones. In each instance, feasibility, sustainability, viability, and credibility hang in the balance. The challenge of securing these cornerstones amounts to balancing competing claims for the project leaders' attention. At some points in the natural contour of projects, one or more of these four challenges will be hard to meet. The best project entrepreneurs find a way to hold these complex endeavors together by attending to—at different points in the project cycle—each of these essential cornerstones.[12]

Managerial attention on a building project must be focused on two critical axes. The first can be thought of as connecting internal decisions to external considerations. The other axis connects financial return and social return on investment. By forcing organizations to look inside and outside and to focus on margin and meaning, these major additions to arts infrastructure demand a lot of attention and commitment over an extended period. In the end, there is simply no substitute for having the right person driving the project forward and keeping an eye on all its different dimensions. Without a person committed to literally willing a project into existence, no matter the roadblocks, there are just too many ways in which projects can fail.

The Stages of the Building Process

When is the best point to intervene in projects that are on a pathway toward misalignment? How do capital projects in the arts usually develop? A naïve conception of the decision-making process for capital projects in the arts would assume that the projects proceed in clearly delineated stages, starting perhaps with the project definition stage and proceeding to design development and then funding and then construction, with decisions made during each stage serving as inputs for decisions in the next. A more realistic view, however, would conceive of decision making as highly iterative, with previous decisions constantly reevaluated and refined as unforeseen events occur and new information is encountered. The exigencies of the fundraising process or the architectural design process may force a reconsideration of the project definition. Decisions about funding and design are frequently made simultaneously, often by separate teams, even though these decisions are interdependent on a basic level: capital project price. In other words, decision making about building projects is rarely linear.

In their large international study on similar decision-making processes in large engineering projects, Roger Miller and Donald R. Lessard call these iterations of decision making "shaping episodes." In these shaping episodes, decision makers confront challenges and their own false expectations, engage stakeholders, build coalitions, find and evaluate solutions, and then come to a temporary closure. At this temporary closure, the shape of the project once again seems clear, but only until the next shaping episode prompts another reconsideration. Though the temporary nature of the decisions reached through this process may strike some as perilous, Miller and Lessard stress that postponing final decisions until the right moment is how leadership teams create value. Unexpected events and discovery of new information are nearly a certainty for these projects. No one knows which obstacles will remain hypothetical risks and which will present themselves in reality. By creating closures that are temporary, teams leave themselves options for dealing with unexpected challenges and gain greater certainty in key assumptions and models over time.[13]

To the extent that all capital projects can be divided into phases, those phases are marked by temporary closures that signal an escalation in commitment of resources.[14] Iterative shaping episodes take place during each stage. At first, projects exist as dreams, sometimes dreams held by arts groups for decades, until a promise of a large gift makes the dream seem feasible in the near rather than distant future. These gifts usually come from large donors or local governments, and to secure them sponsoring arts organizations frequently commission expert studies to test their project concepts and speculate on project success. These studies require a relatively small investment of funds, and many organizations receive a grant for these efforts. These studies create a bureaucratic aegis of plausibility—for projects that are usually far from being fully defined. These ideas are bound to evolve if they proceed, thus eventually rendering all the expert findings obsolete. Many projects are abandoned or shelved at this stage because the organization does not find the resources to pursue them further, and a few projects are able to skip this phase by virtue of their sponsors' clout and scale.

The next phase begins with the first sign of project plausibility, which is usually a large gift of money, land, or existing building from either a private donor or a (local) government. For the leaders, the commitment of these resources is the first sign of life, the first hint that their project will get off the drawing board. Once the gift is public, opponents and competitors may come to the fore, arguing that the proposal will have a negative impact or staking a claim to the same resources. These opponents may range from community groups worried about parking and traffic to other community arts organizations who would like to benefit from the plan. The galvanizing gift will help the sponsoring organization attract supporters as well, though some will make their gifts and approval conditional on changes in the vision. To proceed to the next stage, the planning effort has to become more detailed and concrete, and as issues are studied in greater depth, new information and more refined analyses are likely to emerge. In response, the project is likely to evolve through one or several shaping episodes. During one of these shaping episodes, a project may cease to seem plausible and be abandoned.

The next milestone in the escalation of resource commitment is the commitment to an architectural design. Usually, this is signaled by the production of construction drawings. The architectural design and all the consulting work that goes along with it are the first major investments in the capital project life cycle. The farther along the architectural design process is, the more difficult and costly it becomes to make changes. The organization begins to be locked into the shape of its project and has less and less freedom to continue to shape the building and influence the price tag as well as the costs and benefits of the building's postopening operations. With a physical design in place, many estimates and plans can become more concrete at this point, and the decision-making group can still engage in the shaping of business models, community engagement, artistic vision, and operations. At the point when the architectural design is complete, the project has already incurred large sunk costs and becomes emotionally difficult for decision makers to abandon. The cognitive bias toward irrational escalation of commitment becomes an ever-greater liability. The accuracy of cost estimates improves because of the availability of the specific physical details, and the cost forces some organizations to abandon the project nonetheless, or to backtrack and commission a different design. Other projects are stopped because of exogenous factors, like the broader economic situation. More commonly, organizations tinker with the designs for the sake of either bringing down costs or improving on the ideas. They also continue to secure community support and resources to start the final stage of commitment escalation—the actual construction.

The start of project construction is the point at which most of the resources required for the project are fully committed. Project abandonment becomes unlikely. Delays and costly last-minute physical design changes become the tools of responding to surprises. For organizations that wish to avoid such measures, reserves are extremely helpful. If still incomplete, nonconstruction tasks like funding and operational planning increase in intensity and pace, with shortness of time eliminating many of the previously available solutions to the challenges encountered. Shaping episodes still happen, but within the context of a scarcity of available solutions. Some organizations do however build escape hatches into their project plans, arranging for their construction to proceed in phases. The products of these phases can be sold or leased should the sponsoring arts organization decide not to occupy the building upon completion. Yet even in these situations sunk costs weigh on the decision makers, influencing them to proceed despite failing to meet the milestones to which they had previously committed. (Sunk costs, or the money already spent, should of course never enter into decision making about a project's future. Options should be evaluated based on their likely harm or benefit and any remaining costs.) For a sponsoring organization that maintains its commitment to the project, the construction phase ends with the facility's opening. See figure 1.3.

Based on this definition for phases of a building project, we can discuss the best points for project intervention. During the early phases, the least resources have been committed. Therefore, reshaping a project at this point will prevent the majority of the capital investment and time from being misspent. Also, many of the decisions have not reached the state of permanent closure, and therefore, more options for resolving misalignment are available. In later stages, project reshaping may necessitate the abandonment of investments like blueprints. A new architectural design will of course require a new fee, thus increasing the investment required by the project. Still, intervening at this stage is less expensive than intervening after construction has already begun—or after opening, when few physical aspects of the building can be altered without embarking on a new capital project or a renovation. However, uncertainty can also diminish as the project proceeds, enabling leaders involved in later shaping episodes to choose options on the basis of better information.

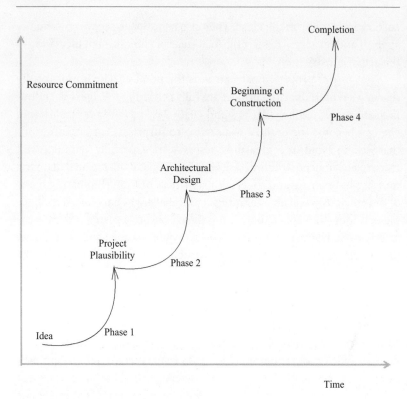

1.3 Phases of Cultural Building Process

Study Methodology

The research presented in this book was part of a two-year, multi-university effort to study the recent cultural building boom in the United States.[15] In the first part of the project, our colleagues Joanna Woronkowicz, Norman Bradburn, and Carroll Joynes conducted a census of the new cultural infrastructure investments in the United States between 1994 and 2008. To accomplish this, they used building permit data, which captured 745 projects in the visual and performing arts with capital costs of over $4 million each. They supplemented these data with additional public source research to understand the dynamics that underlay the cultural building boom.

In the second part of the study, the research team chose 58 focal projects for a more in-depth look. At least one leader of the capital project was interviewed for each of these projects, and detailed financial and organizational data were collected. This information allowed our colleagues to derive common characteristics of these capital projects in the arts. Researchers also analyzed the financial data to derive some conclusions about factors that influenced sponsoring organizations' financial health.

The findings from these two phases painted a provocative picture of the cultural construction in the past two decades. A cultural building boom started in the late 1990s and continued into the early 2000s. Overall, over $16 billion has been spent on new buildings, expansions, and renovations of museums, theaters, symphony halls, opera houses, and centers for the performing arts. An average project took over nine years from start to building's opening.[16]

Building on the broader work of the research team, we developed in-depth qualitative case studies. Eleven projects were the subjects of intensive field study. Seventy-eight interviews about these projects were conducted with current and former executive staff, trustees, public officials, and artistic and community leaders for a kaleidoscopic, comprehensive view of the decision-making considerations and challenges of each project. We wanted our work to cover a range of possible outcomes, and since subject collaboration in a research effort like this seems tied to project success, we also compiled case studies about less successful projects on the basis of the public record. Public record and internal documents were used for case studies on the projects that were subjects of field visits, to supplement our interviews. Twelve case studies appear in this book. Of them, nine are based on our field research and three are based on public sources.

These case studies include museums and performing arts venues. Among performing arts venues, we found the differentiation between projects for performing arts centers and projects for producing organizations useful. Performing arts centers act as landlords to local producing organizations as well as presenters to acts from outside the area. Producing organizations that own and program their own performance venues operate on an entirely different business model. Therefore, these projects differ substantially in their goals, governance structures, and funding models. Overall, the projects we selected represented a diverse set of regions of the country as well as governance and leadership profiles. All of them involved projects within visual or performing arts that cost over $25 million to complete. To ensure that the people interviewed could remember important details, only projects that opened (or would have opened) in 2006 or later were studied. (See table 1.2.)

A third component of the broader research effort collected data from thirteen cities in which large projects were built by interviewing the lead-

Table 1.2. Case Study Selection Grid

| | **Metropolitan Statistical Areas** | |
	Small (<2.5 million people)	Large (≥2.5 million people)
Museums	• Taubman Museum of Art, Roanoke, VA • Austin Museum of Art	• The Art Institute of Chicago • Contemporary Art Museum of the Presidio, San Francisco • Lorton Workhouse Arts Center, DC Metro • The Spertus Institute, Chicago
Performing Arts Centers	• Gerding Theater at the Armory for Portland Center Stage • Long Center for the Performing Arts, Austin, TX • Sandler Center for the Performing Arts, Virginia Beach, VA	• AT&T Performing Arts Center, Dallas • Harman Hall for Shakespeare Theatre Company, DC • Cobb Energy Performing Arts Centre, Atlanta Metro Area

ers of local cultural organizations to understand what spillover effects, if any, these large building projects might create for smaller arts organizations. In seven of these survey cities, data were collected about our case study projects. These served as a useful point of triangulation between community and decision-maker perceptions of the same events. Our goal in this book is to focus on the synthesis of concepts and motifs about strategy and decision making that emerge from all our fieldwork as well as related research.[17]

In the chapters that follow, we consider the ways in which all these concepts play out in different circumstances, and in the process we refine our analysis about the nature of strategic design of cultural facilities. We begin with another look at the question of whether an arts organization should pursue a new building in chapter 2, by considering key dimensions of physical facilities. Assessment of key needs for both existing facilities and hypothetical future ones is essential to making a decision about building. Moreover, understanding which aspects of the physical space matter to arts groups, and why, also underpins any strategy for successful building design.

The considerations of the physical design of any building are deeply intertwined with strategic planning, and in chapters 3, 4, 5, and 6, we consider each component of our strategic alignment framework in turn. We begin by considering key aspects of funding decisions in chapter 3, then proceed to key decisions regarding the project's relationship to its community in chapter 4, address issues of human capacity in chapter 5, and look at mission recalibration in chapter 6. In each of these chapters, we focus on how several organizations dealt with challenges presented during building projects within each conceptual domain. In chapter 7, we look at how these four elements interact and exert pressure on organizations by analyzing two projects' pathways through stages of alignment and misalignment.

Finally, we conclude with a chapter of normative recommendations for practice. Here we present a list of specific tactics and strategies that we believe enhance the chances of project success. Overall, the myriad of issues that present themselves to arts leaders embarking on a construction project require intense and exhausting focus and commitment. We hope that the conceptual frameworks presented here help to prioritize and structure the process of decision making.

2 | *Elements of Building Decisions*

Plans for ideal arts buildings are easy to find—particularly in filing cabinets and dark storage rooms. As one arts executive told us, ruefully, during an interview about his newly opened performance hall: "I have the drawings for a whole other dream back there." Such plans get abandoned because they are impossible to build, run, or fund, and yet the mere process of creating the plans can whet the participants' appetite for perfection. In reality, such perfection in physical design is difficult to achieve, but those who try tend to focus on five attributes: size, location, aesthetics, program-related capabilities, and public spaces. Each of these physical attributes can help or hinder an artistic organization, and they all must be considered during facility design. However, these attributes are deeply intertwined with the organization's strategic blueprint in a way that complicates all attempts to make decisions about facilities on the basis of physical attributes alone.

With regard to sizing, cultural organizations frequently take the Goldilocks approach: facilities that are too small and facilities that are too large are considered inadequate in different ways. This issue is complicated by the fact that growth in the size of cultural facilities takes the form of a step function rather than a straight line. Expansion requires large sums and long time frames. Therefore, at some point all arts organizations are likely to find themselves in facilities that are not a perfect fit.

The issue of size affects arts organizations in a variety of ways. The number of seats in a performance hall and the square footage of a gallery will limit daily attendance. The run of the play or special exhibition can be extended to accommodate a larger audience, but this extension will pose operational challenges.[1] First, an extension will change the funding requirements, since rents, performers, stage hands, utilities, and loaning institutions will need to be paid for a longer period. An extended time frame for a popular program will bring in additional revenue, but since many nonprofits run their programs at a deficit by design, these marginal operating revenues may not cover the marginal costs. An extension will require additional funding from philanthropic sources, corporate sponsorships, or earned income from other activities.

Besides this additional burden of funding, scheduling may be a problem, since special exhibitions and performers are booked far in advance. Thus, an extension is likely to wreak havoc on the events that follow in the organization's programming and venue's booking schedules. If a program is on tour, then adjustments to calendars elsewhere may be required as well. Few organizations can be flexible enough to make such extensions work.

Thus, an organization with a facility that is too small is likely to be required to compensate for this lack with adjustments in its funding model, its programming schedule, and the availability of tickets or admission times to the community. The choices available with respect to funding, community, and mission are constrained by the need to align these strategic imperatives with an imperfect facility—unless of course a different facility, entailing a different set of balancing acts, is secured.

Venues can also be too large. An audience of five hundred in a five-hundred-seat theater is a full house and is seen as a success. The same audience in a 2,500-seat opera hall is a sign of failure. Such considerations may influence the mental state not only of the audience, but also of the performers, thus negatively affecting the quality of the programming. The larger the hall, the harder it is to ensure that the stage can be seen clearly from the farthest seats. Design features required to dampen audience noises like candy wrappers and screeching chairs, as well as to make an unamplified performance sound crisp at the farthest reaches of a hall, increase with size in cost and complexity.

For museums, the key questions about size are gallery dimensions and space.[2] Sparse audiences are less of an issue for art museums, where some patrons will appreciate the experience of contemplating a statue or a painting in solitude, just as others will enjoy the buzz of people and activity in a gallery that is full. Still, museums may wish to change the flow of the people through the galleries. Additionally, gallery walls must still be filled, and specific exhibitions may or may not fit and fill a specific organization's facility. Ceiling height is an important consideration in planning exhibitions of certain objects. Curatorial decisions about how objects are presented and which are presented together may be affected by the size of each room. Last but not least, museums may outgrow their exhibition and storage facilities as the result of actively adding to their permanent collections. Thus, arts organizations have a strong preference for venues large enough to accommodate their audiences and programs, but not so large that they sacrifice other attributes, like acoustics or sense of immediacy.

For arts organizations, location choice is one of the ways to court a community.[3] Ease of access, the neighborhood's availability of amenities like parking and restaurants, and perceptions of safety can all become either barriers or incentives to attending a program.[4] By their nature, arts organizations should excel at creative problem solving, and indeed, many creative solutions to these problems have been tried. When Shakespeare Theatre Company first moved to Penn Quarter of Washington, DC, some still considered the neighborhood seedy. The company hired security to stand on the sidewalks outside its new venue on performance nights, helping create a perception of safety. Valet parking is a tried and true (and expensive) method of making parking scarcity and tough neighborhoods palatable. Recent years have seen performance halls experiment with dinner service in the lobbies before the show, and almost all arts facilities offer food of some kind to draw people to the facility before show time. Many community and arts leaders believe in the ability of an arts organization to reshape the neighborhood adjacent to its facilities over time. Shakespeare Theatre Company, for example, saw Penn Quarter quickly redevelop after its Lansburgh Theatre's opening. Other theaters had followed them there, turning the neighborhood into a theater district and attracting other businesses like restaurants and bars.

The aesthetic appeal of the facilities to the public also plays an important role in venue decisions. At its root, architecture is about the shaping of space, yet in the world of cultural building, architecture is considered a tool for other goals as well, like enhancing the reputations of the institutions as well as trustees, particularly those whose name will be borne by the building. Millions are spent on architect fees and ornate lobbies because of the belief that such investments will lead to increased prominence, prestige, and attendance.[5] In the early 2000s, the experience of the Guggenheim Bilbao—and the enormous importance attributed to its architecture in changing the fortunes of both the city of Bilbao and the museum—was a guiding light for many cultural infrastructure projects. The

Guggenheim Bilbao opened in 1998 to instant acclaim from the architectural press, and newspaper stories across the globe soon followed, extolling the transformation of a small Spanish town into a world-class tourist attraction and an economic dynamo. Many commentators attributed this change to the architectural grand statement of a museum designed by Frank Gehry and to the worldwide interest this design inspired.[6] Perhaps no one has written about the cultural change that the Bilbao marked more astutely than Deyan Sudjic, whose book, *The Edifice Complex,* is a witty, cynical, and provocative account of the function of architecture in our society today. Sudjic describes the Bilbao effect as follows:

> Everybody wants an icon now. They want an architect to do for them what Gehry's Guggenheim did for Bilbao. . . . Sometimes it seems as if there are just thirty architects in the world, the flying circus of the perpetually jet-lagged consisting of the twenty who take each other seriously enough to acknowledge the presence of another member of the magic circle when they meet in the first-class lounge at Heathrow and another ten running on empty, who have been rumbled by their peers but who for the time being can still pull in the clients on the strength of past glories. Taken together, they make up the group that provides the names that come up again and again when yet another sadly deluded city finds itself laboring under the mistaken impression that it is going to trump the Bilbao Guggenheim with an art gallery that looks like a train crash, or a flying saucer, or a hotel in the form of a twenty-storey-high meteorite. You see them in New York and in Tokyo, and they are, with just two exceptions, all men; they are on the plane to Guadalajara and Seattle, in Amsterdam, and all over Barcelona of course. . . . Why has this happened? Partly because architecture has managed to make its mark on a wider culture in a way that it has never done before: buildings get noticed. The trouble is that given the sheer weirdness of so much contemporary architecture, how can their clients tell that their particular train crash, meteorite or flying saucer is going to turn out to be the landmark they are looking for, rather than the pile of junk that they half suspect it might be?
>
> The answer is that they can't. So they rely on that list of thirty names drawn from the ranks of those architects who have done it before. They are the ones licensed to be weird. Commission one of them and you can be confident that nobody is going to laugh at you.[7]

One problem with decision making about architecture in boards' design committees that Sudjic identifies is some trustees' fear of losing face.

Taste in art and architecture is still connected to our assumptions about social status, and this leads cultural organizations to pay large premiums to secure architects who have already gotten the stamp of approval from the taste-making authorities.[8] Needless to say, an architect chosen for this reason alone may not be the most suitable for the specific project.

Further complicating the picture for the role of architecture and the new arts facility's potential to be the next Guggenheim Bilbao, Gehry himself downplayed the degree to which the museum's architecture alone was responsible for the citywide rejuvenation.[9] The museum's construction was after all part of an integrated plan of the city's overall infrastructure development. Still, even if an obsession with the Bilbao effect has led the cultural sector to overstate the importance of architecture in the ultimate success of projects, an aesthetically exceptional building will improve the patron experience. Many aspects of the building can be improved with renovations, but bad geometry cannot be easily fixed. At its best, architecture is capable of transforming the relationship between a community, a cultural facility, and its programming. Moreover, an astounding design can be seen as integral to the mission of an art-presenting institution.

The fourth category of decisions about a capital program involves the various program-related capabilities of a physical space. For a musical organization, like an opera or a symphony, the acoustics of a hall—the nuances, color, sharpness, and fullness of the sound in the audience chamber as well as the ability of musicians to hear each other well on stage—are pivotal.[10] Classical companies believe that subpar acoustics of their halls can limit them artistically while superb acoustics will allow for unbounded artistic growth. The extent to which an average member of the audience can differentiate between good acoustics and great acoustics may, however, be doubtful. Achieving acoustical perfection in a building is an expensive enterprise, both to design and to build. For a dance or theater troupe, sight lines are key. Other qualities of performance halls—like distance from the stage to the farthest seat, depth of the stage, rigging and lighting systems of the performance space, and dressing rooms for the performers—also elicit strong opinions. In the museum world, a similar pivotal role in the artistic experience is played by gallery light, height, and proportions. "Backstage" facilities like storage and conservation areas as well as halls and elevators used for transporting artifacts make a large difference in an organization's ability to fulfill its mission.

While the programmatic capabilities of a space are one of the top priorities for people in charge of artistic programming, managers who oversee the budget prioritize spaces for generation of earned income. The list of such spaces includes gift shops, catering kitchens, cafés, restaurants, meeting rooms, and ballrooms. The connection of these spaces to an organization's mission is frequently tenuous, and the financial return on the capital invested in these facilities' construction dismal. In many cases, the return is lower than the return an organization would expect from an endowment—a fact that makes a strong case for investing the money there instead of in a new café. Yet in reality arts leaders rarely have the option. Capital campaigns offer arts organizations a unique access to funds they will not otherwise get. Using the money to build an endowment rather than a gift shop is not always possible. As Deyan Sudjic puts it in *The Edifice Complex*, quoting a director, "The people who give money have a sense of confidence about the worth of a building."[11] Endowments—and the ability of arts people to manage them—do not always inspire the same. Moreover, some organizations make sound arguments for why these public spaces are critical to their long-term visions for patron experience and community relations.

Thus, though much of the discussion during planning focuses on a myriad of questions regarding physical dimensions of the facility, these physical dimensions are in fact connected to and sometimes overshadowed by strategic considerations. In general, we can group the bulk of the issues of physical design into five categories: size, location, aesthetics, program-related capabilities, and public spaces. All of these frequently become points of contention among decision makers about facility design. As we have seen, these questions are also connected to strategic priorities, like decisions about the mix of revenues that will fund programs and artistic directions. None of these decisions about facilities can be made on the merits of the physical design alone, since all are linked to the strategic dimensions of the building process: funding, capacity, community, or mission.

To examine the principal decisions about building design, it may be useful to consider the cases of two cultural organizations, the Atlanta Opera and the Taubman Museum of Art in Roanoke, Virginia. The leaders of both believed, with good reason, that the inadequacies of their facilities were depleting their organizations' vitality. Both organizations had already relocated multiple times. Both were in cities experiencing cultural building booms, with multiple campaigns raising money for multiple new cultural facilities. These planned facilities promised to redefine the civic identity of their communities, to transform them, to draw worldwide attention. Capital projects were a consideration for both organizations, though the ultimate decisions they made could not have been more different.

The Atlanta Opera and the Search for a New Venue

When it came to venues, the Atlanta Opera had the chance to examine its options several times. The Atlanta Opera was founded in 1979, after the Metropolitan Opera of New York City stopped regularly sending its production to Atlanta on tours. In 1995, the 1,800-seat Symphony Hall at the Woodruff Arts Center, where the Atlanta Opera had been performing, closed for renovations. The opera moved its performances to another downtown venue, the recently renovated Fox Theater, a former movie palace with 4,518 seats.[12] The Fox was a sumptuous hall, with ornate lobbies and a performance chamber decorated in the Moorish style. The patrons loved coming there, and during this second decade of its existence, the Atlanta Opera experienced an enormous growth spurt. In 1993, the Atlanta Opera was selling about fifteen thousand tickets each season. By 2003, the number of tickets sold tripled, to 45,000. Subscriptions more than doubled—from 3,400 in 1993 to 8,300 in 2003. The budget grew as well, but the Atlanta Opera now had trouble controlling it. In 2002, the organization spent $5.5 million, staging five productions. Its revenues for the year were only $5 million, and its deficit of $500,000 pushed its debt past $1 million. In financial straits, the Atlanta Opera began to consider major changes, including a relocation.[13]

Like most performing organizations, the Atlanta Opera depended on three principal sources for support: its audiences, which bought $2.4 million worth of subscriptions and tickets; its donors, who contributed $2.3 million; and grants, which added roughly $300,000. At this point, the Atlanta Opera productions were meeting with mixed reviews. Commentators claimed that the company was underperforming artistically, with regard to its budget and community. The success of the Atlanta Symphony Orchestra, long recognized as a premier regional orchestra, suggested that the city of Atlanta had both the residents with the taste for and the caliber of talent necessary for classical music programs. Critics rattled off names of other regional opera companies that spent less on performances deemed better. These comparisons were not always fair, since the other companies were older or had more community resources at their disposal. For the fiscal year ending in 2002, the Atlanta Symphony Orchestra had an annual budget of $25 million. Since the 1960s, the Atlanta Symphony Orchestra has been nurtured by the Woodruff Arts Center, which provides the company with rent-free performance space and operating support. The Atlanta Opera meanwhile struggled to prove its worth even to its own supporters. In an interview with a local paper, its founder and then-head, Alfred Kennedy, bemoaned the fact that wealthy donors' annual checks to the Metropolitan Opera of New York frequently dwarfed the same people's checks to their local ensemble.[14]

The Atlanta Opera had a bifurcated structure, which many blamed for its problems. Alfred Kennedy was a scion of a patrician Atlanta family, and his principal role at the opera was to raise money. His cofounder Francis Scott was the artistic director. Instead of subordinating one position to another, the Atlanta Opera had both Kennedy and Scott report to the board. As the company grew and its financial complexity increased, a general manager was hired in 2001 to handle challenges other than fundraising, but he resigned within two years and the company did not look for a replacement. The two-headed structure that diffused responsibility for the company's direction among multiple people remained.

Financial statements show that after a $500,000 deficit in 2002, the Atlanta Opera made several changes in the following year. First, the company decreased the number of productions to four. Second, they spent $500,000 more on these productions than they spent on five operas the previous year. They also spent more on their fundraising efforts, and the total budget rose to $6.4 million. Both their ticket revenues and donations rose as well, also to $6.4 million. Third, in October 2003, the Atlanta Opera moved from the Fox Theater to a different venue, the Civic Center.

The move proved to be a critical turning point in the Atlanta Opera's fortunes. The main reason for the company's relocation was scheduling difficulties at the Fox. The theater was operated by a local nonprofit, Atlanta Landmarks, which had as its mission the preservation and promotion of this historic building. Atlanta Landmarks also booked and promoted some of the shows, as well as funded a free ticket program for inner city students. Their large, popular hall was a hit with for-profit promoters like Broadway tours, and from these the Fox made millions. In 2002, its annual budget was $9 million, with a $1 million operational surplus. The Atlanta Opera paid rental fees much lower than the commercial promoters. Unlike road shows, the local Atlanta Opera needed the Fox Theater to close to the public so they could rehearse. The opera patrons spent less on drinks at Fox Theater bars. As the result of all this, the Atlanta Opera's every performance date presented the Fox with a huge opportunity cost. Though the Fox was happy to help a local nonprofit when the space was available, they refused Atlanta Opera's requests to expand its performance calendar and to sign contracts several years in advance so that the opera could secure better-known performers. See figures 2.1 and 2.2.

2.1 Fox Theater in Atlanta. Photo by Scott Ehardt.

By contrast, the city-run Civic Center had a wide-open calendar. The Atlanta Opera could have whatever dates they liked. They could expand their season and offer more performances of each production, which the company hoped would lead to both financial and artistic growth. Of course, the Civic Center was less popular than the Fox for a reason. At 4,591 seats, the two venues were about the same size. But unlike the ornate Fox, the Civic Center was a cement box with a nondescript interior that resembled a lecture hall. The Civic Center's neighborhood was grittier—some opera subscribers feared it was less safe. Backstage, however, the Civic Center was significantly more functional, with more dressing rooms and a deeper stage that would finally allow the Atlanta Opera a greater flexibility with its sets.

On the other hand, both the acoustics and the sight lines were ham-

2.2 Boisfeuillet Jones Atlanta Civic Center. Photo by Scott Ehardt.

pered by the hall's size, just as at the Fox. The Atlanta Opera's leaders thought the Civic Center's acoustics were slightly better than Fox Theater's, but they remained a handicap. The Atlanta Opera would have certainly preferred a hall that fit its audience snuggly, but, incredibly, the city of Atlanta had no performance space that sat more than 1,800 but fewer than 4,000. For a long time now, the company had hoped that someday they could build one. But in 2003, with scheduling issues forcing them out of the Fox, the Civic Center seemed like the only option the Atlanta Opera had.

The patrons hated the move. In October 2003, the Atlanta Opera held its first performance there, of *Aïda*. The *Atlanta Journal-Constitution* ran several generally positive articles about the relocation, but noted that the Atlanta Opera's inaugural weekend at the space was marred by lines for parking, concessions, and bathrooms, as well as general havoc among patrons who could not find the building or their seats.[15] "Despite a Few Glitches, Atlanta Opera Fans Take to Troupe's Move to Civic Center," proclaimed the *Atlanta Journal-Constitution* headline. This proved to be wishful thinking. With every performance, attendance dropped.

"The audience was disappearing faster than the speed of light," said trustee Mott Dinos in an interview. "That whole thing was a fiasco." By the time the opera's second production in the Civic Center started, the organization was forced to cancel one of its four scheduled performances.[16] A marketing strategy firm the Atlanta Opera hired in 2006 pointed out that this and other cancelations put the opera in the position of having to publicize and explain the low demand for tickets, rather than focus the organization's energies on their programs' promotion. The stodgy surroundings and location made going to the opera a much less attractive proposition. Besides, the Fox Theater was using the dates vacated on its calendar by the Atlanta Opera to book other opera acts, usually touring performers based in other cities.

Its new landlord's more liberal scheduling policy, however, allowed the Atlanta Opera to dabble in for-profit performance promotions. Its marketing director booked three pop acts: Harry Belafonte, Andy Williams, and Kenny Rogers. These performers were paid fees, and the Atlanta Opera planned to pocket the surplus box office proceeds. Yet the events lost money instead—somewhere between $200,000 and $500,000. Instead of liberating the Atlanta Opera from constraints on its earned income, the Civic Center's relatively free calendar led the organization only further astray.[17]

By summer 2004, at the end of its first season at the Civic Center, the Atlanta Opera was hemorrhaging money. The attendance and box office revenues had plummeted. Half of the subscribers opted not to renew their season tickets for the next year.[18] Gifts decreased too. By June 30, halfway into the year, the organization had already spent $3 million and taken in only $2.5 million. Worse, a cash flow crisis was looming.

In June 2003, the organization had received a $700,000 grant toward a cash reserve and endowment. They also had a $600,000 endowment, which allowed them to borrow $440,000 more from Wachovia on a line of credit. Kennedy watched the problems mount and felt uncertain that he wanted to continue working long enough to solve them. In March 2004, he announced his resignation, hoping the board could find an immediate replacement. He would retire the moment the right candidate could start.[19] His cofounder, Scott, resigned later in the same year, after the new leader was given the oversight of the opera's budget as well as its artistic programming.

Their replacement was Dennis Hanthorn from the Florentine Opera in Milwaukee. A positive and direct man, he once quipped that his opera philosophy was the kind that required balanced budgets. For 11 years, balanced budgets were exactly what he managed to achieve in Wisconsin. In Atlanta, his budgetary approach would prove to be iterative—he would revisit forecasts and revise budgets throughout the year, as expectations changed. Yet he combined this pragmatic outlook with significant artistic credentials. He trained as a brass player at a conservatory. In Milwaukee, his company attracted positive reviews in the national press, despite limited financial resources. He said that in coming to Atlanta he was looking for a new challenge and offered a rehabilitation plan for the opera: First, they'd balance the budget. Second, they'd pay off the debt, preferably by virtue of new gifts. Third, they'd consider their long-term strategy for organization and staff. Then they would work on a long-term vision for the company as well as a new venue.

Hanthorn was supposed to start in October 2004, but that summer the Atlanta Opera was already tottering on the brink of insolvency. The organization's outlook for the next year was impossibly rosy—they projected a $6.8 million budget and a surplus of $500,000. Given the organization's recent performance, these expectations seemed unrealistic. In August, Hanthorn intervened at the board's behest, cutting $1.3 million in expenses from the plan. Hanthorn cut production expenses by 14 percent and made much deeper cuts to the organization's administrative budget. He kept all four of the planned productions, but shortened their runs. The number of Atlanta Opera performances during his first season would be twelve again, just like it was at the Fox Theater before the move, back when performances would occasionally sell out.

Soon after arriving, Hanthorn started to consider the question of relocating. No immediately available options seemed attractive. He made some changes to how the Atlanta Opera operated in the Civic Center with the hope of making the patron experience more pleasant—installing and opening tents on the plaza to serve patrons drinks, for example. This did little to staunch the bleeding. "Acoustically, it was pretty good," Hanthorn reflected on the Civic Center. "It was just in a part of town that no one wanted to travel to. You can put a bow on a pig and give him a bath, but it's still a pig, in their minds. It didn't matter what I did about their experience to come there, I was still losing attendance." A different venue seemed like the only potential solution. Soon after arriving in Atlanta, Hanthorn went on what he termed a "theater safari" around town.

Returning to Fox Theatre would be difficult because of that venue's scheduling restrictions. Besides, Hanthorn disliked the venue on the basis of its artistic merits. "Fox Theater was no place to produce opera," he said. "It's the way it's acoustically built—it doesn't flatter the voice."

Another previously used venue was the Robert W. Woodruff Arts Center Symphony Hall. At 1,844 seats, that venue was now too small to accommodate the Atlanta Opera's audience (an average of over 3,000 a night in the heydays at the Fox). This made the Symphony Hall an imperfect fit, but the Atlanta Opera could extend its season to accommodate its audience by staging performances on more nights. Moreover, the Woodruff Arts Center was motivated to bring the opera back. The Symphony Hall's principal tenant, the Atlanta Symphony, was in the midst of a $300 million campaign to build itself a new 2,200-seat venue. Their plan had been scuttled once, in 1999, after the symphony could not raise enough money in time to gain the approval of the Woodruff Arts Center. That original plan called for a $115 million theater. Now the symphony had a design from Santiago Calatrava—the ceiling would move, the performance hall would have "cathedral acoustics," and the project would cost them $300 million. The project would also empty a significant swath of space on the old Symphony Hall's calendar once the Atlanta Symphony Orchestra moved, and so the Woodruff Arts Center made overtures to the Atlanta Opera.

The costs of renting the space were, however, much higher than the fees paid at the Civic Center, and the Atlanta Opera was already suffering from overruns and cash flow problems. Moreover, Hanthorn did not want to feel like a second-class citizen. The Woodruff Arts Center had not charged the Atlanta Symphony and instead provided them with operating support. Hanthorn wanted the same deal. Woodruff Arts Center wanted a rental payment.

One option suggested by trustees was building a new hall. "When I was hired, they told me they wanted to build a new theater," said Hanthorn. "Of course, their cash flow was so far down that they couldn't even talk about it. And talk was cheap. I asked, 'How much do you think it would cost to build one?' And they said, 'Oh, about $35 million.' And I said, 'Well, that will pay for the architect, the design, and maybe get a start on the lobby, but not the theater.'"

Fortunately, other organizations were also planning venues of about 2,000 seats for the Atlanta area, and Hanthorn seriously considered the possibility of collaborating with one of them. On the basis of his decades of arts management experience, Hanthorn figured the cost of a new performance hall would be about $100 million. If his organization could in fact raise $35 million, perhaps the state would contribute some funds as well. Another partner—a local government, another performing company, a university, a developer, or some combination of these—could potentially supply the rest.

"I was looking to develop—to get the state to give us the money," Hanthorn said. "I was fully aware that money was available from the state." The state of Georgia would, however, expect the opera to contribute something. "I would go to my donors and say, 'Guess what? We can have a new theater if we raise $35 million.' And I did not know at the time if I had the capacity to do that."

Hanthorn met with everyone who expressed the slightest interest about collaborating on a new facility. He spoke to private developers about including a theater in their new projects. Few of them seemed interested in the nonprofit opera and its relatively small audiences, however. He also spoke to the mayor about the prospects for a new municipal performance hall. She seemed to think that the money to build a new municipal venue could be found, but she couldn't see how the venue's operating budget could be sustained.

The search unearthed two more enthusiastic partners: the suburban Cobb County's convention center authority and Georgia Tech University. Cobb-Marietta Coliseum & Exhibit Hall Authority was a real estate organization run by a board of Georgia General Assembly appointees. Their broad mission was to provide facilities that would promote "cultural growth, education and welfare." Of these, the Cobb Galleria Centre, a convention facility, was one, and a nearby upscale mall was another. Over a decade earlier, the government of Cobb County instructed the authority to look into building a performance venue as well, and the authority had been planning ever since, setting aside $36 million of its profits for the project. Cobb County also provided $57 million in revenue bonds from the hotel/motel tax proceeds. The authority was also seeking private philanthropic funds for the project and planned on a total budget of $125 million. Their plan did not require the Atlanta Opera to raise any money. After opening, their facility would operate as a rental house, with the goal of accelerating the economic development of Cobb County and improving its quality of life with arts offerings. The location was about twenty miles from downtown Atlanta. A groundbreaking was planned for early 2005.

Georgia Tech University was planning to build downtown, on their campus. Their main performance venue, Ferst Center, was aging, and the College of Visual & Performing Arts was looking to develop "a major arts center" or "arts campus." They had invited both the Atlanta Opera and the similarly ill-housed Atlanta Ballet to discuss the possibility of collaboration.

Just like the Cobb-Marietta Exhibition Hall & Coliseum Authority, Georgia Tech University hired consultants to gather a detailed list of the Atlanta Opera's programmatic needs for the potential space. How many seats did the orchestra pit need to fit? How deep did the stage need to be? How many dressing rooms did the company desire? How highly did they value sight lines and acoustics? In fact, the convention center management and Georgia Tech hired the same consulting firm, Theatre Projects Consultants, to conduct two separate feasibility studies.

The 2005 consultants' brief described the Georgia Tech project as follows: "The theater and public spaces in the project are intended to create an excellent environment for the creation and presentation of music, opera, drama, and dance. This requires ensuring that the auditorium and technical areas support a dynamic, intimate, living relationship between artist and audience while at the same time providing good facilities for artistic production." In terms of findings regarding this proposed venue's feasibility, two seem particularly pertinent: First, the extensive wish lists of the opera and the ballet for the stage, sight lines, and acoustics were likely to make the venue expensive. "The combined building program appears to be cost prohibitive," Theatre Projects Consultants told Georgia Tech bluntly. On the basis of the required size and quality, they estimated the construction cost to fall between $80 and $120 million. This was an estimate of the hard costs, not the total costs, which would also include payments made to architects and acousticians, as well as expenses of the capital campaign, moving, and grand opening. Second, Theatre Projects Consultants cautioned that all the venues being planned for Atlanta would entail a highly competitive environment once they were completed. "One or both of these buildings must be viewed as a potential source of competition for funding, patron base, and talent draw," they wrote. The potential for this highly competitive environment, they warned, required "full support" from Georgia Tech and the classical organizations who would be resident there. To be successful, it also required a distinctive vision that would differentiate this new hall from all the others.

With multiple projects on the drawing boards at various organizations in Atlanta, the future of the competitive landscape in the city was far from certain. How many of them would proceed to the next phase? Did each plan need to take into account the prospect of future competition from these other proposed new buildings? Would they all compete for the same audiences and acts? The feasibility of each venue depended on the uncertain plans for all the others.

For Hanthorn, the plans' uncertainty was a key decision factor. The Cobb County facility was the most advanced in its plans and fundraising. Yet it was also the farthest geographically, and he knew the move there would be resisted by many of his trustees. Atlanta Opera's previous experience with moving its performances was hardly encouraging. What if this time subscribers and audiences abandoned the opera in even greater numbers? The trustees were fearful. About half of them opposed the move to Cobb County when the idea was finally presented to the board. "He was not afraid of this, of moving out of Atlanta. He didn't know about how the Atlanta people are," said Dinos. "They're very provincial. If it has the Atlanta name on it, they want it to be in the city."

Hanthorn had no strong preconceptions about the need for prestigious classical companies to perform within the dense city core. He was not from Atlanta and did not share the residents' strong emotional attachment to Midtown as the only appropriate neighborhood for upscale cultural events. "It was a very easy decision for me because I have always lived in the suburbs. My wife wants a nice house. I have three kids," he said.

Yet he also knew that many of his wealthy subscribers and supporters lived in the affluent neighborhood of Buckhead, which was much closer to Midtown than to Cobb County. Moreover, the Atlanta Opera audiences had proved fickle during the organization's previous move from the Fox. "My first reaction when Dennis said that was, 'Dennis, don't do this. You'll kill the opera,'" said Mott Dinos.

The Taubman Museum and Three Extraordinary Gifts[20]

The Taubman Museum of Art in Roanoke—then known as the Art Museum of Western Virginia—was also struggling in its existing venue. The museum began as a sort of club where local artists taught, took classes, had galleries, and exhibited, first at a former restaurant they had renovated for $250 (equivalent to about $1,800 today), then in the basement of a former church, then in a donated mansion in the tony neighborhood of South Roanoke. Eventually, the museum began to amass a collection by virtue of gifts from local art buyers. Still, the collection remained focused on the work of regional artists and in the early 1990s had few works worth over $100,000. The museum's South Roanoke home lacked the humidity and temperature controls necessary for storing art. Moreover, the board began to believe that its suburban location prevented large portions of the Roanoke community from coming to the museum. They sensed that South Roanoke was both physically removed and seen as an enclave for the wealthy and the wealthy alone.[21]

Thus, in the late 1970s, the museum was considering relocation. Simultaneously, a downtown business league was leading a planning effort on how to revitalize the blighted commercial center of Roanoke. The plan called for a cultural facility, and an old warehouse was bought and remodeled for $7.5 million. This cost was funded by a combination of private gifts, government grants, and bonds. The facility—named Center in the Square and operated by a foundation—would provide free space to select cultural organizations in Roanoke. These tenants would not have to pay for maintenance, security, or custodial services. Center in the Square would also provide some marketing for the programs housed there. The hope was that these free services would help the tenants eliminate entrance fees. Though the art museum considered pursuing an independent facility construction project even then, the deal offered by the Center in the Square was too attractive to turn down. When the Center opened in 1982, and the museum took up residence on the first two floors, four other organizations—the Science Museum, Mill Mountain Theatre, Roanoke Valley History Museum, and the Arts Council of the Blue Ridge—occupied the rest of the building. Forty thousand people came to see the place on opening weekend, and in the decade that followed, the downtown around the Center became a vibrant area filled with amenities and pedestrian activity, with Center in the Square claiming most of the credit for this transformation.[22]

By the late 1990s, Center in the Square started planning an expansion. Four hundred thousand people, 100,000 of them K-12 students, were entering its doors every year.[23] Of these, only a small portion (50,000–100,000, depending on the year) went to the art museum. Having grown in the decades since opening, its existing tenants wanted more room, and the Center itself was expanding to provide services to more local organizations. A space use study concluded that they needed 80,000 square feet of additional space.[24]

Simultaneously, reports of fissures between the Center and its tenants were emerging in the press. The Center now had an annual budget of over $2 million and a staff of 22, dwarfing each of its tenants, many of whom felt they deserved more control over how the Center spent money on their behalf. Jim Sears, a recently hired executive director for the Center, had a brash personality, and the tenants felt overpowered in interactions with him. Anonymously, they told local reporter Kevin Kittredge that they feared a decrease in private donations would follow any expression of dissent. They felt they could not trust the Center's leadership to advocate with key leaders on their behalf. Sears called these accusations ridiculous and said the tenants were excessively sensitive to his suggestions for changes.[25]

The museum, too, was anxious for an increase in space, but despite the tense atmosphere at the Center in the Square, museum board member and key benefactor W. Heywood Fralin claimed an expansion independent of the Center was not something the museum would consider.[26] Eventually, however, an independent building project, with all its attendant benefits and additional costs, was exactly what the museum came to pursue.

The primary reason for the museum's desire to expand was the promise of an extraordinary gift. In the 1990s, in secret, Roanoke resident Peggy Macdowell Thomas, grandniece of painter Thomas Eakins, promised to leave her collection of art to the Taubman Museum. Worth millions, her treasure trove had 20 paintings, most by her famous relative, as well as prints and photographs. The local press described her as "eccentric," "vain," flirtatious, and funny.[27] She loved having curators and museum directors from across the country visit and fawn over her, asking for a peek at her collection or its bequest. "Peggy loved to be courted in general," said Sandra Lovinguth, a former Taubman executive. [28] This meant that the Taubman Museum was not completely certain she would keep her promise to leave the collection to them until her will was read after her death in 2001. Board member Jenny Taubman said, "We were all very dubious, because she had changed her mind several times. There were many people who were romancing her for those paintings."[29]

Still, even the mere promise of the Thomas collection was sufficient to transform the museum, which had been struggling to define a vision and a strategy. The board had fired longtime executive director Peter Rippe in 1988 because he refused to broaden the museum's mission beyond serving and collecting Blue Ridge Mountain artists.[30] Since then, the institution had been led by a quick succession of interim directors and outsiders, who were brought in after rigorous, nationwide searches and who, a few years after getting to Roanoke, resigned to take positions at more prominent institutions in larger cities. But with the Thomas gift, a museum with a haphazard, unedited collection of inexpensive paintings by local artists had an opportunity to develop an excellent niche collection focused on turn-of-the-century American art. Then, more good luck came: a local foundation, the Fralin Trust, responsible for overseeing the philanthropic legacy of Horace Fralin and headed by his brother Heywood, stepped in to fund purchases of masterworks from that period.

In May 1999, Kittredge came with executive director Judy Larson on one shopping trip to New York, where her days were filled with galleries and paintings brought out and placed on a velvet-draped easel for her critical eye. She knew many gallery owners from her days as the curator at the High Museum in Atlanta, but still, a few treated her with disrespect, perhaps owing to her affiliation with an unknown museum in a small, working-class town. One dealer discussed the redecoration of his Los Angeles home on the phone while she waited, and several were not available to see her until Fralin, a wealthy man and a collector in his own right, arrived. Fralin—now so important to the museum's future—visibly discombobulated Larson, who became less certain around him, even, at his suggestion, acquiescing to add to the collection a painting by Irving Wiles that she had wanted to take a pass on. Fralin financed purchases at auction for the museum, including Childe Hassam's *Across the Park* for $1 million and Winslow Homer's *Woodchopper in the Adirondacks* for $900,000. Back in Roanoke, they joined recently purchased paintings by John Twachtman, Edward Potthast, and Mary Oakey Dewing.[31] Over the next few years, a John Sargent, a Norman Rockwell, and other paintings were added to the collection as well. Fralin Trust paid for all of them.

Thus, before the new building was even contemplated, the museum was a growing institution. In 1995, their budget was $500,000. By 2003, the operating budget had risen to $816,000, with an additional $1 million–$2 million a year being spent to acquire art. Before 2001, $325,000 in annual funding was received from the state. Admission was free, and therefore the museum's earned revenues were insignificant. Attendance was on the rise, increasing from 55,000 per year in 1988 to 86,000 in 2007. Before Fralin's involvement, the museum's largest private gift had been a $238,000 endowment received in 1994. From FY1999 to FY2003, the Fralin Trust had contributed nearly $8 million—65 percent of all contributions.[32]

The Taubman Museum entered the twenty-first century with a newly crystallized mission to collect works from almost exactly a century earlier. Decades of growth had resulted in financial stability, new donors, growing attendance, a financially beneficial partnership with Center in the Square, and a promise of acquiring a distinctive specialized collection. Yet this new collection seemed to require better and larger space, and problems that seemed to stem from a lack of recognition, like the inability to retain key staff, remained. The board also had feared that the inadequacies of their physical space would lead Peggy Macdowell Thomas to change her mind about leaving them her collection. The museum's home, Roanoke, was also striving to get noticed, and to retain and attract information age companies and young, educated professionals and creative individuals. When the idea for a brand new museum finally surfaced, both the museum and the city were ready to saddle the fledgling initiative with dreams for national acclaim and community transformation.

Another extraordinary gift took the museum one step further toward its metamorphosis. In 1998, a local, family-owned chain of furniture stores moved one of its shops to a better location. Knowing of the Center in the Square's desire to expand, the family offered that nonprofit its 64,000 square foot downtown building as a gift. That morning, Judy Larson ran into board member and future president Heman Marshall in the local bagel shop. "She said, 'Have you seen the paper?' The two of us started talking over bagels and said, 'We need to talk to somebody quickly,'" said Marshall.[33] Soon, said Larson, the museum got into "the buffet line" for the building.[34] After consulting with the donor, the Center encouraged the museum to proceed with preliminary planning for a new facility at the Grand Home Furnishings and Piano location. Along with its other recent windfalls, the gift of this building and its fortuitous timing seemed to empower the members of the museum's board. "The stars seem to be aligned for us right now," one told the local paper.[35]

With the Center's permission, the museum hired Boston's E. Verner Johnson and Associates to conduct an architectural feasibility study on transforming the donated building. Half the consulting fee was funded by a $145,000 grant from the state. In addition to considering what would be required to make this space meet the bare minimum requirements for serviceability as a museum, like heating, ventilation, and air conditioning systems, the firm included in its plans changes that were highly desirable, like increasing the height of ceilings to accommodate visiting exhibitions and changing the order of the rooms. The firm released its findings in August 1999. They found one of the most difficult challenges with this adaptive reuse project to stem from the history of the Grand Home Furnishings building, which was in fact five different buildings constructed over time and hidden under the same "brick skin." This made HVAC controls required for art display and storage difficult and expensive. Fire safety, as well as the maximum load allowed by the floors, were additional concerns. Johnson estimated the total building renovation price tag for both the absolutely essential and the highly desirable features at $20 million–$25 million. For that much money, the architects pointed out, the museum might as well build a new building. Then Verner Johnson and Associates finished their presentation with a concept sketch that illustrated a design they might produce for such a new building, if hired.[36] The modernist lines of the Johnson concept sketch produced a minor uproar in the Letters to the Editor section of the local paper, thus beginning an unusually lively, protracted, and occasionally rigorous community discussion about architectural aesthetics and monetary value.

Even though museum officials said they were looking for a "better" concept than what Johnson had produced, his suggestion that the museum build anew took root. The idea of a building perfectly and exactly built to the museum's specifications, for a price that did not exceed the cost of renovations, was tempting. The Grand Home Furnishings store would need to be razed for the museum to build there. The building itself was no longer of any use to the museum, and its leaders started considering other sites, including those not in need of expensive bulldozing. The fortuitously timed gift that seemed to make the museum's dreams possible only a year before no longer seemed necessary to bring those dreams to fruition. The sites the museum's leaders considered included Mill Mountain Park, a green space that was the home of the Roanoke Zoo, and a city-owned downtown parking lot situated just a few blocks away from Grand Home Furnishings and the Center. The parking lot— known as the Billy's Ritz site after a nearby restaurant—was larger than the Grand Home Furnishings lot and visible from Interstate 581, where 75,000–90,000 cars drive by daily. It was also across from Hotel Roanoke, a local landmark and conference center.[37]

At this point, the Taubman Museum story takes a slight turn to the bizarre because the city already had plans for the Billy's Ritz site, wanting to build an IMAX theater on that spot. A 1997 study by Wide Image Theatres Corporation found that once attendance stabilized in year three of operations, 250,000 people would come to an IMAX theater every year—about 50,000 more than required for the theater to break even on operating expenses. Assuming an adult ticket would cost $7.50 and a children's ticket $5, the study projected an annual operating surplus of $360,000 a year. The study also projected that construction costs of the building would reach $7 million. The mayor first announced that the city was looking for an organization to take on the building and operations of such a theater in 1997, saying the project would give an economic development boost to the downtown area. Many leading organizations, such as Center in the Square, said they liked the city's proposal. However, they all declined to lead the effort, even after the mayor promised $1 million in funding.[38]

Once the museum expressed interest in the site intended for the IMAX, Brian Wishneff, an economic development consultant attached to the IMAX effort, proposed merging the two projects. A profile of Wishneff in the *Roanoke Times* described him as someone not very good at the social niceties of small talk, but extremely adept with complex financing structures and the intricacies of applications for public funds intended for economic development.[39] His pitch to the museum and Center in the Square leaders stressed the plan's financial practicality. "You need only one heating system and one lobby and one ticketing area," said Wishneff. The IMAX operating surplus would also help the museum. The mayor's office was also very interested in seeing the IMAX project get started.

The museum leaders were stupefied by the suggestion of adding a novelty theater most frequently used to screen 3-D nature films to a museum intent on being taken seriously for its art collection. "They were kind of taken aback," said Wishneff about the reaction.[40] Larson said: "I think my first response was, 'Hey, wait a minute. How do these go together?'"[41] Eventually though, she acquiesced. "I was sort of talked into the idea that film was an art form, that it would add interest and accessibility to the museum. I thought, 'Why not?'"[42] In August of 1999, the merger of the museum and the IMAX project was announced by the mayor—along with the gift of the Billy's Ritz site and a grant of $4 million from the city government. To fund this subsidy, the city planned to issue bonds.[43]

From the point of view of the design, the merger was another baby step toward a giant price tag. As museum leaders knew, IMAX cinemas require several stories worth of vertical space. Indeed, to accommodate the IMAX, their proposed size changed from 65,000 square feet to 100,000 square feet, and the expected construction budget rose from $20 million–$25 million to $30 million–$35 million.[44]

Buy, Rent, or Share

At this point in their decision making, both the Atlanta Opera and the Taubman Museum were anxious to improve on the quality of their existing spaces. The Atlanta Opera was focused on the number of seats, public amenities, acoustics, and sight lines, while the Art Museum of Western Virginia was intent on increasing gallery size and visibility. The focus on these factors had tremendous implications for the health of these organizations. During the first stages of planning of capital facilities, both of these organizations were asked to produce lists of their building needs. This building program was a result of an iterative process of thought and discussion with expert consultants on physical facilities. The artistic companies were required to consider their needs with regard to size, location, aesthetics, and programmatic space quality.[45]

What we can see from these narratives, however, is that for the leaders of one of these organizations, a highly critical factor about facilities was about control, not facility characteristics. Did these two organizations want to buy, rent, or share their facility with others? How much ultimate control over the specifics of the building program, scheduling, and operational policies did these arts organizations want, and how much were they willing to pay to attain it? Did they want to partner with others—and if so, whom, and on what terms—or did they want to strike out on their own?

The ownership and management structure of a facility greatly influence the terms of its use by an arts organization. The needs of a presenting organization like the Atlanta Opera can be orthogonal to the needs of the organizations charged with operating facilities, like the Fox Theater. This often leads to conflicts over tenancy costs, scheduling, and policies about needs like rehearsal time. These problems—all related to ownership and management structure—in turn lead artistic organizations to search for a hall of a different size, or a hall with fewer tenants. Patrons may hold a presenting organization at fault for facility operator oversights like parking difficulties and box office lines. Facility operators like Center in the Square must choose between the demands of their varied users, who may find their lack of clout in this decision-making process frustrating. Meanwhile, even in a project undertaken by a single organization independently, funding partners dictate their own terms. Complete control of a facility has its drawbacks too, requiring an artistic organization to secure funding and develop human capacity for facility maintenance and operations. How would leaders in Atlanta and Roanoke resolve these tensions? Very differently.

The Atlanta Opera Moves Again

Under Hanthorn's leadership, the Atlanta Opera's financial situation was stabilizing, but challenges still remained and the Civic Center location posed a continuous problem. Hanthorn kept looking north, to Cobb County, for a solution. Once the ground was broken on the construction of the performing arts center in Cobb County in early 2005, the venue was on track to open for the Atlanta Opera's 2007–2008 season. The Cobb project's leaders secured a sponsorship deal with a local company, and the venue would be named the Cobb Energy Performing Arts Centre. The Georgia Tech project was still in the discussion stages, and the new Symphony Hall's capital campaign seemed stalled. In September 2005, Hanthorn asked his executive committee for an authorization to

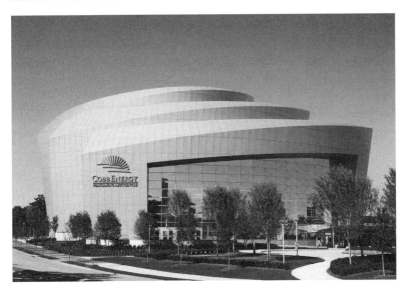

2.3 Cobb Energy Performing Arts Centre. Photo by J. Glover, Atlanta, Georgia. Creative Commons Attribution-Share Alike 3.0 license.

negotiate a contract with the Cobb Energy Performing Arts Centre. His presentation stressed the new facility's attributes like "exciting patron experience," "state-of-the-art technical systems," "priority availability," and "competitive costs." See figure 2.3.

The board was not enthusiastic. About half the board opposed the move, with long-time supporters Mott Dinos and Nancy Bland among the detractors. Hanthorn took Mr. and Mrs. Bland to the Cobb Energy Centre on a hard hat tour to convince them that the venue could work. "The biggest objection was, We're the Atlanta Opera, and we're going to be in Cobb County. That was the biggest objection," said Dinos. "It would be perfect if this theater were downtown."

The trustees realized, however, that the Atlanta Opera was hampered by performing in the Civic Center and that the problem with the facility had to be resolved. Slowly, they came around. "We discussed it, rationally," said Dinos. "Everyone knew something had to be done. Everyone was so disenchanted with the opera at the Civic Center, they were willing to try anything. My thought about it was emotional to begin with, but then I changed, I rolled with the punches." Eventually, Nancy Bland also came around. "It became apparent that the opera was just going to die unless we did something," she said. "Kicking and screaming, I went."

The issue of how much say the Atlanta Opera would have in its venue's decisions was critical for convincing reluctant trustees to authorize the move to Cobb. "They were so eager to have us," said Mott Dinos. "Of course, that was when it was just open. They were thrilled to death to have some big charitable organization want to come and do our thing out here. I don't know if that will ever change or not, but if so, it'll be a long time."

By January 2006, Hanthorn had board approval to begin negotiations with the Cobb Energy Performing Arts Centre. Soon, a contract was in place for the Atlanta Opera to perform at Cobb beginning with the fall of 2007. As predicted, some subscribers protested that the move would be yet again catastrophic, and Hanthorn commissioned a poll of current and lapsed subscribers from the Gallup Company. He wanted to have a response for his critics. Gallup found that 78 percent of the subscribers were likely to renew their tickets for the season at Cobb. At about the same time, it had become increasingly clear that Georgia Tech would not proceed with its plans for a new facility, at least not in the near term. Hanthorn's facility choice, made by a newcomer with no emotional attachment to a downtown location, was looking wiser with every moment.

The Gallup poll was part of a strategic planning process to ensure a successful move to the new venue. Since the Cobb Exhibition Hall Authority was doing all of the design and building oversight as well as the venue's operational planning, the Atlanta Opera could focus all its energies on its own plans. The Atlanta Opera had twelve months before the move to get ready. In that time, they wanted to persuade their ticket buyers to try going to the Cobb Centre and to reach out to the lapsed buyers from the Fox Theater days. On the basis of other companies' experiences, they expected a two-year period of a honeymoon with their public to follow their move. During this time, they expected higher ticket sales and more receptive donors. They hoped to persuade some of the new or returned donors or attendees to stay past the two years. To maximize the extent to which they took advantage of this honeymoon effect, the Atlanta Opera planned to focus on building its fundraising and marketing capacity. In November 2006, they launched a $10.9 million capacity campaign. They also secured corporate sponsorships for their performances in the new venue. These steps may have been impossible had the company been responsible for any portion of planning or fundraising for the construction itself.

On the eve of the move, the uncertainty among subscribers about going to the suburbs was still high. "You wouldn't believe some of the questions that I got when we were going to Cobb," said Bland. Some of her acquaintances were still unconvinced that a stellar audience experience would be possible so far away from central Atlanta. "They wanted to know if we would have more adequate restrooms and whether there'd be one on every level. I just couldn't believe it," said Bland.

People who had never attended the Atlanta Opera performances before came in droves. Fifty percent of the subscribers for the inaugural 2007–2008 season were new to the company. Twenty-five percent of all subscribers were now suburban dwellers from Cobb County. In the first and second seasons, 70,000 people attended the opera performances—exceeding even the records set previously at the Fox Theater. In the first year, the Atlanta Opera still ran a $1 million deficit, taking in $6 million and spending $7 million. In the second year in the new venue, their revenues finally caught up with their expenses, with a budget of $7 million and a surplus of $660,000. For both years, ticket revenues were about $2.5 million, with contributions accounting for the rest. In the third year, the ticketing revenues declined, to $1.9 million, and the opera once again faced a deficit. Then in 2011, a major bequest of $9 million started the company on a path toward building a significant endowment.[46]

Overall, the Atlanta Opera's leaders are happy with the new home. So far, the Cobb Energy Performing Arts Centre management has been open to working through the usual conflicts over scheduling and prices. Nancy Bland has come to enjoy aspects of the suburban location. "You look back at the city, at the lights," she said. Still, whenever questions about Atlanta Symphony's ambitious plans for a new, Calatrava-designed venue—since canceled—came up, she grew wistful. "I wish we could afford that, to have a hall like that."

Choosing an Architect, Raising Money in Roanoke

As the Taubman Museum prepared to leap into a capital project, the cultural landscape in Roanoke was undergoing significant changes. Competition for gifts from the private sector was increasing. A study for the Funders Circle, a group of Roanoke's most generous philanthropists, found that cultural institutions in the area alone were in the midst of $63 million worth of fundraising campaigns.[47] Donors complained that the spate of campaigns showed few signs of awareness of other organizations' efforts or coordination. In addition to that, the year 2000 brought the first rumors from Richmond of reductions in state funding for the arts. In 2001, the legislature cut all funding for cultural institutions not owned by the state and sent established Roanoke institutions—like the Science Museum, Mill Mountain Theatre, Center in the Square, and even Taubman Museum itself—scrambling to cut expenses, sometimes by eliminating hours or jobs. With state cuts, the fundraising competition grew even more cutthroat.

This was the fundraising climate in which the museum began the quiet phase of its capital campaign as well as its search for additional public funds. The chair of the capital campaign was Jenny Taubman, a native of Romania, a former model as well as a former officer in the Israeli army. Taubman was fluent in six languages and ran her own personal image consulting firm. Her husband, Nicholas Taubman, headed the only *Fortune* 500 company still remaining in the Roanoke Valley, Advance Auto Parts, which had been founded by his father. In 2001, Jenny Taubman confirmed that Advance Auto Parts made a pledge of $4 million to pay for the naming rights to the IMAX theater. The museum was also successful in getting Virginia Governor Jim Gilmore to request $10 million for the new building in his FY2002–2003 budget.[48] But the governor's request for funding was denied by the legislature, and for years, no further public announcements of any gifts were forthcoming.

* * *

If the board of the Taubman Museum felt at all deterred by this fundraising climate, their plans for the new building did not show it. The board appointed 11 trustees to an architect selection committee led by Deanna Gordon, a former school superintendent.[49] Of high concern to them was ensuring that they accomplished something great for their city.

From the beginning, the Bilbao effect—or the belief that if a great museum were built, the audience would come—became a touchstone in the architect selection committee discussions. One of the Taubman Museum's trustees, Damon Littlefield, wrote in March 2000 in the *Roanoke Times*, expressing an idea often mentioned by project leaders in other editorials and interviews:

> If we want to move Western Virginia further up in recognition, we need to create a new art-museum facility that will be immediately recognized by world citizens. As an example, consider the Guggenheim Museum in Bilbao, Spain, designed by architect Frank Gehry. Had anyone ever heard of Bilbao before that museum was built? Not many of us can say that we did. But, now, we know Bilbao because Bilbao has a new world-recognized art-museum facility. We can do the same.[50]

Attracting the kind of attention that the Taubman Museum wanted would require that their building make a grand architectural statement, but at the beginning of the process, not everyone on the committee agreed: "I guess I thought it should look like what we've got," said Heman Marshall about his viewpoint early on.[51] What Roanoke already had downtown was a preponderance of brick mid-century facades—like the Grand Home Furnishings building. A reporter describing her visit there wrote: "Until now, the prominent features of Roanoke's skyline have been neon: a Dr Pepper sign, a giant star atop Mill Mountain and an animated coffee pot that pours its contents into a cup. Not far away, 'Jesus Saves' glows in red from a hilltop church."[52] Eventually, however, Marshall and all the other skeptics on the board were convinced by their peers that the Taubman Museum needed to create a building of architectural distinction downtown, something grand to symbolize Roanoke's new identity as a city that was looking ahead toward a bold, new era of innovation, rather than backward to its coal and railroad roots. In interviews, members of the committee said they reached this consensus through a process of familiarizing themselves with contemporary architecture. The names of top architects in the world were divided among the committee's members for research and presentation. Valetta Pittman showed the board the work done by Renzo Piano, who later declined to be considered for the project. Pittman told a reporter that for her, a primary criterion in selecting an architect was ensuring that the building was a work of art in and of itself. Others were concerned with additional questions. "Does this person stay on budget?" asked executive director Judy Larson.[53] In the end, the committee reached an agreement that they would look for an architect who could produce a bold design that hopefully would also attract the attention of the national and international press.

In 2000, the Taubman Museum sent invitations to a select group of architects to submit applications for the museum's open selection process. The applications required the architects to submit their qualifications rather than asking for preliminary designs.[54] In December 2001, the finalists—Michael Graves, Verner Johnson, Antoine Predock, and Randall Stout—came to Roanoke for their interviews with the board. Stout was the youngest in the group. As an associate at Gehry's firm, Stout had had a hand in designing the Disney Performance Hall in Los Angeles. "Randall came totally prepared. He actually brought a tabletop model of the market area," said Valetta Pittman. He used the model to give the board members an idea of where each part of the building would be situated on their unusually shaped site. This was in contrast to architects who "spoke in generalities, or gave dry architecture lectures." Jenny Taubman, a trustee and chair of the capital campaign, said: "It came down to Predock and Randall. [Predock]'s very experienced. He's already a star. I think he was also going to give us a beautiful product." Stout was described as charming, but relatively young and inexperienced. Larson did not see this as too much of a drawback. "You just know you're going to get 200 percent of that person. It's always a risk. Anybody would have been a risk. I like the idea of giving younger people a chance."[55] In May 2002, Stout's selection for the project was officially announced.

In July, executive director Judy Larson resigned to take a job in Washington, DC, and yet another search for an executive director began. Stout finished a design concept quickly, even assembling and sending a model for use in the capital campaign in the fall of 2002. After this, and despite numerous inquiries from the newspapers and letters to the editor pillorying it for secretiveness, the museum refused to show the public their new design, insisting they must first convince key donors. Neither the design nor its costs were made public for three years.

Up until this point, the project had proceeded without encountering much resistance, but now several challenges arose. First, Stout's design cost more than the $35 million project budget allowed. The board solicited the advice of a developer on cost in 2003, and then proceeded to attempt to trim the capital budget. Yet they found compromising on any facet of the design exceedingly difficult. One telling example was their consideration of cheaper building materials. Stout's original design called for Italian travertine marble in the lobbies. When the board began considering cost-cutting measures, Stout suggested a trendy sealed concrete finish on the floors instead. In the end however, the board went back to the costly travertine because they thought a marble lobby would look a great deal better.[56] Lacking resolve, the board found the value engineering process difficult.

The second challenge was the operating plan for the expanded museum. A closer look at the IMAX audience projections made the board fearful that instead of boosting the museum's bottom line with operating income, the cinema would run a deficit instead. Moreover, finishing the space was costly, and the board had trouble finding the money in the capital budget. Finally, in 2005, they announced they would not include the cinema in their new museum, though Stout's design already included the space and was difficult to modify. With Stout's design finalized, a revision to reallocate the space intended for an IMAX projector was never completed. The built museum has 5,000 square feet of unfinished, unusable space originally intended for IMAX equipment on its gallery floor.[57]

Another difficulty with the operating plan was the projected quadrupling of the annual budget. The estimate for the annual operating budget in the new building was $3.75 million. This figure made other cultural groups in the city fearful that the museum would suck up all the available funding, in the end causing all but the strongest of them to struggle for their very survival. The museum planned to make this annual budget manageable by earning $1.25 million in revenue, raising $1.5 million from private and government sources, and meeting the rest of their annual funding requirement by drawing on a $20 million endowment they planned to raise once the capital campaign was complete.[58] Former president of the board Valetta Pittman spoke about the process of coming up with a business plan in an interview. "There have been some spectacular public failures. I think we've learned from that. We keep testing the numbers over and over again."[59] However, as the capital campaign foundered, the endowment goal was reduced to $10 million that was to be raised by 2012.[60] By the time it opened, the museum had $2.7 million in its endowment fund.[61] "Until we build that endowment, we're going to have issues with the operating budget," said executive director Georganne Bingham in an interview after the endowment target was reduced.[62]

The issues with the capital campaign were the museum's third principal challenge between 2002 and 2006. From the beginning, the campaign struggled to raise the large gifts that form the foundation of a successful fundraising effort. By opening day, public records showed that only four donors had made gifts over $1 million: the Taubman family (approximately $25 million gift according to press reports), the Fralin Trust (over $8 million),[63] Advance Auto Parts ($4 million), and the Mary "Peggy" Macdowell Thomas estate ($1 million). Approximately $8 million came from government sources. The rest of the funds (about $7 million by opening day) had to be raised one small, five- or six-figure gift at a time, from about 200 other donors. The campaign was grueling enough that acquisitions of paintings had to grind to a halt, with the Fralin Trust's annual $1.5 million–$2 million in contributions redirected toward the new building.[64] Unconvinced donors or the insufficiency of funds in Roanoke could have been the root causes of these difficulties. As capital campaign chair, however, Jenny Taubman assumed most of the responsibility. She said: "It became necessary for someone to come up with additional funds to make this happen. It just so happened it was us. Because I couldn't get anybody else to give it except for Nick."[65]

Finally, the museum's fourth challenge was intense community resistance to Stout's proposed design. In 2005, shortly after the design's public unveiling, the *Roanoke Times* commissioned an independent poll of residents. Thirty-one percent said they disliked the proposal, 28 percent said they liked it, and 34 percent were not familiar enough with the design to comment. The margin of error was 4 percent. The fact that the community was so deeply divided over the proposal was not surprising. What seems shocking, however, is that 66 percent of the respondents were engaged enough to look at the drawings. In fact, community passions over Stout's postmodernist concept ran so high that Roanokers began to express their opposition with car bumper stickers.[66]

Those who disliked the proposal attacked Stout's project for one of two reasons: either they believed the design was too modernist to fit well within Roanoke's downtown landscape and local culture, or they believed that the design was not avant-garde enough. The first group pointed out that most of the downtown had simple mid-century facades made of brick, and that an angular titanium edifice would be out of place there. They nicknamed the design "A Wreck of the Flying Nun."[67] The second camp's most vocal member was Virginia Tech architecture professor Dennis Kilper. He accused Stout of "expensive mimicry" of Gehry's ideas rather than true innovation. Because the design was imitative, it would fail at being a visionary project, he said. In fact, the *New York Times* wondered if the design constituted an act of architectural plagiarism. Kilper also questioned why so much money would be spent on the multiple planes of the design's exterior walls and roof. Each additional plane, Kilper wrote, increased the cost of both construction and operation.[68] Yet every letter from a detractor like Kilper was answered in the paper by another museum supporter. The community debate continued in spurts for years—so much so that local cartoonist Chris OBrion wondered if anyone cared about any facet of the plan other than the architecture.

Despite these challenges, in April 2006, one year after its original planned groundbreaking, the museum chose to begin construction. Fralin, board president at the time, announced that work would begin as soon as possible because every month of waiting was costing the museum $400,000. The delays due to design decisions and fundraising progress had cost the museum millions because prices of raw materials had skyrocketed while they had been waiting. The hard costs of construction were now $40.5 million, with $66 million needed to cover the project's total costs. Of this money, $46 million had been raised. In order to begin work immediately, the museum secured a credit line with a limit of

Table 2.1. By the Numbers: The Impact of the Taubman Museum's New Building

	Before New Building	Aspirations for New Building	Year the New Building Opened
Museum's Resources			
Facilities			
Total space	~ 20,000 square feet	66,000 square feet	81,000 square feet
Gallery space	8,000 square feet	20,000 square feet	15,000 square feet
Seats in theater	0	150	150
Employees	20	55	17
Art acquisition budget	$1 million–$2 million per year		$60,000 per year
Public programs budget	$537,000		$800,000
Hindrances			
Long-term loans	$0	$0	$17 million
Annual fundraising requirement	$0.7 million	$1.5 million	$4.4 million

$20 million from Wachovia, SunTrust Bank, and the Virginia Tech Foundation. The museum planned to raise the remaining $30 million needed to complete the capital and endowment campaigns while the construction was ongoing.[69]

Yet another increase in the target of the museum's capital campaign was cause for an outcry from other cultural organizations. Since 2001, the fundraising climate in Roanoke had not improved. The competition had gotten so fierce that two different ballet companies presented two different *Nutcracker*s—a reliable revenue generator for ballets across the country—and feuded in the press about which production was the best. Some companies, like the Roanoke Symphony, blamed the art museum's capital campaign for their inability to run campaigns and endowment drives. In addition, they said they were seeing reductions in giving, with donors explaining that they were giving less owing to commitments to the art museum. By 2006, the increased competition for both fundraising and audiences was resulting in program cuts and deficits at Mill Mountain Theatre and the Jefferson Center for performing arts. In 2009, with the onset of the recession exacerbating the theater's situation even further, Mill Mountain announced it would close.[70] (See table 2.1.)

By the time of the new museum's opening in November 2008, $53 million of the $66 million needed had been raised. An 81,000 square foot building now belonged to the museum. Visitors entered a 4,600 square foot atrium that stretched the entire height of the building. The building had three floors, with a gift shop, café, catering kitchen, auditorium, theater, and education center on the first floor; galleries, storage, and the space planned for the IMAX projector on the second; and offices, as well as a board room and an events terrace, on the third. The first floor was below the flood plain and could not be used to exhibit art. The museum now has 15,000 square feet of gallery space—7,000 more than the gallery space at the Taubman's disposal at Center in the Square. This was in contrast to the original aspirations, which had called for 20,000 square feet of galleries in a 66,000 square foot building.[71]

In the first month, attendance was encouraging, reaching 20,000, but then the number of visitors declined. The total number of people who came to the Taubman Museum in the first year was 130,000—far below the projected 240,000–250,000.[72] Simultaneously, the cost of operating the facility exceeded expectations. By the end of July 2008, $14.4 million had been borrowed for construction. In the first year of expanded operations, an additional $2.8 million had been borrowed. This $17.2 million loan cost $945,000 in interest payments in FY2009, further stressing the budget. In FY2010, another $14.3 million in cash toward the building was raised and collected through a concerted effort of board and new leadership. Additionally, a loan of $4.4 million from trustees and other philanthropies permitted the museum to retire the construction loan in its entirety. Some of the benefactors do not expect to ever be repaid. Yet even with the loan retired, the museum still struggled to pay its expenses. The museum's cash flow statements reflected that cash produced by operating activities and contributions was $3.4 million less than cash spent for FY2009 and $1.3 million less than cash spent for FY2010. These shortfalls were covered by payments on the capital campaign intended to repay the building refinancing loans from donors and other foundations, who consented to the arrangement. The entrance fee was raised from $3 before the expansion to $10.50, then dropped again to $7 after community members expressed dismay. Four rounds of layoffs followed, reducing the staff from 52 employees at opening to 17 employees in September 2010. In that same month, citing family reasons, Jenny Taubman left the museum's board.[73] In a few short years, the museum had gone from a financially stable and accessible museum with a growing specialization in American paintings to a fiscally challenged institution that owned a large building. See figure 2.4.

The extraordinary expansion in the Taubman Museum project scope

2.4 The Taubman Museum of Art. Photo by Timothy Hursley/Taubman Museum of Art. Courtesy of Virginia Tourism Corporation.

thus came as the result of a gradual drift by small increments away from the original purpose. From attempting to preserve and display works of art, the trustees turned to attempting to create a piece of architecture that was art. From a project the purpose of which was to best display a small but distinguished group of paintings to their best advantage on the inside, the museum turned into a showcase of modern architecture, best enjoyed from without. The project, which started as a modest proposal to renovate a building in order to have a larger and leak-free exhibition space, turned into a quixotic quest to draw the eyes of the world to a small town in Western Virginia.

* * *

How well an organization handles the challenges of planning for its building needs has a profound impact on its vitality. A building project should be contemplated only in situations where the fit between community support and artistic offerings is already sound, to the mutual benefit of the artistic organizations and their host cities. Frequently, a new building is instead conceived as a method of making the community and artistic organizations fit together better—to furnish new sources of operating support, or to raise an organization's cachet in the philanthropic community, or to attract a better caliber of artist or collector with a new facility. From the cases we have studied, new buildings rarely fix these problems and frequently exacerbate them by taxing the organization with a heavier burden of operating and sometimes even interest expenses. However, in cases where the fit between the community and its arts programming is right, the cultural organizations may still face challenges that must be overcome to maximize impact. Tickets to performances might sell out quickly, but only to the loyal followers willing to pay top price, thus precluding a continued expansion of the organization's reach. Galleries may become too crowded. Backstage facilities and storage might become increasingly cramped, sometimes to the point of hampering further artistic growth. These problems are in fact best fixed by a well-managed and soundly envisioned new construction—assuming that inadequacies in the physical plant are the true barrier to continued mission attainment and growth.

A building's ability to accommodate an arts organization's needs is characterized by five traits: size, location, aesthetics, program-related capabilities, and revenue-generating spaces. Yet the degree to which any building will fit the needs of an artistic organization is contingent on its ability to realign its strategy to the facility. An assessment of the suitability of existing and planned facilities in the area to the current needs of an arts organization is the first step in cultural building planning. This process can unearth options for relocation or partnerships that had been ignored in favor of pursuing a dream of a new home. These options should be rationally evaluated and compared with an organization's needs. Many cities have plentiful cultural facilities to accommodate the true physical plant needs of the local arts organizations.[74]

The catalyst for many arts projects is often something other than these facility issues. The recent building boom suggests there's something inherently attractive to US arts organizations about building, and that the instinct to start is a deeply rooted one. Some organizations embark on projects because of gifts of money or "free" real estate, as in Roanoke. Others start because they receive gifts they consider small, and the organization's leaders believe they'll do better in a new, more prestigious building. Some projects start because an arts organization runs out of space and cannot accommodate its growing audience. Others start because attendance is sagging, and leadership believes this to be the fault of the building rather than programming, even if studies suggest that appeal of programs outweighs other considerations in decisions to purchase tickets.[75] In other words, instead of achieving community fit and strategic alignment through a recalibration of strategy, some arts organizations attempt to achieve these goals by risking their viability on a new building.

The idea that arts buildings should be built only in cases where the artistic offerings of the prospective beneficiaries and the community support for the arts are both at high levels is hardly revolutionary. Yet it is not reflected in practice. In some situations, the development of strategies designed to improve the fit between art and community is an appropriate first step. This may take time and effort, and require that building dreams be deferred. In cases where this match between the arts and community already exists, and when the facilities both existing and planned are deficient for the beneficiaries' needs, a building effort has a chance to deliver its promised impact.

Should the project proceed, its leaders must revisit periodically the nature and scope of the facility needs of the arts organization. The organization needs to test—and retest over time–the feasibility of its facility wish list and the soundness of its strategic alignment. In these deliberations, one of several central factors will be funding availability and requirements, a topic we take up next.

3 | *Seeking Funding*

Within the process of seeking strategic alignment in a cultural building project, money—its availability or its inaccessibility, for both construction and operations—is a force that can introduce many distortions. In many cultural infrastructure projects, the task of fundraising becomes so overriding and all-consuming that it eclipses or at least lowers in priority all other concerns.[1] Funding is at once the critical ingredient in all ambitious building programs and the greatest distraction to an organization seeking to maximize the quality and integrity of its work.[2]

One of the most crucial determinants of the funding process is its interaction and dependence on the process of physical design. For the purposes of funding, the most important outcome of the design process is its price tag, which commonly depends on project ambition. The decision making about facility requirements can be sensitive to changes and decisions in the funding situations, such as implementing cost-cutting measures or incorporating design elements that had previously been shelved to save money. The success of these two processes and how well they function in concert determine whether the organization opens its new or expanded facility with unanticipated debt obligations or fully in the black, perhaps even with a large operational reserve.

What imperils sound decision making for arts projects is the widespread forecast inaccuracy. In the world of megaprojects outside the arts, forecast inaccuracy is endemic. Previous studies on megaprojects suggest that underestimations of costs, both capital and operational, and overestimations of use and revenues are so prevalent that any given forecast is more likely to be wrong than right. In multiple studies, Bent Flyvbjerg has argued that these inaccuracies are strategic. He found that as many as 90 percent of megaprojects had forecasts that underestimated the true costs of construction. Meanwhile, overestimation of costs occurred very rarely, suggesting that there was a systematic bias toward underestimation. Moreover, accuracy has not improved over the past few decades, despite advances in forecasting methods. Therefore, Flyvbjerg concluded that forecasts of construction costs and future benefits are purposefully misleading, meant to persuade decision makers and key stakeholders to approve a project on the basis of spurious information. Flyvbjerg argues that this behavior is enabled by opportunism among project boosters and professional forecasters.[3]

A trend toward forecast inaccuracy can be observed within the world of the arts as well. In the broader research team survey of managers, most projects found that after opening, operating costs were above estimates and operating revenues below expectations.[4] Throughout the case studies we researched, the initial rough estimate for what the project would cost was usually an order of magnitude below the true cost of the project. The effect of this lowball estimate was predictable: It made the project seem feasible, and after the project team was committed, a realistic price tag was introduced after further study. The well-known cognitive bias toward irrational escalation of commitment seemed to be in play frequently, as even the most skeptical leaders chose to stay the course despite mounting costs.

Forecasts are based on many assumptions, and through these, cognitive biases and self-serving agendas enter the equation. Donors and other powerful stakeholders like local governments scrutinize finances, ask for construction and operational forecasts, and then reward optimism with grants.[5] In this environment, instead of being used as tools for operational planning, forecasts are used as tools for fundraising. Meanwhile, professional consultants who are counted on to provide objective opinions depend on the sponsoring organizations' recommendations and endorsements for securing their next jobs. All of these forces conspire to distort forecast reliability.

One subconscious bias at play here is the "planning fallacy," or the tendency toward optimism by insiders making "intuitive forecasts," first described by Daniel Kahneman in his Nobel Prize–winning work.[6] Indeed, most cultural sector forecasts are based on intuition. Frequently, forecasters take either a "top down" or a "bottom up" approach. A "bottom up" approach will be based on a set of assumptions, such as cost to build per square foot or the average ticket price. Some "bottom up" models are extremely detailed. For example, they may factor in the average amount spent by each patron on parking and concessions. This detail frequently makes the models feel more trustworthy and substantial, even if in the end they are based on insider guesswork—in other words, precisely the sorts of "intuitive forecasts" that Kahneman demonstrated to be vulnerable to subconscious biases. "Top down" models are similarly flawed. They usually begin with some baseline—like current season's sales—and assume improvement or growth (or sometimes decline). Assumptions about the rate of growth are prone to the same bias.

Benchmarks are sometimes used to substantiate forecasts. Thus, the assumptions about forecast model line items like cost per square foot or revenue growth in the year after opening are compared with the actual performance of organizations with completed projects. This practice is a move in the right direction, since benchmarks can provide the much-needed outsider view to temper insider bias toward optimism. Yet the benchmarks selected are usually few and selected in a subjective manner. Naturally, everyone wants to emulate successes and not failures, so successful projects are used as reference points. But a more realistic forecasting methodology will take into account a broad array of potential outcomes.

One forecasting methodology advocated by Flyvbjerg and now endorsed by the American Planning Association is reference class forecasting. Reference class forecasting depends on first identifying a "statistically meaningful" number of already completed projects that are comparable with the project under study. Second, forecasters tabulate a probability distribution for this reference class. Thus, they establish, for example, that construction cost overruns of 15 percent or less were experienced by just 5 percent of similar projects, while overruns of 50 percent or less were experienced by 15 percent of similar projects. This probability distribution helps forecasters determine the "uplift factor," or the percentage by which the forecast offered by insiders should be increased to achieve the desired certainty about total project costs. The purpose of this exercise is to eliminate conscious and unconscious bias from analysis by basing the forecast on known performance of comparable projects.[7]

Several barriers to sound forecasts are sector-level problems that will require leadership or coordination to solve. First, reference class forecasting requires accessible and reliable data to make a difference in forecast accuracy. Second, Flyvbjerg also suggests over a dozen new regulatory and market mechanisms for greater accountability for forecasts, including peer review and financial responsibility for forecast inaccuracies. These initiatives could result in better forecasts sector-wide.

What also contributes to the difficulty of construction cost forecasts is the simultaneity of the forecasting and design efforts. What usually happens is that different teams, whether composed of trustees or staff or a mix of both, undertake the capital campaign, the architectural design and building management, and the operational planning separately. With simultaneous design, building, fundraising, and operational planning efforts proceeding on parallel tracks, the average cultural sector building project takes about a decade to complete. If these decision-making processes were staggered, so that funding is secured before the architectural design process starts, and the operational costs are clear before the capital campaign is begun, these projects would take even longer, perhaps decades. This timing issue with phased development is joined by considerations of the relative uselessness of cost and operating estimates made years ahead of time and never again adjusted, as well as the infeasibility of asking for commitments from donors before the organization is seen to fully commit to a specific concept. Thus, the processes are simultaneous and highly iterative, with each round of the preliminary results of one decision-making process causing the need for course corrections in the other. The boards that embark on these projects must become accustomed to ever-shifting, mutually dependent, and uncertain plans.

Thus, one of the first and most critical decisions to be made with regard to funding is settling on a target budget and campaign goal for both processes to work toward at the outset. Both over- and underestimates of funds available and building program requirements are potentially perilous for project success. Artistic groups are incentivized to tailor a project's budget to the available funding. A building program far out of reach of its community's financial means risks at best the failure of the building effort to get off the planning board, or, at worst, the financial collapse of the artistic groups as the result of construction debt. The troubled births of the Adrienne Arsht Center in Miami and the Overture Center in Madison, Wisconsin, are infamous and well-known cautionary tales about how a project can bring an organization to the brink of extinction by far exceeding the affordable budget. The Taubman Museum case detailed previously is another example of how perilous overly ambitious goals and project scope can quickly become.

Yet, in its most extreme form, thrift at all junctures of capital planning also poses at least three significant risks. First, compromises on the project's scope—unnecessary in cases of an abundance of funding—can cause fissures in the community and lead to operational deficiencies. Too much economizing may drain the spirit of enthusiasm and diminish civic pride and commitment, with a "sensible design" disappointing some who want to make a grander statement. Second, a design with unnecessary compromises that cause operational deficiencies will hasten the time when this risky capital project process will be contemplated again. An organization must get it right the first time or risk needing to ask for a redo in the not-too-distant future. Third, a capital campaign that is too timid is a lost opportunity. In the current landscape, capital campaigns allow organizations to access otherwise unavailable sources of funding, and the stakes for capturing as much money as possible are high. This is especially true because capital campaigns provide opportunities to fund endowments and operational reserves for the new buildings in addition to the buildings themselves. A building allows the organization to claim a larger set of concerns, from community rejuvenation to civic pride, and these are of interest to a larger circle of funders.[8] The campaign can also add urgency and an attractive cause to appeals to long-time supporters as well as provide access to capital improvement grants from local, state, and national governments. In today's environment, a capital campaign is sometimes the only way of capturing these funds.[9] The opportunity cost of leaving money on the table is high, and the ideal project will be scoped to capture every dollar available.

Across many of the projects we examined, we found that most projects follow one of four possible paths with regard to balancing the funding and design equation. When funding is tight and where the project budget is modest, organizations execute small "lily pad" projects that meet an immediate critical space need and have a very clearly defined scope from the start. At a later time, when a higher level of community commitment is achieved, the resident organizations may leap from this lily pad to a larger project. When money looks to be plentiful and the project budget is pegged at a high number, arts organizations work toward the realization of a dreamlike "palace." Such facilities are usually designed to afford their resident organizations room to grow. When ample funding is potentially available from the community but the organization settles on a limited scale project, a "compromise" project results, one that could have achieved more if only the vision were broader and more ambitious. Finally, there are certainly many instances when substantial funding is simply not available but where the organization nevertheless plows ahead with a high-budget project, resulting all too often in a failure, where financial and operating crises plague the organization from Day One as it

Table 3.1. Aligning Funding and Project Scope

		Program Scope / Budget	
		Low	High
Funding Availability	Low	Alignment on a small "lily pad project"	Danger of project and organizational failure
	High	Risk of unnecessary compromises	Alignment on an ambitious "palace for the arts"

attempts to pay debts, meet payroll, and operate a facility that is simply unaffordable.

While it would be tempting in the name of conceptual hygiene to assert that projects start and end in one of the four quadrants in table 3.1, the reality is that projects have a way of starting off in one cell only to migrate to another cell over time. Sometimes this is due to inaccurate projections of the giving potential in the community. Sometimes it is a function of unrealistic budgeting that fails to come to terms with the expensive tastes of those planning the project. A modest "lily pad" project can turn into a "failure" when extra windows are added, when a second staircase is thrown into the plan at the end, or when expensive acoustic baffles are ordered as a final addition to the plan. Just as common is the mutation of a "palace" for the arts into an abject "failure" when fundraising falls off after ground is broken or when consultants overestimate giving potential and a star architect comes up with a design that is too expensive to build and operate. Other mutations across the cells of the table are possible too. Suffice to say that the critical interplay of funding availability and project budget will predict a great deal about what happens over the course of a complex and arduous building project.

The ways in which arts groups specifically access the capital market increase the difficulty of deciding on a budget. Outside the cultural sector, most buildings have a budget determined by known financial figures like a homebuyer's savings and salary, or the expected return on investment for a new for-profit production facility. Inside the cultural sector, the preferred sources for funds are gifts and grants. For any given project in the cultural sector, the total amount that an organization can afford to spend is determined by the inclinations, shifting economic fortunes, and political considerations of hundreds if not thousands of potential funders.[10] How many of them will give once asked and how much they will give are large unknowns. In any capital campaign, surprises are par for the course. Thus, unlike organizations and individuals in other sectors, arts organizations rarely start their projects knowing exactly how much they can afford to spend. Yet both the fundraising and the architectural design processes demand that at least preliminary budget and capital campaign targets be set in the beginning.

Faced with large commitments to architectural design and construction costs and frequent struggles to meet them by their capital campaign committee, many organizations look to loans.[11] Financing is usually available only to the largest and most well-established arts organizations, those with large assets like other buildings and endowments already on their balance sheets. Smaller organizations can access loans often only through the intercession of governments or wealthy benefactors willing to provide guarantees. Once a campaign is underway, however, a loan against gifts already pledged becomes possible. In many cases, private donors will make large gifts that are paid over a period of up to five years. Loans against these signed donor pledges can be an effective method of managing cash flow—they can ensure that the money to pay the architects, professional consultants, and construction contractors is available at the time it's needed, rather than years later when it's scheduled to be paid. For larger projects, such cash flow management methods may be essential. However, the danger in this approach is the temptation to use their abundance of cash to become less stringent with their expenses. During the latest building boom, many organizations used these types of loans to increase their project budgets above what they could reasonably raise. In the heyday of the early 2000s economic boom, some even counted on making money on their financing deals as the result of arbitrage between returns on investing their cash in the stock market and the low interest loans they could secure through municipal bonds. Actual market performance over the past decade led several such schemes to end in financial disaster. Even without plans to get rich in the stock market, loans that will not be covered by gifts and grants secured by the capital campaigns before the construction is complete pose a significant burden and risk for the cultural organization. The best case scenario is interest exerting stress on operating budgets, and fundraising efforts that must remain focused on closing the capital campaign to the detriment of operating funds and endowments for years to come. The worst case scenario is insolvency.

Preparing for the impact of the capital project and campaign on the long-term financial health of the organization and its stakeholders is essential within the fundraising and strategic planning processes.[12] As in the case of the Taubman Museum of Art in Roanoke, capital projects can land previously stable organizations into states of financial crisis. Even if an organization manages its campaign and the design process well enough to permit opening their building without taking out large loans, new buildings tend to lead to operating deficits. The most pessimistic arts leaders we interviewed believe that all new construction leads to deficits. The best-planned projects set targets for operational funds to be raised during the capital campaign to cover shortages from the very start. For some, these operational funds take the form of building an endowment.[13] Others raise a reserve fund that will be available to cover several years of deficits after project opening.[14]

Regrettably, even in the few campaigns that incorporate such operating funds into their targets, they are usually prioritized last. When they also end up being raised last, the practice of multiyear payment schedules on pledges means that the cash is not actually paid in time to make the money available during the crucial years directly after opening. The discipline to reserve some portion of every dollar paid into the capital campaign for operations *as it comes in* could have a profound positive impact on organizations' fortunes. The same could be said for donors who make their pledges conditional on such practice. In any case, what is certain is that capital projects require funding not only for the bricks and mortar, but also for the organizational resources that will be required to make any capital project a success after all the construction is complete. To manage the risks of undertaking a capital project, the raising of operational funds should be an integral part of every campaign.

A Tale of Two Capital Campaigns: The Art Institute of Chicago and the AT&T Performing Arts Center in Dallas

Over the past decade, two arts organizations have distinguished themselves by the scale of their capital campaigns and their ambition.[15] The AT&T Performing Arts Center (once known as the Foundation for the Dallas Performing Arts Center) had a capital campaign target of over

$300 million for new facilities downtown. The Art Institute of Chicago set its campaign goal for a new wing even higher, at over $400 million. Yet in pursuit of these comparably ambitious goals, these organizations sometimes made divergent choices about strategy and method. In Dallas, an early—and modest—estimate of donor giving capacity was rejected because it did not fit the intended scope of the project. In moving ahead with a project where funding and budget seemed initially out of alignment, the leaders in Dallas gambled that fundraising and feasibility study estimates were in fact too low. In Chicago, as the project budget grew with the addition of a pedestrian bridge and an extra building floor, there was a risk of financial overexposure and the question of whether adequate operating funds would be raised to operate the expensive new building once it opened.

How much money can be responsibly sought for the project? How should the campaign be led and structured? What role does preparation for funding future expanded operations in the newly (re)opened building need to play in planning? For every project, these decisions are pivotal. Each of our two organizations' answers to these questions are crucial not only to meeting the fundraising goal for the specific project, but also for the organization's long-term strategic alignment and success.

Project Genesis and Decisions about Scale

For the first few years, the goal of creating a new Dallas performing arts center was advanced actively by just three people. All three were trustees of either the Dallas Opera or the Dallas Theater Center (DTC), and two of them, John Dayton and Bess Enloe, had once been presidents of their boards. The two companies had explored the idea of building a new joint home before, in the 1980s, but gave up because of adverse conditions. Now Dayton and Enloe, who had been friends for decades, had been asked to study the project again. They met in their living rooms. Except for personal assistants employed by individual members, the project was being run by volunteers without any professional staff. They did, however, eventually retain multiple top-tier professional consulting firms to help them plan the effort.

In early 2000, their professional consultants informed the nascent board of a $100 million chasm between their ambitions and their means. The project cost was estimated by Donnell Consultants at $265 million. This budget projection was based on a preliminary building program written by the board, with the assistance of other consultants, after two years of conversations with future resident groups and other community stakeholders. The AT&T Performing Arts Center (PAC) planners knew that the costs of running the campaign, acquiring the land, clearing the site, creating parking, paying for construction bonds, starting an operational endowment, and staging public events like groundbreaking, as well as other miscellanea, would increase that budget further. Meanwhile, another consultant, the Brakeley Company, thought the AT&T PAC capital campaign could reasonably expect to raise no more than $160 million in private, philanthropic support. The city of Dallas expected to fund some of the costs with municipal bonds and would eventually make an $18 million investment in the AT&T PAC, as well as furnish some land. Yet the gap between expected costs and expected funds remained large.

Just as the consultants delivered their reports, the AT&T PAC hired its first staff member—the founding president and CEO, Bill Lively. Lively had a master's in education and started his career as a member of the faculty at the Southern Methodist University in Dallas, where he eventually became the associate dean of the arts school and then the vice president for development and public affairs. In that capacity, Lively had designed and directed a campaign that raised $280 million for the university before his departure. A native Dallasite, a gaunt man, and an avid mountain climber, Lively knew Dallas and its donors; he was a singular fundraiser with a lifelong passion for music and football. "I don't think he ever sleeps," said Enloe.

One challenge accepted by both Lively and the board in his hiring was his lack of experience building, programming, or operating a performing arts venue. The board chose him and he took the job since during his tenure at AT&T PAC he would have one main responsibility: raising money. "I didn't want to run the center. I wanted to build it," said Lively. "Bill wanted to raise the money for what we wanted to build," said AT&T PAC and DTC trustee Deedie Rose. "He didn't want to tell anyone what to build or how to build it. That was the kind of CEO he was." Lively was conscious that the organization needed to face other challenges, like planning its operations and its finances, but both he and the board thought that the majority of his time needed to be dedicated to devising and executing a strategy for the capital campaign, and that others—including trustees, professional consultants, and other staff, once they were hired—would do the bulk of the work necessary for success after opening. Once the center approached its first season in 2009–10, a new president would be hired to oversee programming and operations. Lively would move on to work his fundraising magic elsewhere.

The disconnect between cost and funding projections was one of the first questions Lively had to address. The board's certainty about key aspects of the building program limited the prospects for a reduction in estimated costs. They were committed to building a campus of two buildings: an opera hall and a dramatic theater. They also felt strongly that the architecture had to be distinctive and that certain technical standards with regards to acoustics and backstage capabilities had to be met. These characteristics were nonnegotiable because both the Dallas Theater Center and the Dallas Opera already had performance venues. To them, the most important aspect of the future facility, the aspect that would justify the expense, was an improvement in the artistic capabilities of the new space.

Both the opera and the DTC wanted to move owing to the limitations of the venues in which they performed. Founded in 1957, the Dallas Opera was recognized as a leading regional opera company and aspired to become one of the top opera companies in the nation, a peer to the Lyric Opera of Chicago and the San Francisco Opera. This aspiration required the company to grow both financially and artistically, but in its home, the Fair Park Music Hall, further growth along either dimension seemed unlikely. "It is a roadshow house," said Dayton about the Music Hall, "meant to receive traveling Broadway shows, not a facility that had anywhere near the stage capabilities to support a regional opera company. It's a cinematic auditorium, meaning it's fan-shaped, clearly designed for amplified sound, not for raw voice. The symphony got out as soon as they could, and the opera wanted to follow close on their heels."

In addition to limiting the quality of the opera's productions with its poor acoustics, small stage, and cramped backstage, the city-owned Music Hall also prevented the opera from expanding its season, and therefore its budget and audience. In 1998, the opera had an annual budget of about $9 million, roughly twice its size a decade earlier. About 40 percent of its revenues came from ticket sales, and about 50 percent from contributions. Its seasons consisted of five productions with 21 performances. It had 11,000 subscribers and filled an average of 90 percent of the Music Hall's 3,420 seats with paying ticket-buyers. The percentage of the total seats sold had flatlined in recent years. Expanding the season seemed like the only way to continue growing, but the Music Hall's schedule was full, with performances by Dallas Summer Musicals, a Broadway series, and the Texas Ballet.

For all these reasons, the opera wanted a new home. However, it could neither mount a successful capital campaign of sufficient size nor fill a venue's schedule on its own. "Dallas Opera was an institution that couldn't justify a facility of this size and cost by itself. It would need to partner with other cultural institutions to make this a viable, long-term operating facility," said Dayton.

A partnership with the DTC—a seasoned group with an artistic reputation and financial stability on par with the opera's—seemed like a logical choice. The Dallas Theater Center was founded in 1959 and had since become an acclaimed regional theater company with a professional resident troupe of actors. In 1992, DTC had sold almost 100,000 tickets; by 1997, that number was down to 82,000. In 1998, the DTC had a budget of $3.9 million, with ticket sales of $1.4 million and contributions of $2.4 million, but the general trend in ticket and subscription sales was still one of decline. The DTC curtailed the number of performances, but still the overall percentage of capacity sold declined, too.

"We've had the same artistic director for 15 years, and things around here just got stagnant, with our programming and our fundraising and our ticket sales. There was no enthusiasm, no excitement, there was nothing building for this place," said the managing director of the DTC, Mark Hadley. "We were in a 50-year-old building designed by Frank Lloyd Wright, which was very comfortable for the patrons, but backstage, it was very hard on us to produce theater. It boxed us in in terms of what we could do."

Unlike the opera, the DTC had complete control over the operations and scheduling at its two venues, the Kalita Humphreys Theater and the Arts District Theater, both of which it managed. In the Kalita, the company was severely handicapped by the theater's technical limitations, and in the Arts District Theater by financial ones. The Kalita's backstage areas were dark, cramped, and in need of repair. Frank Lloyd Wright had been opposed to elevators in principle, and only one was installed for transporting sets to the stage from the loading dock. According to legend, the elevator had to be hidden from Wright by stacks of boxes when he came to visit. The flyhouse could support only a limited weight and had just nine lines for flying in sets, though the DTC had jerry-rigged some extra ones over the years. The house had 491 seats. Of these seats, for the previous decade the DTC had filled just 61 percent. Because the DTC had built the theater, the city allowed the company its almost exclusive use for $1 per year. The DTC offices were next to the Kalita, as were the homes of many of the company's wealthy subscribers, who lived in Highland Park. Hadley thought the proximity of this affluent enclave made the DTC seem elitist, whereas a downtown location would make the theater seem more accessible. Attendance at the temporary Arts District Theater confirmed this suspicion.

Overall, embarking on a plan to build the performing arts center represented a risk for the DTC. In initial discussions, a seating capacity of 700 was floated for the theater, and the company wondered whether it could fill all those seats. Eventually, the capacity was revised down, to 575. The rent would certainly be higher than the $1 per year paid at the Kalita Humphreys. Yet a flexible, technologically advanced new theater would offer the DTC a blank canvas. The excitement around a new, marquee building in downtown Dallas would give the company an opportunity for rebirth.

This context shaped the AT&T PAC leadership team's approach to finding and evaluating solutions for the projected gap between design cost and available funding. The opera house would be built first, with the $160 million in philanthropic funds projected by Brakeley. A multiform theater for the DTC would follow in a second phase. However, the DTC feared that the first phase would exhaust funds and community enthusiasm for a new performing arts facility. Enloe had even asked her friend and the DTC chairwoman at the time, Deedie Rose, to join the AT&T PAC board so as to prevent the phasing plan. "The Theater Center is the smaller nonprofit, and we'd help the opera hall get built, but then the theater would never happen," said Rose. After the phasing plan was scrapped owing to the DTC's objections, the board was left with only two options for dealing with the gap between cost and funding estimates: discarding either the project or the Brakeley study. "If we do believe the report, we shouldn't start this project, because there's not going to be enough money to build it," said Lively.

The Brakeley Company's approach to quantifying a reasonable goal for the Dallas capital campaign was to conduct confidential interviews with Dallas donors. In these conversations, Brakeley shared a preliminary case statement for the proposed performing arts center and asked its interviewees about any potential causes for hesitation, as well as the size of their potential gifts and their expectations about who else would give and how much. In its report, Brakeley outlined the key considerations that could limit the size of philanthropic pledges and concluded that the scope of the project needed to be revised and the capital campaign goal set at $160 million.

In the end, Lively chose to think of the Brakeley report as limited in its conclusions about the availability of funds among traditional arts donors. "That study was addressing predominantly reliable sources who had some history giving to a project such as this," said Lively. "We knew we had to identify a whole other legion of donors." A project like the AT&T PAC had never been attempted in Dallas before, and some of the donors the center needed to involve had never given in Dallas or to the arts. Thus, their future gifts could not be captured in a study, and Lively's approach to establishing a realistic target for fundraising was based on a best guess, combined with his knowledge of Dallas and his experience fundraising there. For him, there were two key questions. First, was there enough wealth in Dallas to pay for the project? The answer to the first question was a resounding yes. Second, could the AT&T PAC motivate a sufficient portion of the individuals, foundations, and companies who held this wealth to fund their project? "You can't scientifically quantify that," Lively said. "A capital campaign is a psychological exercise, and if you doubt you can do it, you can't do it," Lively said. "Was it risky? Absolutely."

"I walked into the first meeting, and I said, here's where we are, board members," Lively remembered. "We have a vision. We have us. And we have a feasibility study that was developed by the Brakeley Company, and that feasibility study says, 'We might be able to raise up to $160 million to build a world-class center.' But you can't rebuild the Meyerson next door for that. So this study is of no use to us." Lively continued, "Can we do this? Absolutely. We have to believe in it and have to be faithful to the mission, and here we go."

That day, the trustees voted to proceed with a campaign to raise $275 million. Following the meeting, Lively got each of his board members a copy of Stephen Ambrose's *Undaunted Courage*, a book about Lewis and Clark's exploration of the American West. He asked them all to read it that night. "If [Lewis and Clark] could do that, we could do this," he said. A year later, he gave them copies of *The Devil in the White City*, the story of Chicago's 1893 World's Columbian Exposition, another building project that at first seemed daunting. That book began with a quote from Daniel Burnham himself: "Make no little plans; they have no magic to stir men's blood."

Deciding on Project Scale at the Art Institute of Chicago

In Chicago, the capital campaign for the new wing of the Art Institute of Chicago was equally ambitious, but the approach to the capital campaign target differed in several critical ways. First, unlike the Dallas PAC, the Art Institute of Chicago was an existing institution that had to simultaneously face the rigors of the capital campaign and continue its uninterrupted daily operations. Second, in Chicago the board considered the physical requirements of the building more flexible than their building budget; in fact, they changed direction, concepts, and scope at several junctures. Still, the capital campaign target was a shifting goal too, contracting and expanding, frequently in lockstep with the US economy. Third, the Art Institute made an addition to its endowment to fund the new wing's operations part of its capital campaign target from the start, which increased their target and fundraising pressure.

At the Art Institute of Chicago (AIC), the Modern Wing was a project born of opportunity. In the late 1990s, a handful of Chicago philanthropists who had long supported the Art Institute of Chicago told the museum's president and CEO, James Wood, that they were ready to contribute to another capital project. "It's quite Chicago, in a way," said Wood in an interview. "Loyal supporters of the institution saying, 'If you're getting to that point, we'd like to try to help, but we're not sure what the amount could be.' It was the first inkling that people to whom we would go for money wouldn't be averse to the idea." Wood was responsive to the suggestion. The US economy was booming. The high-tech sector was growing at a particularly quick rate, churning out initial public offerings and overnight millionaires. The economic situation boded well for funding an expansion.

Former board chairman John Bryan described the idea as first mentioned to him as follows: "Jim Wood had an idea that he wanted to do a small, jewel-like building on the south side of the railroad tracks there. Not quite sure what for, but it was time to build." Bryan added: "He [Wood] was not an expansionist. . . . He was not someone who wanted to do something grand. He wanted to do something reasonably small and high quality and was very interested in the architecture." Indeed, architecture and travel were two of Wood's great pleasures in life. Now, as he was approaching the end of his career, the board would offer him a chance to do both.

There was also an ever-present internal rationale for building: the need for more gallery space. "It was clear given the scale of our collections that we desperately needed more space to do justice to the things you'd like to have on view relatively permanently," said Wood. "There's this sense of responsibility—are we making the most of our collections?" The Art Institute's encyclopedic collection was one of the most renowned in the United States, certainly the best in the Midwest, with only a portion of its approximately 225,000 separate objects on public display at any given moment. The majority of these objects belonged to the fragile photography, print, or textile collections, items that could be displayed only for short periods in order to comply with conservation guidelines. Some had significance but were not of the caliber that justified permanent display. According to a former senior administrator at the institute, the consensus among staff was that the AIC's space was sufficient for most collections, but that the African and pre-Columbian collections had a critical need for more gallery space. Also, additions to the collections would inevitably lead to a space shortage at some point in the future. For these reasons, the curatorial staff was enthusiastic about the initial plans for a small addition to the museum. After an interview with the official spokeswoman, the *Chicago Sun-Times* described the Art Institute's view of itself as "not overly cramped but can always use more room." In other words, the Art Institute had a long-term need for an expansion but was not suffering acutely from a shortage of space or its imperfections at the time they started planning to add more. The expansion was a capital project waiting for the right timing.

An additional reason to build was ensuring the continued relevance of the Art Institute and its renewal. "I think if we hadn't done that, we would be in the class of the venerable but not very exciting," said John Nichols, another past chairman of the Art Institute board of trustees. The Modern Wing project began during Nichols's tenure, and he was both an advocate and a donor for whom a bridge leading to the new building is named. All around them, the city of Chicago was changing. The museum building boom in Chicago and across the United States also influenced the decision to build. "Certainly, the environment everybody knew was okay," said Bryan. "I must say that I think a lot of it is that you'd look a bit lazy if you didn't [build] at that time because it was popping out all over. The museums in Chicago—all of them—did something to their infrastructure in that period of time. Museums around the country were announcing here and there. And Jim [Wood] sort of caught the fever." Wood in turn thought that the optimistic spirit of the time influenced the board: "This was in a climate where many museums were contemplating expansion. . . . The board was confident they could do something. Then the question was really going to be to define the scale of the ambition."

The first step in moving the project forward was selecting an architect. Bryan believed that Wood, whose taste he fully trusted, was better qualified to select an architect than a committee of trustees. Bryan had seen the board committee model misfire at Chicago's Museum of Contemporary Art, where a new building—picked by a committee—was savaged by the architectural press. After seeing museums built across the world and meeting with architects, Wood settled on Renzo Piano, who had just won the Pritzker Prize in Architecture in 1998.

Before Piano's involvement, Wood and the staff thought the building would be about 70,000 square feet. A site development study conducted by Skidmore, Owings, and Merrill in 1996 identified three potential sites for additions, and Wood and his team chose one of them—an extension of the existing building southward of Gunsaulus Hall. The new wing would sit on a platform over the rail lines, thus providing both additional gallery space and a loop for visitors to take while seeing the galleries on both sides of the tracks. However, all of these ideas would be subject to alteration during the collaboration with Piano. Even the programmatic vision for this addition—which collections would go where, how much gallery space there would be, and how the new galleries would alter the flow of visitors through the museum—would be up for discussion.

Like most visionary architects, Piano arrived at the project with his own set of expectations. "He certainly had no interest in a jewel-box stuck on the side of the Art Institute," said Bryan. In interviews with the press, both Piano and fellow Pritzker Prize winner Frank Gehry joked about their buildings competing with each other from the two sides of Columbus Drive—Piano with his Art Institute addition and Gehry with his Millennium Park.

From the start, Piano pressed Wood to expand the scale of the museum's ambition. Piano wanted to give architectural definition to the museum's labyrinth of galleries and to create a "magical" public space to anchor the maze. "I still believe," he wrote to Wood in 1999, "following my visit and our conversations, that you need to establish a general vision at the urban scale (as well as, of course, at the functional and cultural level). You need to give 'unity' to the entire complex in the general 'diversity' so well expressing the museum's growth and history. My feeling is that by solving the connection across the railways, you need a Piazza or a Courtyard that may become a self-orienting centre of gravity."[16]

The different goals that a new addition could achieve and the many architectural concepts that could be used to achieve them became the focus of years of meetings and presentations. Over the course of this process, the project's goals expanded and evolved. James Cuno, the man who followed Wood in Chicago, wrote:

> It is difficult to overestimate the investment of emotions involved in developing and refining a design scheme. Every participant has a strong view as to the potential of the project. The architect sees the larger picture and cannot easily limit his concerns to just a part of it . . . The director, on the other hand, must always maintain the balance between what is needed—or at times *desired*—and what is affordable, financially

and politically. Ultimately the director has to convince the Board of Trustees that the project justifies the risk to be undertaken in funding it: what once was discussed as 70,000 square feet and later revised to 75,000 square feet has now become 197,000 square feet and easily more than twice as expensive. Why had this happened? Because the more one learns about a project and a site, the more one understands what needs—indeed *ought*—to be done. With every iteration of the design, with every workshop meeting, the project gets larger and more expensive, as well as more desirable and convincing.[17]

Eventually, Wood and Piano settled on a wing of approximately 290,000 square feet. After the first design, built over the railroad tracks that bisect the museum, proved prohibitively expensive, they started over again at a different site on the Art Institute of Chicago campus, but now with an agreement on an expanded scope. However, Wood was nervous about the size. As early as the railroad tracks plan, he wrote to Piano that he wanted a plan that would allow for the construction to be staged "so that our Board of Trustees will have choices as to how much we would need to commit at the outset."[18]

This expansion in scope also worried some among the Art Institute staff. When the expansion was first proposed—as Wood's "jewel-box" of a building—the staff was united in its enthusiasm. However, according to a report of a former senior administrator, as the planning continued and the scope and budget for the building expanded, the staff grew increasingly worried. The administrator said that the project always seemed motivated mainly by external considerations, like the nationwide museum building boom and the Millennium Park project, whereas the Art Institute's main institutional need, in this interviewee's view, was the continued building of the endowment. He said that as the project progressed, and its scope expanded, more and more staff became concerned. At this time, museums like the Milwaukee Art Museum and the Cleveland Art Museum were opening new buildings and expansions only to find that their financial projections had been overly optimistic. As a result, they had been forced to curtail programming and lay off staff. Troubled by these institutions' experiences and the Art Institute project's growing size and cost, the staff expressed their misgivings confidentially, to trustees with whom they were close.

From the time of Piano's selection in 1999 to the fall of 2004, the design underwent a number of changes, some small and some not so small. After twelve months of work and eight workshop meetings with the Art

Institute representatives, Piano produced a design for a building sited on the northeast quadrant of the Art Institute campus. At first, five floors were planned for this building, but soon the number of floors was cut to four. The entrance to the new wing was moved from Columbus Avenue to Monroe Avenue, bringing about the first discussions of how to get the pedestrians across that street from the Millennium Park and its new underground garage. A sub-basement meant for preservation and storage purposes was removed from the plans. Many of these changes were made, at least in part, because of Wood's nervousness over the final price and the worsening economy. "Clearly, the building was becoming more rational, as was the program," Cuno wrote in his essay about the design process.[19]

In September 2002, citing the difficulty of fundraising in the post-9/11 economy, Wood wrote to Piano to say that the production of construction drawings would be put on hold.[20] Piano greeted this news with unhappiness but continued refining his concept. He revised continually, producing a new version every few months, sometimes to the consternation of the building committee of the board of trustees, whose members would become concerned over the growing list of alterations, and the impact of these on the construction schedule and budget.[21] Nonetheless, every month of the delay seemed to give Piano more time to sharpen his ideas. "These were not minimal changes, but they were brilliant," wrote Cuno about one such revision.[22]

Whether the price tag rose or fell, then-chairman John Bryan seemed undaunted by the funding task. He thought that "value engineering" efforts—revising a design in order to bring down costs—tended to produce buildings with problems. "I'm not someone who meddles," he said of his leadership style. "I'd rather the professionals do their work and boards find the money."

Finding the money was exactly what Bryan concerned himself with as the design proceeded. Another trustee crucial in the fundraising efforts was capital campaign chair Lou Sussman, whose fundraising experience came mostly from the political world, where large sums are amassed through many smaller contributions that are "bundled" and gifts are solicited and received in a matter of minutes, not months. Sussman had been extremely successful as a fundraiser for both the Kerry and Obama presidential campaigns. He was rewarded with an ambassadorship to Great Britain for his tenacity. Both Sussman and Bryan were helped in fundraising by the Art Institute staff.

The first stage of the campaign was difficult. The Art Institute had

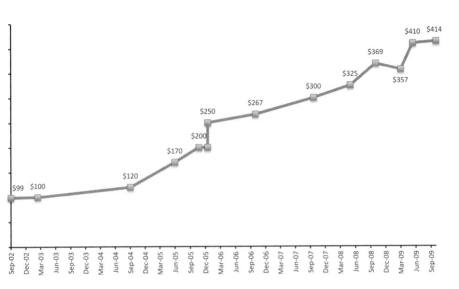

3.1 Art Institute of Chicago Capital Campaign: $ Millions Pledged.

decided to seek $50 million for the naming rights to the new wing, but for years no one stepped forward with a gift of that size. Unlike traditional campaigns, which proceed from the largest gifts to the smaller ones, the Art Institute did not secure its lead gift until 2005—six years after Piano's selection as architect and the beginning of the planning process. The largest capital campaign undertaken by the institution up until this time was the roughly $60 million raised for the endowment and various small projects in 1995. Despite the Art Institute's size and venerability, the Modern Wing capital campaign was thus unprecedented in scale for the organization. After the first $50 million–$60 million was pledged, the money became easier to find, Bryan said. In fact, he said, he was skeptical of the idea that the campaign was affected by the national economy's fluctuations (he once joked to a reporter that the tech bubble bursting did not matter for the campaign because the newly minted high-tech millionaires had not had time to become philanthropists). However, other project leaders, like Cuno and Wood, attributed the acceleration and deceleration in funds raised to the economic situation. See figure 3.1.

Design Progress

Piano was given the go-ahead to produce construction drawings by the board in February 2003. By November, he wrote to Wood, urging that the proposed start of demolition work in May 2004 be approved by the board too. But the board had set a preliminary target of $150 million in pledges that they wanted to be raised before construction work actually started, figuring that having commitments for 75 percent of the building budget would be sufficient for the trustees to feel confident that the capital campaign could be finished by the proposed opening date. The demolition date was not approved.[23] Some trustees sought clearer answers to the questions and concerns.

At this point in time, two events added urgency to the desire of project proponents to proceed. First, the leadership at the Art Institute changed. Second, Chicago and its Millennium Park were selected to host the annual Pritzker Prize in Architecture ceremony. In 2004, Jim Cuno replaced James Wood, who had led the Art Institute since 1980. Just like Wood, Cuno was trained as a curator. He had previously led the Harvard University Art Museums and the Courtauld Institute of Art in London. He had also worked with Piano before, on a new museum for Harvard that was ultimately scuttled. The AIC expansion was begun by Wood and Nichols in 1999, but Wood always proceeded with extreme financial caution. "Jim [Wood] was a great director, but was very conservative on fiscal matters. Jim [Wood] was always very nervous about the money," said Nichols. Jim Cuno "was very conscious of it, but he was more of a builder than Jim [Wood] was." With Cuno joining the leadership team, Bryan was joined by a fellow optimist. "Jim Cuno never saw a building he didn't want to build," he joked. The difference in leadership approaches taken by Wood and Cuno was subtle, yet still added pressure to proceed.

At about the same time, Chicago's Millennium Park, located across the street from the Art Institute's most unseemly side, was chosen as the 2005 site of the Pritzker Prize in Architecture ceremony. Millennium Park was an urban rejuvenation project, a park of manicured gardens, spacious lawns, and displays of public art. The park and its outdoor performance amphitheater were designed by Frank Gehry and built atop a rail yard in the heart of Chicago. Despite public and private rumblings about cost overruns, and an intermittent political tug of war starting in the early phases of planning, Millennium Park became a sensation on opening day. Throngs of tourists and Chicago residents inundated the new facility. In the three days of opening festivities alone, Millennium Park was visited by 300,000 people. And shortly, the international architectural press and some of the world's most acclaimed architects were coming there for the Pritzker Prize ceremony.

Cuno described this moment as follows: "We were less than half money raised, and there was no indication of when we would get trustee approval to go forward with the building. To break ground. To really commence." And now the architectural world was coming to the Art Institute's front door. "We were sitting here, stalled, with this dynamic success across the street, a site from which you looked on to the worst side of the Art Institute—a derelict building on the corner, a loading dock, a railway. It was just not what you wanted to do."

The pace of fundraising was increasing, however, and Cuno was anxious to start. The construction work would take three and a half years—a significant period in which to finish fundraising. Given its financial condition, the Art Institute would be able to secure bridge financing, or a bank line of credit, to cover initial construction costs, a strategy which would help alleviate any cash flow challenges. Cuno believed the capital campaign would pick up speed once construction started. "It's one thing for me to say 'Please support this project—we might build a building someday.' It's another thing for me to say 'Please support this project—we *are* building a building.'"

The most committed holdouts against the immediate start of construction were members of the finance committee who wanted to see a financially conservative plan. Then-treasurer David Vitale summarized their position: "You should raise the money before you commit the museum to that big a financial exposure." His finance committee wanted to see the financial challenges of operating in the existing building—both the severe losses in the endowment in 2001, and an existing operating deficit—fully addressed first. "We had more complexity to the financial situation than just the building of a new building," he said. "We had a bunch of financial stuff that created some anxiety about this project on the part of those who were more fiscally conservative."

In addition, people were concerned that the total cost of the project had seemed like a moving target. How could they authorize starting if they didn't know how large the project was actually going to be? Piano and Wood had kept the cost of the design of the new Modern Wing itself under the initial cap of $200 million, but now additional enhancements and changes, many with unclear costs, were under discussion. These additions included the pedestrian bridge across Monroe Street to Millennium Park. In order to ensure that the bridge's slope was gentle enough for wheelchairs, the new building needed another floor so that the bridge had a viable terminus. And Piano still wanted to include some of the com-

3.2 Winspear Opera House by Andreas Praefcke. Creative Commons Attribution 3.0 license.

ponents of his initial design for the other side of the museum. Notably, this entailed replacing a wall of an existing hall with glass. "Frankly, as the building went on, it started to get more expensive, at least in aggregate," said Vitale.

Last but not least, some trustees were concerned about the overall scope of the campaign. Despite the Art Institute's significant size, reputation, and history, nothing of this scale had ever been attempted there before. The largest campaign to date had been for $60 million. "All of a sudden, the conversation about how much this whole project was going to cost . . . was going well north of $300 [million], and that created some anxiety in people's minds when we'd only raised $50 [million] before, even if we'd crossed $150 [million] at this point," said Vitale.

"There were plenty of people who said we'd never raise over $50-$60 million," said then-chairman John Bryan. "You can't raise $200 million—$200 was the presumed amount. I had letters from the trustees—good friends—saying, 'You can't do this, John. It's not a good idea. Please stop this.' Good friends. And I tried to explain to them that I thought it was okay."

"We pushed hard with the trustees," said Cuno. "John Bryan and a few other key trustees pushed hard, saying, 'We have to do it. Millennium Park is a big success. Look how it looks from Millennium Park. Architectural press is coming in nine months. Let's go forward. We've got to do it.'" See figures 3.2–3.5.

3.3 Wyly Theatre by Andreas Praefcke. Creative Commons Attribution 3.0 license.

3.4 Museum Complex/Grant Park, G32519, © Paul Warchol. Used with permission from the Art Institute of Chicago.

3.5 Modern Wing Façade, G32522, © Paul Warchol. Used with permission from the Art Institute of Chicago.

Donor Response in Dallas

In Dallas, Lively turned the board's decision to thwart convention and expert advice into a marketing tool. The story of exceeding expectations and overcoming obstacles became part of the sales pitch for the AT&T PAC. In interviews, trustees and donors mentioned the decision to ignore the fundraising study with pride. In *Stages*, the AT&T PAC's fundraising bulletin, Lively described the organization as "scaling what often seemed insurmountable obstacles." The narrative of the campaign as Lively shaped it became about accomplishing something unprecedented, ambitious, and unique that surpassed people's expectations of what was possible. The size of the campaign thus became a selling point rather than a stumbling block. This narrative appealed to the locals' perception of Dallas as a city of big ambitions, and the money poured in.

Another factor that featured prominently in the AT&T PAC's ability to raise money was the organizational structure, which afforded potential trustees and donors ample opportunities for meaningful involvement. Lively's main focus was fundraising. The rest of the decisions were delegated to trustees or consultants, or left for future staff.

The consultant plans had anticipated the organization would need multiple full-time employees to start the design and capital campaign, but Lively wanted to run a cheap, lean campaign. (The campaign ended up costing only 3.5¢ for every dollar raised.) "My first year, I was the president and CEO of me. I had a secretary. That was on purpose because we built the model around the cadre of qualified volunteers." At the end of his first twelve months, Lively hired employee number three, a publications specialist to produce marketing materials. After another year, he hired a vice president to manage the construction.

This staffing strategy left the trustees with ample opportunities to get intimately involved with the details of designing the building or generating ideas for revenue strategies. Without staff, the board was never in danger of crossing the line and micromanaging. Each trustee committee charged with a task had leadership with expertise in the area. The head of the architecture committee for the theater, Deedie Rose, for example, had led other architect selection committees before, and the head of the operations committee—responsible for the organization's business plan—had been the CEO of PepsiCo. As with any building project in the arts, many of the committees provided the volunteer trustees with opportunities to learn a new skill rather than use an existing area of expertise. Some trustees, like Bess Enloe and Deedie Rose, even traveled to take executive education courses at Harvard, where they hired their instructor to consult. In general, a coterie of professional consultants with decades of experience were always on hand to provide expertise as well as do the grunt work.

In essence, this organizational structure created the philanthropic opportunities of a lifetime for any Dallas donors who ever wondered what it would be like to be closely involved with a big charitable project. If they wanted to serve their communities directly, they had a chance to be a part of important, difficult decisions. If they felt they had the business acumen to help an arts organization figure out a way to be profitable, there was a place for them. If they had always dreamed of understanding the work of a brilliant architect, they had a place to do that. Dayton, for example, went to London for long stretches of time to work on the design for the Winspear Opera House with Foster and Partners, the architects chosen for the project.

What was also clear was that all of these people were creating a project that they and their friends would want to pay for. All of the people joining the board were expected to make sizable, seven- or eight-figure contributions. In Dallas, philanthropy frequently acts as a social glue. Some business executives join boards of charitable organizations in order to network. Thus, Lively wanted to make sure that all of the trustees were respected members of their communities—"people of integrity" was a phrase he used frequently. He also wanted to ensure that board members belonged to a diverse set of social circles. He wanted representation from a broad section of ages, careers, and business sectors on the board, so that the AT&T PAC could, in fact, make inroads among donors outside the arts community.[24] Moreover, he needed more trustees, since he had started with only twenty. By 2007, the AT&T PAC had sixty-five trustees, many of them new to the arts; $166 million of the philanthropic funds for the project came from members of the board. Lively also recruited a 205-member President's Advisory Council that had a social calendar, but fewer of the planning responsibilities.

"These volunteers came on board with a clear view of the expectations of each of them," Lively said. "I said to each something like this when they were appointed: 'I'm inviting you to join this great adventure and serve and lead and, when I've earned the right, I want you to make a gift of X million dollars. There's no ambiguity about that, and if you don't want to do that, you really shouldn't join. That'd be a waste of your time and ours.'"

Though Lively had a prominent role within the campaign, underestimating the importance of volunteers in the AT&T PAC fundraising would be a mistake. Lively described his role as that of a choreographer and portrayed the capital campaign standard procedure as follows. Three times a week for several hours, Lively would meet confidentially "with people of means" to identify and discuss donor prospects in their friendship networks. First, he would want to know who had the means to make a seven-figure gift. Then he wanted to know what specific reasons would compel that person to make the donation. "We tried to find all of the messages and all of the reasons that someone would support this thing," he said. For most of the potential donors, the primary reason to support the new performing arts center was civic pride. Some of these donors did not enjoy the performing arts at all and in fact dreaded attending theater and opera. But they were impressed with the vision of what the buildings would mean for the city. Of the 133 donors who gave gifts of $1 million or more, most had never given to the arts before. This number was encouraging to community leaders and donors who had expressed concerns over the capital campaign draining all the arts funding.

In his meetings, Lively also wanted to know who knew the person best and understood their thinking about philanthropy. Sometimes, he was acquainted with a donor and familiar with his or her philanthropy from his years running the campaign at nearby Southern Methodist University, but many donors were new to him and to Dallas. Two gifts of $10 million came from people he had not met before.

Lively would also discuss the merits of various settings for the prospect's first introduction to the AT&T PAC, whether the first interaction should be a private conversation, a dinner party, or a reception at the Preview Center with its twentieth story view onto the site and its architectural models. After the first meeting, he'd analyze how the first contact went and plot a course for the second contact. When the time came to make the "ask," he'd discuss which "messages" would be presented to a prospect and which order would make them appear at their most effective. Then he would try to identify the best person to relay these messages and ask for the money. Sometimes, they'd determine who was the best person to ask the prospective askers to do the asking and develop a strategy for getting them to say "yes." They even discussed who was the best person to call for an appointment.

At the meeting with the prospect, the chosen trustee or donor and Lively would discuss the project and stress the points they had previously decided would appeal to that specific prospect the most. The people accompanying Lively to these meetings had already made large gifts themselves and could mention the size of their commitment and their rationales. "They could say, I have done this for these reasons, and I think this is important. Then they would pass the baton to me, and I would describe the project and talk about specific particulars, and then I would make the ask or join a volunteer in making the ask," said Lively. After this meeting, the crucial steps were following up with the prospects to get commitments, and then keeping in touch to inform them of key project developments so that they would feel engaged.

Despite the extensive planning of every detail, the actual interactions almost never completely adhered to the painstakingly developed script. In Lively's view, the most crucial decision for every ask was choosing the asker. "People will give to people, no matter what the project is, if they trust the people," Lively said. "People of integrity will ask people of integrity for a gift and they'll get it, because these guys will trust that the cause is noble."

The AT&T Performing Arts Center also provided its donors with a steady stream of opportunities for recognition. The organization's quarterly newsletter, *Stages,* was a sumptuous, professionally designed periodical printed on glossy cardstock the size of a folded newspaper and filled with profiles and pictures of smiling couples who had made seven- or eight-figure donations to the center. Doubtlessly, this warmed the hearts of the people in the pictures, but this communication strategy also helped cultivate new donors. For some potential prospects, seeing substantial commitments from respected Dallas philanthropists was persuasive. Lively started each newsletter with a column in which he assured his audience, sometimes in italics, that both the construction and the campaign were on budget and on schedule. The dribble of press releases announcing gifts was relentless, creating the impression of the inevitability of success. Sometimes, the announcements of gifts were purposefully delayed, just so these announcements could be staggered. "We went through two economic downturns even before this latest fiasco and two wars, and we just kept chugging along," said one of the founding members of the board, Bess Enloe.

Periodically, acclaimed celebrity performers like Tommy Lee Jones, Sidney Poitier, Dame Julie Andrews, and Hillary Swank would make appearances at the center's lecture series, the Brinker Forum, or at its events. These appearances would be heavily publicized and followed by pictures of major donors with these actors in *Stages*, conveying the social desirability of a membership in the AT&T Performing Arts Center board. For a few years, Chuck Norris was officially enrolled as a trustee. Alas, he rarely came to the meetings.[25]

When doubts about the financial feasibility of the new AT&T PAC did arise during the planning, the doubts focused on the center's ability to sustain its operations after opening. After all, the Dallas organization had set out to raise roughly $300 million for the construction, but planned to set none of that astronomical sum aside for operations. Several of the institutions with a stake in the health of the Dallas cultural sector overall were perturbed by the prospect of a giant new organization entering the competition for the limited public and philanthropic funds for the arts. Dallas arts leaders were also worried about the conditions on which the performance space would be available to Dallas performing groups for rent. A performing arts center that struggled financially could be forced to charge fees and rents that the performing arts groups could not afford. Instead of improving the fortunes of its residents, the new performing arts center could exacerbate their problems. Thus, the bulk of the doubts was focused on the impact of the AT&T Performing Arts Center, with its mammoth capital campaign and operating budget, on the rest of the Dallas cultural ecosphere.

Like so much of the planning, the performing arts center's business model was left to the volunteers on the operations committee of the board. This committee was chaired by Roger Enrico, formerly the CEO of PepsiCo and now the chairman of the board of DreamWorks Animation SKG. He and other trustees served as the principal clients for consultants who studied the issue and returned with reports. One of the goals for the business plan was reducing, if not eliminating, the need for annual giving from individuals and foundations within the annual budget. The hope was that the new AT&T Performing Arts Center could sustain itself on earned revenue and perhaps corporate sponsorships and compete as little as possible with other nonprofit organizations for gifts and grants.[26] Lively thought this could be achieved with some creative thinking about untraditional sources of revenue, like premium memberships that would allow access to the artists and new models for working with corporations on sponsorships.[27] Devising a plan took the consultants and the operations committee a few years. In the end, their model called for an operating budget of $25 million to $30 million, with only $2.5 million to $3.0 million covered through unearned income and the rest covered through earned income sources. (It should be noted that the AT&T Performing Arts Center considers funds from corporations as income earned through its sponsorship programs.) Lively negotiated a contract with the city for $2.5 million in annual operating support and secured a lucrative deal with Lexus, which became the sponsor of the future Broadway series at the AT&T PAC (often called the Dallas Center for the Performing Arts). He also began discussions with other corporations, one of which, AT&T, became the PAC's general sponsor in 2009 by agreeing to contribute an undisclosed amount to its annual operations.

Experience has shown this plan was overly optimistic, in part owing to the economic recession that started nationwide just as the AT&T PAC opened in the fall of 2009. By then, the city of Dallas had reneged on its promise of $2.5 million a year in operating support. After revising its estimates in accordance with these new economic conditions, the AT&T PAC expected an annual budget of $25 million–$30 million with a fundraising requirement of $5 million–$6 million. In the end, both earned income and fundraising fell below expectations, and the center finished the year with a $2 million deficit.

At the time the plan was devised, Dallas community leaders worried about the lack of detail they saw and about the business plan's lengthy period of gestation. The staff at the groups that would perform in the new center wished they had more details. While the volunteers on the performing arts center board were mainly interested in the reasonableness of the annual fundraising requirements, the professional staff at the resident companies was keenly interested in details like the scheduling process, the fees, the policies on unions, and the presence of performing arts center staff at set load-ins. They needed estimates of how much their performances in the new venues would cost, and they wanted them several years ahead of the opening season. The Dallas Opera was commissioning a new work for its inaugural 2009–10 season and had to commit itself financially in 2005 to make this happen. The Dallas Theater Center was making casting commitments. Meanwhile, the programming staff at the performing arts center had yet to be hired; the staffing was still light.

Faced with this uncertainty about operations, the performing companies took different approaches to their first season budgets. The opera asked the performing arts center operations committee and its consultants for absolute worst case scenario estimates of the opera's future expenses. Meanwhile, the Dallas Theater Center simply came up with the cost estimates themselves. Executive director Mark Hadley described this process as follows: "They were working on very broad pro formas that they had developed with outside consultants. It was in very broad strokes. So we had to guess on what some things would be, but honestly, we weren't that far off. We took whatever information we had from them and then threw our decades of experience in."

The Dallas Theater Center also discussed the financial ramifications of the new performing arts center. "It wasn't really an option not to make this happen," remembers Hadley about the discussions taking place among DTC staff. "Here comes the building. It kind of forces our hand. What do we want to be in that building and how do we make it happen?"

Eventually, as construction on the center proceeded, the DTC board looked at its strategic plan. They hired a new artistic director who was a good match for the organization's revised and sharpened vision, and launched an advancement campaign to raise $12 million in support for the productions and increased occupancy expenses for the first five seasons in the new venue.

The business plan's broadness frustrated funders. Bruce Esterline, vice president for grants for the Meadows Foundation, worried about the effect of the performing arts center on the larger cultural ecology in Dallas. "We were concerned about the impact of higher rents on the resident performing arts groups, some of whom were dealing with their own financial challenges at the time," he said. The mayor's office had concerns too. They wanted certainty that the Dallas Center for the Performing Arts (i.e., the AT&T PAC) would not need more than $2.5 million a year in unearned income to operate, and former councilwoman Veletta Lill reported Lively promised to raise an endowment once the capital campaign was complete.[28] Some opportunities to amass funds for the endowment and operations arose throughout the capital campaign, and Lively made use of them, gathering $18 million in pledges for this purpose before his tenure's end.

Yet an endowment campaign never started in full. Lively and the trustees reached their $275 million target a year early, in 2008. The board felt buoyed by this success. Instead of using the time remaining to raise an endowment, however, on the day the final pledge was signed the board voted unanimously to raise the target of the capital campaign to $338 million. They wanted to use the money to pay the architect's fees and construction costs for a park between their new opera house and theater. After all, the capital campaign had already exceeded all expectations. "We were optimistic," said trustee and capital campaign chair Caren Prothro. "We had such big dreams. We've never done this. We had no working manual. . . . I think we fell in love with that economy. We were impermeable."

After this decision, Lively stayed for another eleven months, before leaving in advance of the center's opening as had been always planned. His next job involved raising money for his other great passion: football, specifically the Dallas Super Bowl. By the time of his departure, $327 million had been pledged for the construction costs, but the budget for that construction was raised yet again.

The AT&T Performing Arts Center's grand opening in October 2009 attracted large crowds and attention from the international press. By then, the financial crisis had already begun. At the beginning of fiscal year 2010, in August, new pledges toward the capital campaign stopped coming in. The reported total of capital campaign contributions was still only $330 million. All construction bills were paid by virtue of $150 million in construction bonds issued in 2006 and due for repayment in 2041. As of August 2011, the AT&T PAC was still $50 million short of covering these bonds. Both the sluggish pace of recession fundraising and operating deficits in the first two years of operations contributed to this shortfall.

The operational deficits were exacerbated by the recession. In the first two years, the city of Dallas contributed only $0.8 million a year instead of the expected $2.5 million. This amount was then expected to decrease to $0.2 million for 2012. Early estimates of operating income proved optimistic, and the AT&T PAC began its first year hoping to raise $5 million–$6 million in annual funds. When both fundraising and revenues proved disappointing, the center finished its first year with a deficit just short of $3 million. In the second year, this deficit increased.

The tenants of the new performing arts center have also faced financial challenges. The Dallas Theater Center expected the costs of operating in their new venue to increase dramatically and launched a $12 million advancement campaign to cover the expenses of growing into its new venue. By May 2011, $8 million of the total had been pledged, and these funds have reduced the impact from the economic recession and higher operating costs. The Dallas Opera also found its costs increasing owing to higher facility costs and the more artistically ambitious program that the change of venue had made possible. In its first year at the AT&T PAC, the annual deficit for the opera was $1.5 million, and for the second, $4 million. These mounting deficits forced the opera to cut one of its full-scale productions for the 2011–12 season in an attempt to balance the budget.

For the center, finishing the campaign with the buildings already in existence is proving to be a grind. To some degree, this was due to the recession, but to another, it is due to the difficulties inherent in raising money outside of the building process. Before, the dream for the transformative power of a new performing arts center was easier to evoke for prospective donors. Now, the AT&T PAC is a reality rather than a dream. Its ambitions for transforming Dallas are still there, but daily compromises, large and small, are needed to navigate operational and financial challenges. The new performing arts center is no longer a blank canvas for any and all civic dreams.

Donor Response in Chicago

In Chicago, the crucible of doubts and ambitions was internal rather than external. After all, the Art Institute of Chicago raised over 90 percent of its capital campaign funds from within its "family" of trustees and donors. The Art Institute board was an established organization. Many of its members had served for years. While the Dallas board was trying to create an institution, the Chicago board already had an institution to run. They had other goals and priorities, sometimes orthogonal to the expansion and the capital campaign. Some trustees questioned whether spending $200 million—which eventually grew to over $400 million—on an expansion was prudent. They doubted that a capital campaign of this size could succeed and feared the fiscal consequences of failure. They were reluctant to commit to capital campaign gifts. Meanwhile, Bryan and other proponents of the project advocated in favor of ambitious reconceptualizations of project scale and scope, as well as insisted on the fiscal feasibility of raising money for this vision.

In September 2004, Cuno replaced Wood as president. In Bryan's estimation, Cuno was less anxious than Wood about the ambitious scope of the expansion. From then on, Cuno, Bryan, and Piano all urged the executive committee to approve a May groundbreaking for the project, in part so that the Pritzker Prize ceremony could be leveraged for the project's public relations purposes. But the $150 million the board wanted had still not been raised.

In addition, Piano had continued producing proposals for enhancements and refinements. The latest of these was a design for a bridge and an added floor on the west side of the building. The extra floor was necessary for the bridge to work because of Americans with Disability Act (ADA) requirements for both slope and elevation—otherwise, the bridge would end in a staircase that led down to the building. The new concept was inspired by Piano's first visit to Gehry's completed Millennium Park. The straight, slim bridge was meant to be reminiscent of the hull of a sleek sailing yacht and it would constitute an answer, architecturally, to Gehry's serpentine bridge over Columbus Drive. Piano's bridge would also, Cuno hoped, bring in thousands of new visitors from Millennium Park. The additional floor would hold a restaurant and a sculpture terrace with a view of the city's skyline. In a way, the addition of this floor reinstated spaces cut by Wood during one of the early workshops on the design. For their part, the Art Institute staff hoped these spaces would be popular rentals for hosts of social events, thus boosting the museum's income statement.

The drawings for these proposed additions were not yet final, and the changes had not yet been incorporated into construction blueprints. This, in turn, meant that the board had no reliable way to know the cost estimates for these changes. The trustees thus faced a choice as to whether to delay the start of construction until the drawings and merged blueprints could be finalized and costs estimated, or alternatively move forward now and approve the commencement of construction, knowing that soon costly changes to a plan for a building already in progress might well be required. Cuno wrote: "There was much discussion in meetings of the Executive Committee in February and March over whether we should delay the start of construction until we could integrate the bridge and the third-floor restaurant and sculpture terrace into the project's construction documents to get a single estimate and bid. Some Executive Committee members thought this more efficient and less expensive; others thought just the opposite: that delaying the project would cost more in general conditions by adding a year to the construction schedule."

The process for deciding which of the proposed additions to the scope to include and which to exclude was proposed by Bryan. "They were all very nervous about the notion that we would not have the money raised," said Bryan about his fellow trustees. "So I said, 'Look, what if we get the money from someone who would not have given money otherwise except for the bridge?'" Besides the bridge and the additional floor, Piano was advocating other ideas, like renovating Gunsaulus Hall by stripping its walls down to their trusses and then sheathing them in glass (at an estimated cost of $30 million). The process for deciding whether to proceed with projects like the renovations of the Gunsaulus, in the end, centered on finding a donor willing to pay for that specific component of the expansion. Throughout the process of raising money for these projects, the avoidance of poaching gifts from one facet of the project—like the endowment—to pay for another—like the bridge—was a concern. "Everything had to pay for itself," said the Art Institute's current CFO Eric Anyah. Anyah also projected the costs of operating the additional facilities, estimating a positive impact on the operating statements from the added revenues generated by the restaurant and sculpture terrace and a neutral impact from the bridge, which required little operational funding. Bryan hoped the bridge would in fact help improve the institute's operating statements by bringing more visitors to the museum from across the street.

Faced with these stakes, Piano himself got involved in fundraising. During one visit to Chicago, he went to dinner with the former chairman John Nichols and his wife (and current AIC trustee) Alexandra Nichols. At the restaurant, he drew them a picture on the table cloth of the bridge he wanted to build. "We have a tablecloth all framed at home," said Nichols. The story became a legend at the Art Institute, where many thought that the dinner with Piano was the moment that finally persuaded the family to increase their gift by another $10 million. John Nichols, however, disagreed with this interpretation. "The driving concept for my wife and myself was connecting to Millennium Park. That to me was the driving force more than Renzo. I like the story, but there was more of a rational reason than the wine and the dinner."

In April 2005, once the capital campaign had $162 million in pledges booked, the majority of the trustees of the Art Institute voted to approve a plan for groundbreaking and demolition. Soon, with the inclusion of the bridge and the third floor, the capital campaign goal for the Modern Wing was revised to $375 million, with $84 million of that targeted for the endowment. In addition, the renovations to the old building—including a scaled-down $13.2 million version of Piano's proposal for Gunsaulus Hall, as well as gallery reinstallations—required another $39 million in funding. John Bryan's term as chairman of the board ended in November 2006, and Thomas Pritzker took over the role, overseeing the rest of the project. Now a lifetime trustee, Bryan continued to raise money. In the end, by opening day, $414 million was pledged. Much of the money came in multiyear pledges, which required the Art Institute to borrow $150 million in bridge financing through bonds in order to have cash on hand to pay for construction. At the end of FY2011, the total of its outstanding debt was $296 million.

The new Modern Wing opened in March 2009, to widespread critical acclaim for Piano's understated design. Now the Art Institute of Chicago has the space to display 1,000 additional works of art, with each of the museum's curatorial departments benefiting from the gallery expansion. A longtime curator who was recently appointed president and director of the Art Institute, Douglas Druick, noted that the new and renovated galleries are better suited to the collection as well, with more light and more space. "The Modern Wing allows us to show works to their best advantage, in a thematically coherent arrangement," he wrote in an email.

As of October 2009, $312 million had been contributed in cash and $102 million in pledges were still outstanding. Almost no one reneged on pledges, a fact trustees like Vitale attribute to the campaign largely being kept in the "family," among donors with long-term relationships to the Art Institute.

Financial sustainability is the main challenge for the new wing. "In a way, thank God it's built and done and paid for, but there'll be a struggle now to maintain, particularly until the economy picks up, ability to absorb all the new costs," said Wood. The Modern Wing has cost the Art Institute about $6 million per year to operate. In the first year after opening, the annual attendance for the museum increased, from 1.4 million to 1.5 million, then in subsequent years fell back and held steady at the usual level. The admission fees were increased as well, and admission and membership revenues rose by $4.4 million from FY2009 to FY2010. Overall, even after a decrease in endowment income due to a market drop, operating revenue for the museum increased by $10 million (11 percent year-over-year) in FY2010.

However, a precipitous drop in endowment income loomed on the horizon for FY2011. Owing to market conditions, the endowment had dropped from $842 million at the beginning of FY2009 to $618 million at its end, and FY2011 would be the first time the impact of these losses would be fully absorbed by the annual budget. The additional endowment funds that the Art Institute finance staff counted on to support the expanded building's operations were delayed. Raising the money for the building was always a more urgent priority, and money for the endowment was solicited last. This was why, at the time of the opening, most of the pledges toward the endowment were promised but still outstanding, and the Modern Wing opened with little of its $84 million endowment in cash. This meant that for the first few years, the museum had to bear the expanded cost of operations without the benefit of additional investment income. "Analysis was based on $80 million on Day One," said Anyah. This has been "causing some stress on current operations," he added. "At the point where we collect the gifts, that will go away."

Soon, austerity measures followed. After pay cuts, furloughs, a salary freeze, and other cuts, two rounds of layoffs were still necessary, one in June 2009 and another in May 2010. The first round of cuts was distributed across the departments, with 22 people losing their positions, while the second round of cuts was focused on retail operations, facilities, education, and security. The second round of layoffs was precipitated by the anticipation of a $10 million deficit for the organization in FY2011.

These cuts in costs put the expansion of the Art Institute's organizational footprint, a measure once viewed as necessary to keep up with the expansion of its facility, on hold. Instead of expanding its budget as expected, the Art Institute was forced to contract instead. The museum's total operating costs before depreciation and interest first rose from $74 million in FY2008 to $82 million in FY2009 (the year of the Modern Wing's opening), then dropped to $77 million in FY2010 and FY2011, after the cuts took effect. Approximately $6 million of that $77 million budget was spent on the Modern Wing. Over the same period, interest and depreciation expenses increased sharply because of the new building. Thus, even as the total annual operating budget soared to over $100 million, the financial resources available for programming and other activities stayed about the same, despite the significant expansion in physical size. Overall, the museum finished FY2009 with a $4.4 million deficit, FY2010 with a $1.3 million operating surplus, and FY2011 with a surplus of just $78,000.

The leadership of the organization was also transformed. In June 2010, James Wood died of a heart attack at the age of 69. He'd been coaxed out of retirement to become the CEO of the Getty Trust in 2006 and was mourned by his colleagues in both Chicago and Los Angeles. Yet again, he was succeeded in his job by Jim Cuno, who resigned from the Art Institute in May 2011 to take the top job at Getty. With Cuno's departure, both of the Art Institute directors who had spearheaded the project were gone.

* * *

As we have seen in these cases, project finances and ambition of scope are inextricably intertwined, as well as intimately connected to the organization's financial flexibility after opening. They are linked because they influence the project budget and the target of the capital campaign. Yet they are also connected by their impact on the perceptions of and enthusiasm for the vision. Rather than being mere manifestations of philanthropic and government degree of support for the project, these issues are also major influencers of the grant-making process.

At the beginning of the chapter, we proposed a classification matrix for the match between funding and project scope. In cases where both funding availability and project scope are large, project leaders may find themselves in the enviable situation of being able to afford a palatial new home. In cases where both funding and budget are relatively low, arts leaders may build a lily pad project to use as a place from which to launch the next stage of the organization's life cycle. Yet should the project leaders misjudge the situation, two significant risks present themselves: either insolvency due to project costs or failure to fully capitalize on the building project opportunity. Though the risks of the latter situation are less obvious, organizations that end up in buildings that cost significantly less than the organizations' funding capacity may find themselves needing to build, expand, or renovate again soon. Since each capital project poses a significant organizational risk, project leaders are likely to aspire for maximum fundraising capacity and total project costs to mirror each other closely—at least after operational funds like endowments and reserves are taken into account.

Examples of lily pad projects are found throughout our case studies. Dallas Theater Center used the metal shack of the Arts District Theater for years before attempting to build a new facility. Though the Arts District Theater was razed to make room for the Wyly, the Kalita Humphreys Theater continues to serve as a smaller, alternative theater venue, not only for the Dallas Theater Center but for smaller and younger producing theaters as well. Not only did this theater enable growth of the Dallas Theater Center, but now the theater may serve as a launching pad for other artistic organizations as well. Arguably, the Taubman Museum could have found a state of alignment if a smaller lily pad project had been undertaken in lieu of the museum that was actually built. The outcome of this smaller project may have been starkly different. Though some leaders, particularly wealthy donors, fear that projects with small budgets and ambitions will turn into embarrassments, many lily pad projects become success stories instead, as we will observe in greater detail in the next few chapters.

In contrast, in both Dallas and Chicago, leaders and communities reached alignment on projects that were palaces for the arts—expensive, ambitious, attention-grabbing buildings. The way in which this alignment

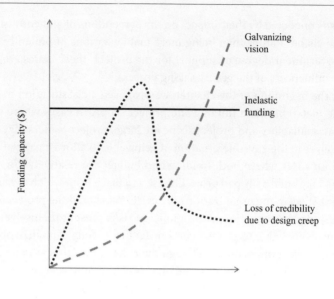

Galvanizing
vision

Inelastic
funding

Loss of credibility
due to design creep

Funding capacity ($)

Building program (cost, $)

3.6 Changes in funding capacity in response to changes in ambition.

was reached allows us to examine how design ambition and funding interact. Indeed, what these two cases demonstrate is that these two variables are interlinked rather than independent.

In certain communities, funding may prove inelastic to changes in design. In other cases, an unexpectedly large and expensive project proposal can cost the organization credibility with voters, donors, and foundations. The trustworthiness of the organization's stewardship of the funds is put into question, causing a decrease in available funding. In rare cases, however, a project with a monumental vision can galvanize donors and inspire giving in sectors far outside the artistic organization's initial reach. Whether an organization's operating plan seems sound plays into this process as well.[29] See figure 3.6.

Shrewd leaders use the project vision as a lever. They increase the availability of funds through a calibration of the plan to key decision makers' desires and dreams. Yet the side effect of this has an extreme negative effect as well—visions, operating plans, and budgets become materials for fundraising. This introduces many distorting effects into what should be an internally focused process of strategic planning.

To a certain extent, the fundraising fortunes of the two projects discussed in depth here, the AT&T Performing Arts Center and the Art Institute of Chicago, followed these trajectories for the interaction between the building design and the community's philanthropic response. At the Art Institute, the initial reluctance to give was attributed in part to key donors' initial doubts about the scale of the project. Once this scale seemed congruent with the progress of fundraising, however, the willingness of donors to give increased. In contrast, the Dallas project seemed from the beginning to be beyond the means of the companies that wished to perform there. This vaulting ambition endeared itself to Dallas philanthropists, who were inspired by civic pride to shower the project with generous gifts. Yet in the end the Dallas performing arts center still began its life saddled with debts as the result of its board's approving too many increases in program scope. Even in communities that respond favorably to ambitious designs, there still exists a danger of overreaching. This is one of the many ways in which the attributes of the community are tightly interwoven with issues of fundraising and strategic expansions for cultural institutions.

4 | *Connecting to Community*

When projects careen dangerously toward misalignment that will imperil the sponsoring organization and thus hamper the cultural vitality of a city for decades to come, local governments and community stakeholders can intervene. Neighborhood activists and local arts groups have scuttled or delayed many a project through civic action and protest. Frequently, these external stakeholders bring useful perspectives or emphasize issues that had been overlooked. From op-eds to speeches at the meetings of planning commissions and the city council, from public marches to social media campaigns, local activist groups today have many tools at their disposal for getting the attention their arguments deserve. Even for projects funded entirely through private philanthropic donations, a public outcry can present a serious obstacle. This is at least in part because local governments always hold power over the building projects within their jurisdictions—sometimes through planning and permits, and at other times because arts groups depend on municipalities to provide resources like capital or operational funding. Grassroots community organization is an effective strategy for sapping municipal goodwill toward any project, and thus causing a reconsideration of key decisions and dimensions. Faced with a seemingly inevitable, privately funded project, conceived by a small group of powerful decision makers operating behind closed doors, community members have many ways to voice opposition, cause delay, and gain a voice in the project. Decision makers, in turn, should take notice of community sentiment. If they fail to engage in a substantive manner, they may find their project in serious peril.[1]

However, not all community input is equally constructive. Just as input offered by parties inside the organization varies in helpfulness, community opinion can be influenced by both conscious and unconscious bias. Competing arts organizations, political groups, or private interests, like developers, can plant seeds of opposition to serve their own interests. On a subconscious level, community agents are subject to the same cognitive biases as the decision makers. Emotional attachments to the way things already are and irrational aversion to risk can lie at the root of opposition. With many potential competing claims emanating from the community, today's arts and civic leaders must have heuristics for identifying the most salient community concerns. And community activists too must be aware of how legitimate their concerns are within the context of so many. Understanding what differentiates salient community stakeholders from the rest will help both leaders at the center of decision making and leaders of external constituencies to devise better strategies for the engagement between arts building projects and their communities.

The process of identifying the most salient stakeholders should begin by identifying who all the stakeholders are. The most encompassing definition of a stakeholder comes from the work of R. Edward Freeman, who defined a stakeholder as anyone "who can affect or is affected by" an organization's activities.[2] Within the arts, the candidates outside the organization are likely to belong to one of three groups: patrons, partners, or the general public. The patrons commonly concern themselves with changes to the experience of attending the programs of a cultural organization, from transportation to admission cost to program quality. An organization's potential partners include other cultural institutions, universities, city agencies, and artists who all actively participate in the same cultural ecology of the community, and their principal concerns about any new project are likely to center on the new building's impact on the cultural vitality of the community as a whole. These concerns could include the challenges a large capital campaign could pose to others' ability to raise funds and draw audiences, as well as the new opportunities opened by the expansion of available facilities. The rest of the general public, including those apathetic toward the arts, will also contain actors who nonetheless have a stake in the new facility. Public funding for the project is likely to draw voter scrutiny, as well as a debate on the merits of the project plan.[3] Neighborhood coalitions, historical preservationists, and environmental groups will pore over a facility plan to gauge its impact on their concerns and commitments. All of these agents together may well offer a cacophony of inconsistent views on how the project ought to proceed.

One approach to prioritizing stakeholders' opinions was offered to private sector business leaders by Mitchell, Agle, and Wood, and their framework can be useful in the arts sector as well. They propose that there are three attributes that can describe any given stakeholder: Power, Legitimacy, and Urgency. Individuals and groups have power if they have the capacity to enact changes despite resistance. Stakeholders' legitimacy is the extent to which their activities are generally perceived as desirable and appropriate. Finally, their claims' urgency is a function of the time-sensitivity of their claims as well as these demands' perceived importance to the stakeholder. All three of these attributes are dynamic—any stakeholder can both acquire and lose any of them over the course of the relationship. These three factors are also continuous rather than binary variables, which is to say that any stakeholder can be perceived as more or less legitimate than another legitimate stakeholder. All of them are also based on external perceptions rather than intrinsic characteristics.[4]

Mitchell, Agle, and Wood posit that the saliency of any stakeholder's claim increases with the addition or intensification of each of these factors. They suggest that stakeholders can be stratified into three groups: definitive, expectant, and latent. Definitive stakeholders have power, legitimacy, and urgency. Their opinions should be considered and addressed. Expectant stakeholders have two of these three attributes, and therefore, a reasonable expectation that their voices are heard. Latent stakeholders possess only one of the three attributes. Their opinions should be considered last—but these stakeholders must still be monitored, for signs that they may acquire one other attribute and become more important. Any agent who has no power, no legitimacy, and no urgent claim should not be considered a stakeholder. In general, the argument is that an organization should set then adjust its community engagement strategy to the fluctuations in the potential stakeholders' characteristics.[5]

This framework for stakeholder saliency may help one understand cases of particularly heated community opposition. Take, for example, the case of the Contemporary Art Museum of the Presidio in San Francisco, which the *San Francisco Chronicle* called "the city's fiercest development battle in a decade."[6] (The Presidio is a park and former military base.) The number of people and organizations involved in the debate was immense. In June 2009, the spokesperson for the Presidio Trust said: "We can easily say there are thousands of comments, from form letters to 60-page documents from public agencies. We'll be stepping back and considering a year's worth of reaction."[7]

The museum—the Contemporary Art Museum of the Presidio, which area bloggers and commentators enjoyed calling CAMP—was suggested by San Francisco philanthropists Donald and Doris Fisher.[8] Donald Fisher had just finished his two terms as a Presidio trustee and thought that a new art museum in the park would be to the mutual benefit of both institutions. The Fishers were the founders of the Gap retail empire, and their fortune was estimated to be worth over $1 billion. Over the course of a few decades, Donald Fisher had amassed an extensive collection of contemporary art. Of the 1,100 paintings in the collection, 400 of these were deemed as important by curators. This private collection included 21 Warhols, 23 Gerhard Richters, 24 Sol LeWitts, 45 Calders, as well as works by Chuck Close, Ellsworth Kelly, Willem de Kooning, Richard Diebenkorn, Anselm Kiefer, Wayne Thiebaud, Roy Lichtenstein, and dozens of others.[9]

The Fisher collection was stored in a warehouse, with select pieces displayed on a rotating basis at the Gap corporate headquarters for the enjoyment of the employees. A *New York Times* article once reported on the Take Your Children to Work day at the corporation, when school-children traipsed down the halls filled with these canvases. Fisher had enjoyed curating these private exhibits, but he also wanted his art to be accessible to the public at large, preferably in his native San Francisco. Both Donald and Doris Fisher were trustees of the San Francisco Museum of Modern Art, and some of their holdings were exhibited there, but after many conversations with the museum's leaders, Fisher felt unsatisfied with the prospect of giving his collection to the museum. At 50,000 square feet, its building was too small for the leadership to make any guarantees about how much time works from the Fisher collection would spend on view rather than in storage. For a philanthropist motivated by a desire to have his collection seen, a new facility was looking increasingly like an attractive proposition. The head of the SFMOMA, Neal Benezra, explained his board members' decision to strike out on their own as follows: "I think we're dealing with a very independent couple, Don, and Doris. . . . Don has been curating the collection for at least two decades in the Gap HQ, and I think it would be foolhardy to think that Don and Doris would give up that much cherished independence. But our position is that we're thrilled it's going to stay in San Francisco, and thrilled it's going to be open to the public."[10]

What Fisher was proposing now was to build a museum at the Presidio National Park. He would pay for the construction of a 100,000 square foot museum with 50,000 square feet of galleries, make a $10 million gift to the park, and give another undisclosed sum toward the museum's

4.1 Artist's rendering of the proposal for the Contemporary Art Museum of the Presidio. © J. F. Mahoney, 2008. candraw.net. Used with artist's permission.

endowment. He would also leave the museum his collection. In his 70s, Fisher was anxious to begin and wanted the construction to start within a year.[11] See figure 4.1.

The plans for the new museum were presented to the public along with a plan to build a hotel within the national park. The Presidio, a former military base filled with historic buildings as well as the site of one of the first European settlements near the San Francisco Bay, at one time had been the most expensive national park to maintain, with an operating budget of $40 million. In 1995, the federal government struck a deal for the newly founded Presidio Trust to take over operations with the goal of the Trust becoming independent of federal subsidies within 13 years. The redevelopment project was part of the effort to draw more visitors.[12]

The public outcry over the proposal was immediate and intense. One leader of a neighborhood group called it a "public uprising." Critics derided the Fishers' taste in architecture (the preliminary design they had funded called for a six-story glass tower). They noted that a museum of contemporary art was not germane to the national park's mission or the Presidio's historical character. The glass box design would ruin the cohesiveness of the surrounding historical site, said the critics. Neighborhood groups were certain that traffic, parking, and green space would all be negatively affected by the museum. Groups dedicated to historic preservation feared the impact of the museum on the historic landmark status and the preservation of buildings as well as potential archeological discoveries at the park. Environmentalist organizations were skeptical. "No preservationist would suggest that most historic places shouldn't continue to evolve. . . . They can be tinkered with. But they [the Fishers] are not tinkering. They are engaging in wholesale alteration of the Presidio," said Anthony Veerkamp of the National Trust for Historic Preservation.[13]

Last but not least, all opponents were incensed by the process the Presidio Trust and the Fishers used to come up with their proposal. By law, the Presidio Trust was required to openly solicit proposals for development, which the Trust did not do until after the Fisher museum was announced. This carelessness about due process incensed all of these public groups who had never been engaged by the planners.[14] Now, they were frustrated by the appearance of the new museum's inevitability. Their opinion did not seem to count. They felt powerless. "In a sense, we're David against Goliath," said Gary Widman.[15]

Over the next two years, the public debate grew rancorous. Letters to the editor about the project were published as far south as Los Angeles. Hundreds came to the Presidio Trust's meetings. Members of the city council started paying attention and several became champions for the community groups' cause. Personal attacks proliferated, with project critics casting aspersions on the personal integrity of key leaders. At one point, an anonymous party printed posters with Donald Fisher's photograph and a label: "Donald Fisher: filthy rich from child slave labor." These posters were pasted on walls around the Presidio and adjacent neighborhoods. A scaled-down proposal for the museum once again failed to please. Both the Fishers and the Presidio Trust cooled to the idea of the new museum, and the project was scrapped.[16]

From the viewpoint of the Power-Legitimacy-Urgency framework, what happened in San Francisco was a failure to engage or consider a group of expectant stakeholders. Expectant stakeholders are those that can legitimately expect to be offered some consideration within the decision-making process because they have two of the three stakeholder characteristics. In this case, historic preservationists, environmentalists, and neighborhood groups all enjoyed a perception of legitimacy. They were all successful in conveying the urgency of their claim that the CAMP plan would harm their interests if implemented. Their urgency and legitimacy should have earned them a place in the discussion and a chance to have their concerns heard and answered before the plans proceeded as far as the architectural design. Their exclusion from the planning process made their claims to legitimacy more credible still, and their ability to organize and attract public attention in the wake of the museum announcement made them more powerful. Finally, as is frequently the case with stakeholders with a claim to legitimacy and urgency, their cause attracted powerful champions, like the San Francisco City Council. The council members had a claim to power and legitimacy, and now, by virtue of affiliating themselves with the community groups, an urgent claim to press within the situation. Eventually, the Presidio Trust caved to these demands.

In an interview, Fisher noted his sadness at the failure of the project as well as his plan to regroup and look for other options for the display of his collection, including sites outside of San Francisco. In the end, however, SFMOMA's Benezra and chairman Charles Schwab were able to persuade Fisher to reconsider their museum. They had just embarked on planning an expansion and could now offer Fisher the things he really wanted—the promise that his collection would remain intact and that a portion would be continuously on display. To accommodate Fisher's paintings, the SFMOMA would expand their proposed addition from 15,000 square feet to 100,000 square feet. The museum would commit to filling 75 percent of specified galleries with Fisher collection artifacts at all times. Donald and Doris Fisher would leave their collection to a trust, which would pay for maintenance and preservation as well as have an exclusive arrangement with SFMOMA that could be renewed after 25 years. The Fishers also made a gift of an unspecified amount to the museum for the expansion. Two days after this ambitious plan was made public, Donald Fisher died of cancer. Six months later, SFMOMA announced that $250 million of the $490 million needed for the expansion and the planned endowment had been raised.

The Power-Legitimacy-Urgency framework does not merely provide guidance for prioritizing the voices of the arts organizations' own stakeholders. The framework also defines how much weight leaders should give to the opinions of the art institution itself.[17] In their relationships to powerful external institutions within the community, arts leaders must remain attuned to the perceptions of their own power, legitimacy, and urgency, since these determine their opportunities to make demands. Their opponents can take advantage of any weakness in these characteristics.[18]

This explains what happened with CAMP. When the Fishers proposed the CAMP project, they had power (as people with ample resources and connections), legitimacy (as philanthropists), and some urgency (as civic leaders attempting to leave a legacy to San Francisco). Yet the legitimacy of the proposal was successfully attacked owing to the perceived lack of integrity in the planning process. The proposal's urgency was also criticized by community activists who saw no pressing need for the museum to be located specifically within the Presidio, arguing that other sites within San Francisco could prove equally attractive. As the Fishers' legitimacy and urgency were successfully attacked and diminished in the public eye, the prominence of their concern in the city's decision-making process diminished as well.

The Fishers seem to have embarked on this misadventure with good intentions.[19] Yet they failed to correctly gauge and anticipate the response from the most salient stakeholders, thus dooming their project. In the end, power, legitimacy, and urgency are all a matter of perception, and appropriate engagement, preparation, and public presentation are vital. Failure in these tasks puts the organization not only in danger of community backlash, but also in jeopardy of losing its own important stakeholder status in the eyes of others.

Though a community engagement fiasco is likely to manifest itself in the decrease of resources available to an organization, like funding or real estate, community engagement can also serve as a tool for achieving strategic alignment.[20] Coming from their positions of power, legitimacy, and urgency, salient stakeholders are sometimes able to suggest strategies for securing necessary resources, advocate for any overlooked legitimate public interests, and identify flaws. At CAMP, for example, the first proposal contained oversights regarding transportation, parking, and environmental impact. Community dissent increased the scrutiny of the project, and as independent experts reviewed the proposal, they suggested improvements. If salient stakeholders had been identified and engaged earlier, this feedback may have engendered a better, perhaps even successful, proposal from the start. Yet not all community opinion is equally constructive. Personal attacks on Donald Fisher during the public outcry over CAMP were not a valid argument against the creation of a museum. Sometimes, a sponsoring organization needs the ability to reject community opinions, though arguably only after understanding them. Another example showing the need for this kind of sorting of stakeholder input is the case we take up next, the planning and construction of the Sandler Center for the Performing Arts.

The Sandler Center for the Performing Arts, Virginia Beach

While the Contemporary Art Museum of the Presidio confronted a unified vocal group of dissenting stakeholders, most arts groups deal with an entire ecology of competing claims. The community response is also likely to come at many stages in the capital project process. The case of the planning, design, and construction of the Sandler Center for the Performing Arts in Virginia Beach highlights some of the challenges inherent in this task and allows us to consider the various approaches to prioritizing stakeholder needs.

Virginia Beach is a city of 437,000 people encompassed within the metropolitan area of Hampton Roads with a total population of 1.6 million. Fourteen miles of manicured, sandy, Atlantic beaches run along the eastern edge of the city. The Oceanfront has a three-mile cement boardwalk along the shore. Several streets running in parallel are filled with hotels, restaurants, shops, bars, and other amenities for the city's annual influx of 2.75 million visitors, who spend nearly $900 million per year here. During the peak tourist season, the city hires musicians, mimes, magicians, theater troupes, and portrait artists to perform on nearly every street corner as well as several outdoor stages at the Oceanfront. The city council is invested in keeping the Oceanfront family-friendly, and the performers are selected with an eye toward entertaining people of all ages. Posted signs warn that cursing is banned.

The city is home to several major military bases, including, famously, the training center and home base for the Navy Seals. The Navy is the city's largest employer. The military's presence is a source of pride for the Virginia Beach residents and contributes significantly to both the tourist trade and civic life. A fifth of Virginia Beach's adult population consists of retired military personnel. Fighter jets fly over the Oceanfront several times an hour to the delight of tourists and many residents.

The journey toward a new theater began in February 2001, when the city council decided to raze the Pavilion Theatre. Opened in 1981, the theater was home to local performing arts groups. Over its two decades, it benefited financially from being attached to the city's convention center, which subsidized the theater's operations. Now, however, the convention center had to expand in order to keep Virginia Beach competitive with other cities as a destination for meetings of large groups. Two architecture firms presented two different plans for the proposed expansion. The first firm, tvsdesign (TVS), suggested adding a wing and a parking garage, expanding the site, and leaving the theater in place. Another firm,

Skidmore, Owings, and Merrill (SOM), called for bulldozing the existing building, including the theater, to enable a newly conceived design with architectural significance and an efficient yet elegant layout. Moreover, this design came with a master site plan that anticipated future expansions. This site plan made this proposal particularly attractive, since the convention industry trend has been toward doubling of facility size every ten years. Hotels and tourism had long been a major industry in Virginia Beach, and the convention center was one of the city's top-priority capital investment projects. The expanded convention center was projected to generate significant revenue for local hotels and other businesses and to increase the city's tax receipts. The expansion would cost $200 million, but was to be paid for by an increase in taxes on hotel rooms and meals, which would also fund an Aquarium plan to build additional parking as well as other municipal projects. In anticipation of the economic benefits of the expanded convention center, the city's hotel and restaurant owner associations supported this tax increase. In comparison to economic growth, the needs of the theater and its tenant artistic groups seemed less important. The city's mayor and vice mayor, Meyera Oberndorf and William Sessoms, studied the plans and enthusiastically recommended that the council choose the SOM proposal.

The Pavilion Theatre would be razed. To compensate the arts community for its loss, the city council would commit to building a new theater that was "as good or better." In order to ensure that the new theater would actually get built, Oberndorf and Sessoms insisted that the city council fund the new theater at the same time it funded the convention center expansion. TVS architects—who specialized in designing convention centers—had previously estimated that replacing the Pavilion Theatre would cost about $20 million, so the restaurant association was going to have to accept an additional increase of 0.5 percent in the meal tax to support the theater replacement. This estimate of costs would soon prove to be not even remotely in the ballpark.

The most powerful advocate for replacing the Pavilion was Mayor Meyera Oberndorf. Mayor since 1988, Oberndorf was a city institution. A lifelong enthusiast for the arts, she possessed a voracious appetite for cultural performances of all kinds—an opportune trait, since her ceremonial duties called for her to attend everything from Russian ballet tours to elementary school plays. Standing five foot tall, the gray-haired, talkative woman was nicknamed "Your Shortness" by one of her colleagues on the council. Oberndorf grew up in the neighboring Newport News, from where her parents frequently took her to New York City to see musicals and plays. She did the same for her children and grandchildren, all the while wishing that Virginia Beach had more offerings in the performing arts. Her commitment to building a new theater was absolute—at a White House reception, she spent the evening convincing the author Arthur Golden to speak in the new theater once it opened. One of her grandchildren once overheard her joke that if she had to, she would sell him and his sister to get the new theater built.

With the city's strong bond rating and favorable interest rates in the credit markets, the additional meal tax revenues netted $35 million in bond proceeds. Since the city soon found that the price tag for a satisfactory replacement was $40 million–$50 million, the additional funds were a boon. Nonetheless, the initial estimate of $20 million as the replacement cost had already been widely reported and the public saw it as the total project cost. With the bond sale, the city commitment was seen as increasing to $35 million. Then the consultants and the architects started speaking about a $45 million project. Within a twelve-month period, the public saw the project cost reported in the media increase from $20 million to $35 million to $45 million. The community became skeptical.

Neighborhood meetings turned acrimonious during discussions of the council's management of this and other public works projects. In 2002, a third of the eleven-member city council either declined to run for re-election or lost, and in at least one campaign, the winner identified the theater as one of the key issues. Council members received record numbers of emails and calls about the new theater. Oberndorf remembers being accosted in public by the project's opponents. At her gym, a man interrupted her on the treadmill to tell her that backing the theater would cost her his vote, and this after twenty years of supporting her. "I took a lot of abuse, verbal threats," she said. It became clear to the mayor and other project supporters that a concerted effort to demonstrate to the citizens that a new theater would benefit large numbers of Virginia Beach residents, and that it had enthusiastic support within the community, was crucial if the new theater was ever to be built.

The public scrutiny brought two issues to the forefront of the decision-making process. First was controlling capital costs. Finding ways to minimize costs or finding partners who would cover them became politically imperative. Second was improving, rather than merely replicating, the Pavilion Theatre model during rebuilding. The Pavilion Theatre had been operating as a community theater, and the primary mission was to provide affordable space to community groups rather than draw large audiences. The Pavilion had 1,000 seats and in 2001, on average, each of that year's 144 events drew just 561 people. The venue collected little in ticket revenues. The higher the cost estimates climbed, the more difficult rebuilding this theater became to justify. Yet if the council could find a way to expand the reach and public benefits of a city-owned theater while designing its physical plant and organization anew, the social returns on the investment would improve, as would the expenditure's palatability to the public. The options considered in this reach for greater legitimacy ranged from building a Broadway-sized road house to incorporating a performing arts high school. Time and again, the city council postponed decisions about the project until one of these new suggestions could be studied.

The primary decision-making body for the project was the Virginia Beach City Council with its eleven elected members. A council-appointed city manager serves as the chief executive, while an elected mayor presides over the council, votes on its resolutions, and carries out ceremonial duties. In FY2003–4, the city had an annual operating budget of $1.3 billion and was spending an additional amount of about $200 million on various capital projects. Since the council members are part-time employees of the city who receive only $28,000 a year for their service, the city manager, Jim Spore, and the professional staff bear the bulk of the responsibilities for all daily operations and the planning and management of capital projects. But they have little decision-making authority beyond that authorized by the council. For the theater project, this meant that the planning proceeded in short bursts. A steering committee chaired by Marcy Sims, the head of the public library system, worked with outside consultants to study various issues and then make presentations and recommendations to the city council during the members' televised weekly meetings.

The city council was unwilling to commit the funds, and such study and planning continued for three and a half years without any final decisions being made about even basic issues like location and size. These questions just kept being debated by various committees—first by the committee of staff, then by committees of stakeholders like artistic groups, then a committee of appointed civic leaders the city council hoped would raise money. None of them actually had the authority to decide anything. City Manager Jim Spore described the process as "excruciating." Oberndorf called it a "nightmare." She said: "It's like having, God forbid, a terminal disease. You're watching little bits of medication being administered, but it's not doing the big steps that are needed."

Community Response

From the beginning, the project had its detractors within the community. The first wave of vocal opposition came from the arts groups themselves. Shortly before a final city council vote on the expansion plan that would doom the Pavilion Theatre, the management of the convention center invited that theater's users for a chat. Here, the news of the Pavilion's demise was met with nearly universal dismay and desperation, and assurances that the theater would be rebuilt did little to assuage the tenants. They were angry and mistrustful of the city's intentions.

The most vocal among them was also the largest, Virginia Beach Symphony Orchestra (VBSO), now known as Symphonicity. The VBSO is an all-volunteer orchestra. "It's what we call amateur, which means that we love music, not that we are bad," said Wendy Young, the company's managing director. The VBSO had a season with four concerts, two performances of each, as well as an annual free concert, the Messiah Sing Along, during the winter holidays. The Messiah usually played to a full house, and the rest of the performances at the Pavilion averaged paid attendance of 700 a night. The annual budget for 2001 was $139,000, of which $31,000 came from donated income, $44,000 from government grants, and $54,000 from ticket revenue. The rest of their revenue came mostly from sales of merchandise. "Our philosophy is high quality, low cost music," said Wendy Young.

For VBSO, the primary objective was "continuity." The company's leaders feared change, and David Kunkel, the conductor and artistic director, was one of the most vocal opponents of the Pavilion's razing. Kunkel and Young summarized their main concerns in a three-page public letter in July of 2001. "It is not an acceptable circumstance for the City to be without a theater for any time at all," they wrote. The city council members had promised to replace the theater, but VBSO did not fully believe them. They pointed to many features of the Pavilion Theatre that VBSO would not find in any other venue in Virginia Beach. In this list, Kunkel and Young mentioned equipment, acoustics, quality of seats, rehearsal space, backstage space, arts group office space, convenience of location, competency of staff, box office, marquee sign, parking, and, last but not least, affordability. If the Pavilion closed before the new theater was finished—or if the council backtracked on its promise to build a new theater or changed the Pavilion model too much—the VBSO would be homeless. With no venues other than high school auditoriums available, the company feared it would be forced to fold.

At that first meeting of the tenants and for many months after, Kunkel and Young rallied their supporters for a campaign of protest calls and emails to the city council. Kunkel met with Sims and other leaders from the staff for lunch. At the September 13, 2001, public meeting on the new theater, about 130 people showed up to criticize the proposal, mostly supporters of the symphony.

The only Pavilion tenant to support the building of the new theater was Jeff Meredith of Virginia Musical Theatre (VMT). In 2001, the VMT had an annual operating budget of $534,000, of which $144,000 came from contributions, $73,000 from government grants, and $317,000 from performance revenues. In addition to some educational programs, Meredith directed four productions every season for a total of 32 performances. Each production attracted three thousand to four thousand people over the course of its eight-day run. Meredith held auditions in New York and also hired some "top notch" local performers to perform in musicals like *Grease* and *1776*. He was committed to shows with high production values.

He remembers the Pavilion as a theater with inadequate dressing rooms, a "cold" audience chamber, and an unsociable layout of the public space with two unconnected lobbies. "It was sterile. You didn't feel like you had come to a place where something exciting in the arts was going to happen," he said. He saw the change as an opportunity to reshape the profile of the performing arts in Virginia Beach. "We want an identity that says this is the performing arts. Not, and by the way, there's a boat show and there's an antique show and there's a theater. Part of your credibility is where you perform and what you're a part of."

Soon, another opposition group surfaced. Cost projections rose as the question of the building was studied, and criticism of using public funds to build a theater grew louder. "We have a lot of other needs of equal importance to the theater. We have pressing needs in transportation, all the time. Public safety is always a priority," said councilman Ron Villanueva about the reasons for his skepticism. Councilman Bob Dyer explained his dissent in similar terms: "This is a lot of money to be investing when there are some needs that exist in other areas." Dyer did not think that the arts were an essential public need that merited government funding. Yet Virginia Beach was also an unlikely location for arts groups and arts facilities to be built and nurtured without public support. The project's champions pointed to positive externalities like economic development to justify city funding. Mayor Oberndorf defended the new theater's right to exist in more emotional terms: "I have always been such a believer in performing arts. It helps your soul when things are the darkest. That is what motivates Man above all other animals, because we can comprehend, we can create, and we can celebrate, and that's why I wanted a permanent edifice in the city where these things could happen."

A third issue voiced by the project's critics concerned the possibility of failure. This concern stemmed either from the fear that the region was already saturated with performing arts venues or from the perception that Virginia Beach was inhospitable to the arts and thus the wrong location for a new theater of this sort. Those concerned about market saturation argued that the larger Hampton Roads region had plenty of theaters. They were concerned that another venue and its events would lead to a situation where the availability of cultural events would outpace the audience's demand for them. "We didn't want to introduce a theater that would be destructive in terms of the cultural art scene in the region," said City Manager Jim Spore.

The metropolitan area of Hampton Roads (formerly known as Tidewater) also includes the cities of Norfolk (population: 234,000), Newport News (population: 180,000), Chesapeake (population: 199,000), and Portsmouth (population: 100,000), as well as the historic towns of Williamsburg, Jamestown, and Yorktown. Located twelve miles from the geographic center of Virginia Beach, Norfolk is home to seven city-owned performing arts venues, including the 2,361-seat Chrysler Hall, the 1,600-seat Harrison Opera House, and two 600-seat professional quality theaters. In Newport News, a 1,700-seat Ferguson Hall was being built at Christopher Newport University, but the traffic at the Hampton Roads Bridge Tunnel was likely to make Beach residents think twice about attending. In Virginia Beach itself, a 750-seat Performing Arts Theater was under construction at Regent University, which was founded by the televangelist Pat Robertson. Sims and the council met with Regent administrators and found them sympathetic to the plight of the soon-to-be-homeless Virginia Beach groups. However, university uses had to come first and Regent representatives could not commit to the number of dates that would be available.

In addition to the availability of venues, project critics doubted that the culture of Virginia Beach would prove hospitable to a new venue and that the frequently amateur groups calling Virginia Beach home really needed a place to perform. Partially, this attitude grew out of cultural snobbery and sibling rivalry between the cities of Norfolk and Virginia Beach. Norfolk had long laid claim to being the more culturally sophisticated of the two, dubbing itself the "cultural capital of Virginia." Norfolk has a small but densely populated city core with shops, cafés, and restaurants. Professional companies like Broadway Across America, Virginia Opera, Virginia Symphony, Virginia Ballet, and Virginia Stage Company called Norfolk home.

By contrast, Virginia Beach had struggled to find the audiences for its one theater with 1,000 seats. A newspaper based in Norfolk, *The Virginian Pilot*, had a sharp-edged columnist, Kerry Dougherty, who became one of the theater project's most loyal observers and harshest critics. She was particularly unimpressed by the Pavilion Theatre's attendance record. She wrote: "The last time we checked, the citys [*sic*] existing theater had tumbleweeds blowing down the aisles. This is shaping up to be yet another Build-It-And-They-Will-Come project. Is the Council simply scared that angry strip-mall dance studio owners will incite tutu-clad mobs to march on City Hall, demanding a public venue for their next recital?" Dougherty was adamant that any new Virginia Beach venue was doomed by the city's cultural inferiority. "If established groups like these in Norfolk are struggling—in a city that strongly supports the arts—what in the world is going to happen at the Beach, where the most notable recent cultural contributions have been Rudy Boesch and Evan Marriott? Fact is, Virginia Beach is not the cultural capital of Hampton Roads. Norfolk is. Always will be."

Yet data gathered by Theatre Projects Consultants complicated this lopsided characterization of Virginia Beach as a cultural backwater. First, for the regional groups, including professional groups of record based in Norfolk like Virginia Symphony and Virginia Opera, the highest concentration of audiences lived in Virginia Beach, not Norfolk. Second, a survey of 75 cultural leaders showed that the region's cultural organizations wanted another venue. Third, a demographic customer segmentation analysis of Virginia Beach and projected growth suggested there was unmet demand for cultural offerings.

In light of this, why wasn't the Pavilion Theatre doing better? The convention center manager, Courtney Dyer (unrelated to councilman Dyer), pointed out that the Pavilion's mission had been nurturing local groups. From this vantage point, the Pavilion had achieved a measure of success, allowing local groups like the Virginia Musical Theatre and the Virginia Beach Symphony to take root and find an audience. He also believed that with a different facility and operating model, the attendance figures would look drastically different. Once, even at the Pavilion, things had been different. When the city made programming there a funding priority, its headliners included Yo-Yo Ma, Itzhak Perlman, the Moscow Ballet, and Joan Rivers. Then the funding for programming was decreased and some newer, technically superior venues like Harrison Opera House and Roper Theater opened in Norfolk, and as a consequence the Pavilion Theatre was less successful in attracting famous acts. The attendance dropped. A better venue could change this. The new theater would be technically and aesthetically superior to the Pavilion, and would provide a better experience for the audience. If removed from the Oceanfront, the theater would have ample free parking. It would also offer the performers and producers an opportunity to reach not only the Virginia Beach audiences, but audiences from the entire region. With a calendar filled with events, the new venue could not only continue to nurture local talent, but also educate and develop the local audiences too. "A baseball analogy," he said. "We'd been in the minor leagues and we wanted to bring it up a level or two and have some offerings that the community would recognize as first class, would want to participate in, want to support, and really take the cultural arts to the next level."

Thus, the new theater faced opposition from both sides of the cultural funding divide from the start. The artistic groups were afraid that the city would renege on its promise to rebuild, or change the parameters of the theater so much that they would no longer be able to perform there. Other critics doubted the probity and the success of a public investment in an arts project in Virginia Beach. The combined weight of these two opposition groups cast a pall over the project. Meanwhile, the project's champions proceeded with planning, optimistic not only about replacing the Pavilion but about improving it too. They would rebuild a home for the displaced local groups, draw national touring shows, and put themselves on a more equal footing with Norfolk.

Yet soon, it became apparent that within the space of one theater several of these dreams were incompatible. National tours of popular acts like Broadway shows and famous musicians consider the total box office revenue potential of a venue when making decisions. Thus, theaters with larger seating capacities tend to win. However, a theater large enough to attract a Broadway tour would be a half-empty cavern during a performance by the Virginia Beach Symphony or Virginia Musical Theatre. Seats would go empty, to the chagrin of both the audience and the performers. The sense of immediacy would be lost. The local groups needed a smaller theater. In settling on the theater's size, the civic leaders of Virginia Beach faced a choice between stakeholders: for-profit promoters and the prospect of large audiences on one side and the entire ecosystem of local groups, performers, and their small number of loyal followers on the other.

Somewhere in Virginia Beach, support for any number of seats between 200 and 2,500 could be found. Governor's School for the Arts wanted a small 200-seat theater for the two annual performances by its students. Tidewater Classical Guitar Society would perform three times a year, preferably in a theater with 500 seats. Overall, ten local organizations said they needed a venue with fewer than 500 seats for 71 performances every year. In addition, six other current tenants of the Pavilion Theatre had an average attendance of less than 500. Together, these six organizations held 56 performances at the Pavilion, though all of them said they wanted a space with seating capacity larger than 500 to allow for future growth. In Spore's opinion, a new 500-seat theater was not necessary, since the new Contemporary Art Center the city built in 1990 already had a small theater of 268 seats that served the same artistic and marketing niche. Still, a theater with 500 seats was the least expensive in terms of capital costs, and the city's finance director reported that the city council had turned to the option at one juncture in an attempt to reduce spending.

The Pavilion's largest tenants, Virginia Musical Theatre and Virginia Beach Symphony, were initially insistent on a smaller theater of about 800 seats, which would better fit their audiences. Young and Kunkel of VBSO mentioned that they wanted a venue that would accommodate their 650 subscribers as well as the 100–150 people who buy their tickets "at the door." (The symphony considered its most important constituents to be its volunteer musicians and its subscribers.) However, Kunkel and Young were aware that both the large capital investment on the part of the city and the operating budget of the potential theater made a larger venue seem more attractive. "We were smart enough to know they needed to make it bigger to make it pay," said Young. In their July 2001 letter, she and Kunkel wrote: "If a way can be found to raise the seating total, with all other things remaining the same, the Virginia Beach Symphony Orchestra would be in favor of it."

VMT's Meredith was also talked into eventually supporting a slightly larger venue once he and his peers looked at the future center's programming during the course of their meetings. "You've got 365 days out of the year. I do 32 performances. What about all those other days in a year?" he says. "That's when the whole idea of bringing in additional acts and having all those seats that were going to economically make that feasible came up. There aren't many people out there who are going to book an 800-seat house given the cost of touring, a musician, or whatever. You have to be realistic about where the venue's going to be eventually."

Yet Meredith's willingness to consent to a larger space was limited. "The number 2,000 came up," said Meredith, describing an advisory committee's deliberations. "That's when all the arts organizations said, that's ridiculous. We'll be all selling to 50 percent capacity." Like most performers, Meredith preferred to have the smallest venue that would fit his audience so as to foster a sense of spatial intimacy between the audience and the performers as well as to avoid actors' looking out from the stage into an audience chamber that was half-empty.

In addition to the support of these core tenants, the midsize theater also had the benefit of being politically defensible. No theater with seating capacity between 900 and 1,500 seats existed in the region, and the city council could claim that the new theater would not be competing with or replicating any existing venue. Without competition, the opposition to public expenditure that Oberndorf suspected of emanating from Norfolk would lessen.

Another suggestion on size was offered by the Norfolk-based Virginia Symphony, which, as Virginia Beach planners discovered, was willing to defect. They saw the creation of a new theater in Virginia Beach as an opportunity. Chrysler Hall in Norfolk served as the group's home, but ever since Chrysler became the home of the lucrative touring Broadway series, Virginia Symphony felt marginalized there. Sims said the group told Virginia Beach planners that it would consider moving to Virginia Beach if a suitable new home were built there.

The Virginia Symphony was the only professional orchestra company in the region as well as a local organization that dwarfed its Virginia Beach siblings. Its annual operating budget in 2002 was $4.8 million, $2.3 million of which came from program revenue. The company also received $300,000 in government grants and $1.8 million in contributions. And it ran a deficit of $245,000 for the year. In meetings with the representatives of the performing arts center steering committee, Virginia Symphony leadership asked for a 1,800-seat symphony hall. They were resistant to making the space a multiuse facility, for fear of yet again being displaced by Broadway. Its desired building would have no orchestra pit for dance or theater performances and no variable acoustics that would make the building work well for other genres. In exchange, they promised to become a resident group, thus lending the facility the aura of its artistic credibility and bringing—or returning—its audiences to Virginia Beach.

Yet another option was a Broadway-sized house, as Mayor Oberndorf had always dreamed of having in Virginia Beach. Multiple civic leaders asked by the city council to study the issue (and then to raise private funds to bridge the gap between municipal funds and projected costs) were fond of the idea of a 2,500-seat house as well. This after all was the size of a theater that would attract performers whom they and thousands of Virginia Beach residents would love to pay to see. "If I could bring the show of *Jersey Boys* here, I can tell you there wouldn't be a ticket left," said Mayor Oberndorf. Still, she was committed to the interests of the local groups.

A rental house model was also attractive from the perspective of funding. "Financially, you would have more people attending. It has the potential to bring shows that many people can't travel to other cities to enjoy," said Oberndorf. Bobbi Melatti, a Virginia Beach show business promoter and member of the city's Arts & Humanities Commission, explained why a larger venue brought these benefits. Melatti has been a presenter of live performances at the Oceanfront for over fifteen years, first with Live Nation and now as part of the local company IMG. When he looks for a venue for a performance he is producing, he wants enough seats to generate ticket sales in excess of the costs of paying the performers and covering production expenses, as well as paying the rent and performing arts center services like production staff and cleaning. He said he would be reluctant to rent a venue of fewer than 2,000 seats for one of his events. "You can't make money," he said. "Even if they gave us the building, it would be hard."

Melatti understood the concerns of the local nonprofit groups but believed such emotional appeals should be dismissed. "Go and ask five experts in the area what size you need empirically—which as far as I'm concerned is the only way to look at things." Sims heard a similar argument from other members of the community. "I certainly hope we are not spending $45 million so that Jill's Dancing School can have a space for its recitals," she remembered hearing. "Maybe we should let social Darwinism take its course," said Melatti.

A different perspective was offered by another producer, Robert Cross, the director of the Virginia Arts Festival, who focused on programming offered by nonprofit groups. He believed the quality of the acts brought to a theater depended more on the annual budget than on its seating capacity. With enough money and a sufficiently equipped stage, a performing arts center programmer could book just about any act through a co-promotion arrangement by underwriting the expenses. In this arrangement, the performers' fees and production expenses are covered by a performing arts center, which then collects all the revenues. The performers care about seating capacity less when their remuneration is independent of total attendance. If the city of Virginia Beach or private supporters were to offer their performing arts center annual financial support for operations in greater amounts, then the performing arts center would be able to afford higher profile performances.

Another consideration in deciding on a 2,500-seat theater was that this venue would compete directly with Norfolk's city-owned Chrysler Hall. Chrysler was built in 1971. The partisans of the Virginia Beach theater said that Chrysler Hall was particularly vulnerable to competition owing to its inferior acoustics. "The acoustics were abominable. I've been to thousands of events, and I've never heard the first words. The [performers] all had to be miked," said Oberndorf. This weakness especially meant that the construction of a large venue in Virginia Beach could have a profound effect on the health of Norfolk's theater. "If you put a 2,500-seat theater in Town Center, we are dead," Courtney Dyer, the manager of the Virginia Beach Convention Center, remembered hearing from John Rhamstine, who ran all seven of the Norfolk city-owned theaters. Though few Beach residents saw harming Chrysler Hall as a worthwhile objective, many of the new theater's advocates felt wounded by the insinuations of Virginia Beach's cultural inferiority to Norfolk. Competing and winning would doubtlessly feel satisfying.

However, the clout of the Norfolk cultural institutions was significant and many of their supporters lived in Virginia Beach. These citizens were concerned about both duplication of public expenditure and competition. Oberndorf thought that Norfolk was clandestinely meddling in the affairs of Virginia Beach by pressing these people to speak out against competition with other venues in the region. She discovered this when she began having conversations with her city's arts donors about the prospect of private funding for the new theater. "They're subtle," she said about Norfolk groups. "They line up their givers who live at the Beach and they march them in to explain to us why we don't need to—quote—compete with them." She saw the same phenomenon at neighborhood meetings. "Somebody will stand up and go, 'But we have a perfectly good theater in the region!'" In the end, Norfolk institutions and their supporters' resistance to a 2,500-seat theater decreased its political and financial feasibility.

* * *

Ultimately, the Virginia Beach City Council decided to proceed with a medium-sized theater of 1,200 seats, a capacity that would eventually increase to 1,300 in deference to concerns about revenues and programming. This was a compromise solution, one seeking to cater to both the fans of the local groups and to big name acts from outside the community. Oberndorf returned home from this meeting to face yet another critic—her husband, who questioned how a 1,300-seat theater could ever be financially viable. "My own husband, when I got home said, 'That was a dumb decision.'" He had watched the evening's meeting on TV. Oberndorf saw the 1,300-seat theater as the only politically feasible and defensible solution. "We're doing it to make it affordable to the nonprofits," she told her husband. "We're doing it not to tick off Norfolk. We're doing it not to make Pat Robertson angry."

In October 2004, with the design complete, the council hesitated yet again, this time to authorize the actual construction contract. Mayor Oberndorf estimated the chances of the theater's being approved during that vote at about 50/50. She knew any further delays would doom the project. With Pavilion Theatre's demolition only a few months away, the performing arts groups and the Town Center's Central Business Development Authority rallied their supporters for an email and phone campaign. Even then, Oberndorf thought the theater vote could still fail if not for ten-year-old Annika Jenkins, who asked to speak during the televised public hearing portion of the meeting, then played her violin and presented a glass jar full of coins she collected from her classmates for the new theater. Oberndorf said: "And I looked up—because it was a podium where an equal amount of council was on either right or left—and I looked down the table on both sides and I said, 'I'd like to dare any of you to vote against it now.' So a couple of the men got up and went to the men's room to caucus." The televised vote followed a week later, and the theater was approved, 9 to 2. In 2005, the naming rights to the new theater were sold for $5 million to local developers, the Sandler brothers, who chose to name the new venue after their parents. See figure 4.2.

The opening of the Sandler inspired much civic pride. Itzhak Perlman played to a sold-out hall during the ceremonies. "This place is lit up. There are cars, limos, everyone's decked to the 9s. The businesses love it," said Linwood Branch, now the chairman of the Sandler Center foundation, in reference to the center's events. During the first season, the center's attendance reached 70,000, then 80,000 during the second season. In roughly the first two years of being open, between November 2007 and June 2009, the Sandler Center hosted 266 performances and 42 rehearsals on the main stage. The rehearsal hall held 79 events and 149 rehearsals, while 37 other events were held in the Sandler Center's main lobby and 50 in its upstairs classrooms, which are popular with corporate

4.2 The Sandler Center for the Performing Arts by Craig McClure. Courtesy of the Sandler Center for the Performing Arts.

meetings. The city government also now uses some of the meeting spaces at the Sandler, though the city's use is not included in these statistics. The Sandler Center budget for FY2008–9 was about $1.5 million, with $500,000 allocated to funding programming. The city gives the Sandler Center an annual subsidy of $1.2 million–$1.3 million.

The Virginia Musical Theatre, supportive of the new theater from the very beginning, struggled with the move. After the Pavilion's razing, the group had to move to the 268-seat Contemporary Arts Center of Virginia theater at the Oceanfront. Its shows had to become smaller, its operating revenues decreased, and operational deficits mounted. Once the Sandler opened, Meredith found the new management less welcoming than he expected—there was no office space he could rent for the company and the Sandler Center required him to rent and install a dance floor so that his tap dancers would not damage the wooden floors installed for corporate and fundraising banquets in the rehearsal space. Meredith usually raised $300,000–$400,000 each year, but now his annual fund pledges dropped by 50 percent. Some of his most reliable donors said they had already given that year, to the Sandler Center. His operating costs increased as well, since he was now paying for services like on-site paramedics that at the Pavilion Theatre had been covered by the convention center. On the other hand, attendance in the first year increased by

20 percent, but then dropped during the following year due to the recession. By summer 2009, fundraising recovered. Meredith's productions also became better in the new venue. He was uncertain whether that success was caused by the move. "Sometimes, the casting gods are with you," he said. In the end, however, owing to two years of homelessness, dampened fundraising, increased costs, and the effects of the recession, his company was running a deficit, and in late 2008 the city gave the VMT a $200,000 emergency loan.

The Virginia Beach Symphony Orchestra, now known as Symphonicity, also saw its fortunes changed by the move. At the beginning of the planning process, the company was fearful and resistant to the idea of the new venue, and in anticipation of change, Symphonicity leadership wrote a business plan in 2004 and undertook a board building effort. The company ramped up its fundraising to increase the organization's budget from $140,000 to $250,000. With a new, prestigious home, Symphonicity found a corporate sponsor. Its audience increased from an average of 700 at the Pavilion to 850 during its first season at the Sandler. Symphonicity has also found that its new professional venue attracts a better class of musician to its all-volunteer orchestra. Both the acoustics and the change in constitution have made the performances aesthetically better. The change to the new venue, once so feared, proved to be a boon. Filling seats is still a problem, however, especially given that the 2008–9 season saw the audience drop to 600. To make the house look full for the benefit of its performers, Symphonicity now gives away 50–100 tickets per night. Expressing an opinion seconded by every leader involved with the project, Young said, "We'd like to sell more tickets."

Thus, the facility built in Virginia Beach was a compromise solution to a conflict between stakeholders that has so far failed to please any one group fully. The heads of programming there struggle to book acts and fill seats. For-profit promoters are contemplating a different, privately funded venue, one that will probably serve the summer tourists at the Oceanfront. The local nonprofit cultural groups wrestle with a half-empty theater. At some level, each of these stakeholders also benefits from the availability of a venue and is happy that a new theater has been built. Yet many in Virginia Beach are measuring the success of the new venue in the number of sold-out shows, and so far the new theater has struggled to find the programming niche for its seating capacity. Confronted by diametrically opposed groups of community stakeholders, the decision makers in Virginia Beach chose the middle ground. And the middle ground they chose to accommodate the desires of many satisfies the true needs of few.

From the standpoint of the Power-Urgency-Legitimacy framework, the flaw with the Virginia Beach stakeholder engagement process was treating a large number of stakeholders as equal. Few definitive stakeholders were to be found outside of the city council, and even within it, several of the members failed to make their opinions seem urgent. The artistic groups were stakeholders with legitimate and urgent claims but little power, which put them in the expectant stakeholder tier. Critics of runaway public spending enjoy the perception of legitimacy, though in this case, their ability to make their claims seem urgent varied over time. Few other stakeholders had the same level of salience. For-profit producers had power, but little legitimacy or urgency within the eyes of the community. The Norfolk Opera was an institution with a great deal of legitimacy, but little power, given its deteriorating financial state, or urgency, given its ability to continue to use the Ferguson Hall. Annika's violin performance was an emotionally charged request that seemed to succeed in having the community acknowledge its urgency. Yet no matter how fine a violin player, a ten-year-old is unlikely to see her demand for $45 million in public spending be accepted as legitimate. Thus, the most salient of the stakeholders offering a view on the theater were the local artistic groups and perhaps the critics of public spending. These were the views that needed to be taken into account and balanced against each other. The consideration of the calls for a 2,500-seat theater during this project—and the eventual compromise on 1,300 seats—may have unnecessarily protracted the debates and arguably has hindered this fledgling performing arts center from performing at its full potential.[21]

Assessing and Understanding Community Response

The topic of competition between arts groups and the impact of a capital project in the cultural sector on bystander organizations always arises whenever community role and impact are discussed. As part of the larger research project on cultural infrastructure, a series of community surveys was conducted, reaching a total of 444 arts leaders in 13 cities where large projects were undertaken. The subjects were selected at random from a list of cultural organizations within a metropolitan area to assess external perspectives on these building projects. In 7 of 13 selected cities, the respondents were asked about one of the case study projects, and the insights gained from these interviews have been incorporated into our analysis throughout this book. The only case study cities where the surveys were not conducted were cities with an insufficient number of cultural groups to draw a large enough sample. Most of the time, we had already interviewed the other cultural leaders there in greater depth. Several important themes about stakeholder assessments of these projects emerged from these surveys.

First, surprisingly few community cultural organizations report any negative impact on their attendance or fundraising during and after a capital project. In our case study field interviews, we heard occasional reports from community organizations outside the project who have found their donors giving less because of the competition from a capital campaign. The survey suggests only a small minority of groups perceive any negative effect on their contributions, and that a few organizations even report a general increase in their fundraising as the result of a completely unrelated capital project. A few organizations noted their relief over this outcome, since at the start of the project they had been worried. "I was quite concerned about the impact it might have on us," said one respondent in Atlanta. "The end result is that it's either increased or we've held steady. It hasn't been huge." Another aspect of increased competition that surfaced as a subject of concern during case study interviews was increased competition for audiences. Our survey found that 10 percent of our 444 respondents saw a decrease in audience size in the year following a grand opening of a capital project in the arts. A far greater portion—35 percent—saw their audiences increase, suggesting that the attention drawn to the arts within a city by a grand opening of a cultural facility benefits even the groups with no connection to the new building. An analysis by our colleague Bruce Seaman found that these assessments seem to correlate with general economic growth—organizations in cities with growing employment are more likely to report a positive effect, while organizations in cities where employment is growing less rapidly are more likely to report a negative one.[22]

Second, our survey indicated that community sentiment toward the project evolved over the course of its planning and execution, usually improving. Only 45 percent of our 444 respondents believed that the capital project was really necessary before a project had started, and 38 percent believed the project to be unnecessary. After the project was completed, 72 percent believed that the project had in fact served a vital community need, and only 15 percent continued to doubt the wisdom of the capital investment. A similar revision of sentiment for the better was observed with regards to specific community aspirations, like economic development. During initial planning, stakeholders were more dubious about the project's ability to impact the community than they were after the project was complete. Both of these results paint an optimistic picture of the impact of cultural building projects on their communities, even when the projects themselves struggle. One possible explanation of this result is that community response is a powerful force and usually, but not always, acts as a check against projects that would result in catastrophes. This hypothesis cannot be tested with our data at present, yet communities wield significant power in project discussions, a power that needs to be understood and harnessed.

The complex ecosystems of the patrons, partners, and general public within which arts organizations operate produce a dizzying array of potential stakeholders. Meaningful engagement with all of them frequently proves impossible. Yet understanding and incorporating the perspectives of a select group of the most salient stakeholders is likely to be beneficial to a capital project in the arts. Power, legitimacy, and urgency together are the key to triaging stakeholder needs, as well as to determining an arts organization's own weight in other institutions' stakeholder negotiations. In the hands of the right leaders, a sound approach to community engagement may well become a tool for achieving a higher degree of strategic alignment.

5 | *Growing Operational Capacity*

In 2003, late one evening, the new executive director of Ballet Austin was discussing the future Long Center for the Performing Arts with the other directors of the artistic companies who would perform there, as well as consultants helping them shape the building's program. The project was an adaptive reuse of an existing building, which imposed many constraints on the facility. The construction budget was tight. One problem that was particularly difficult to fix without increasing the budget was the crossover. Essentially, if the center were built as then planned, the performers would have no way to get from stage right to stage left backstage. To exit the stage on the right and then re-enter on the left, a dancer would have to run outside and around the building—in costume. There were only two ways to solve this problem. The first was to sacrifice about fifteen feet of stage depth. This way, there would be enough room within the existing structure for the crossover. Yet neither Cookie Ruiz nor the other performing company heads wanted to give up stage depth, which they needed to be able to rent sets. The only alternative was building a "bump out" to expand the existing facility by about fifteen feet—at the cost of about $5 million.

Finding this $5 million was the subject of the conference call. What could be cut? The heads of the artistic organizations and the consultants reviewed every facet of the program: the dimensions of the stage, lighting systems, rigging, backstage areas, and a myriad of other things that define the performance capabilities of a venue. The call continued for four and a half hours.

Before coming to the ballet, Cookie Ruiz had served as the president of the local chapter of the Junior League. She had a background in fundraising. The arts, however, were entirely new to her. "I was new to my job. I was still amassing knowledge," she said. The technical needs of the stage behind the footlights were still arcane to her. One of Ballet Austin's technologically savvy dancers came up with a solution: Ruiz was speaking by phone to the other members of the design team and to her production director and electrical crew manager through instant messages on her computer.

The consultants would ask her about Ballet Austin's requirement for something like the depth of the stage and she would say, "Let me think about that for a moment." She'd type the question into her instant message window for her staff to answer. "Hurry, hurry," she'd type. "65.3 feet," they'd type back. "Let me see," she'd say into the phone. "I think we'll need about 65 feet."

Ruiz stayed with the building effort for the Long Center from its beginning to the grand opening and has kept her ballet company in the black through the recession. "Every time I cross from stage left to stage right, I just smile and think of that phone call and think of those two guys who made a very green executive director sound very intelligent for four and a half hours."

The learning curve of staff, trustees, and volunteers at the center of the decision-making process for a building project—or how they come to acquire the necessary new skills and knowledge—is one of the most decisive factors in determining the project trajectory.[1] The leadership team required to steer a construction project differs radically in its skills and frequently even composition from the team that oversaw a successful arts organization before the project, and the team that will oversee the same arts organization after opening. During the planning and execution of capital projects, unique fields of expertise become required. Existing organizations need to develop strategies for building capacity to both continue operations and accomplish the large array of highly iterative decision-making tasks. New organizations have to develop from scratch the capacity both to build and to operate.[2] This capacity involves selecting and developing people and processes to best handle the turbulence that is par for the course in large building projects in the arts.

In the world of cultural building, human capacity is destiny. When faced with challenges, leadership teams fall back on their strengths. As Abraham Maslow once noted: "It is tempting, if the only tool you have is a hammer, to treat everything as if it were a nail."[3] Instead of seeking out new tools specifically suited to their problems, arts organizations frequently try to use the capacity already at their disposal. Thus, the diversity of the expertise profiles represented on the leadership team plays a large role in determining project success.

The two most important dimensions of the leadership team as a whole are its breadth and depth of expertise. When the leadership team can rely on only depth or only breadth of expertise, the organization may be successful at pushing the project forward, but will undertake certain risks. Organizations that have members with a deep and thorough knowledge of one of the skills pertinent to capital projects can rely on that capacity to compensate for weaknesses. Thus, organizations with a strength in fundraising (like the AT&T Performing Arts Center under Bill Lively) will use that strength to avoid dealing with their other issues, such as artistic and operating plans after opening. Organizations with a capacity spike in debt financing can get a building erected without ever embarking on a capital campaign. Then, like the Taubman Museum, they face a postopening reality of unsustainable and crippling budget deficits that make proper staffing impossible. More common still are organizations that start the project with a sound strategy, but then find fully executing their vision a challenge. Organizations that do not already have capacity in the areas required by cultural building projects and that cannot recruit staff, contractors, or volunteers may simply fail to get a project past the conceptual stage. Arguably, this can be another explanation for the failure of the Fishers' Contemporary Art Museum of Presidio to get off the ground, despite a surfeit of resources. On the other hand, organizations with human capacity spikes in one or more fields of expertise required by a building project may find they are successful in completing their projects, only to discover themselves in a state of misalignment because operating a new facility requires skills different than planning and building. This inability to anticipate problems and their solutions results in these organizations being blindsided and even crippled when problems arise—problems that others with the requisite skills may well have been able to avoid and resolve with ease. The four potential organizational states for human capacity and the balance of expertise depth and breadth within the leadership team are shown in table 5.1.

What this diagram makes obvious is that the right balance of expertise cannot be found by recruiting a single capable leader. The key lies in recruiting a diverse leadership group and then instituting processes that tap this talent effectively.[4] A study of megaprojects found that diversity of skills within the project governance team is directly related to that

Table 5.1. Risks and Benefits of Balancing Expertise

| | | Breadth of Expertise among Leaders | |
		Low	High
Depth of Expertise among Leaders	Low	Potential for failure to launch	Blindness to risks
	High	Shortcomings in execution	Foundation for success

team's ability to generate creative solutions.[5] In this way, the wealth of approaches that a diverse team, with a variety of fields of expertise and backgrounds, can bring to any given challenge can offer a significant advantage in problem solving. Leadership diversity also helps ensure that the multiple strategic prerogatives of the organization sponsoring the project are all protected, even in the heat of a capital project.

One key aspect of ensuring that the organization takes full advantage of the strengths of its leadership team is keeping all the necessary experts engaged.[6] A silent trustee who does not voice a potential objection might as well not belong to the decision-making group at all. Conflicts are frequently seen as a sign of trouble, yet in our fieldwork, we have seen several projects put back on track toward alignment after a disagreement among leaders about the right course.[7] The expansion at the Art Institute of Chicago, for example, led to a dispute between top fundraisers and the finance committee. These two powerful groups disagreed on the right time to begin construction. Optimism is a prerequisite for any capital campaign, and the leaders of the fundraising effort were naturally optimistic about achieving their fundraising targets. Having the construction underway would also help in fundraising, they believed, and so they felt there was some urgency to begin building. Meanwhile, the finance committee was mainly concerned about the impact of the project on the annual budget, cash flows, and balance sheet. The trustees there were more fiscally conservative. On both sides of the debate, key leaders believed the concerns of their committees were of paramount importance. Unlike in Dallas, where the capital campaign committee was far more active than the relatively dormant operations committee, in Chicago leaders were active and engaged on both sides of the debate. Their difference of opinion over which potential risk was the greatest—and how that risk needed to be anticipated in the strategic plan—resulted in a plan that was ultimately more sound. Leadership teams are reluctant to admit to any conflict, yet in the end, a constructive disagreement between leaders with diverse backgrounds and perspectives, followed by a rational process for resolution, is the best way to ensure project alignment.[8] Rather than a sign of failure, such internal debate is frequently the early indicator of good decision making.

Understanding Leadership

Beyond building a strong team, leadership involves another dimension: the capacity to move an organization when need be. Leadership has traditionally been a misunderstood element of an organization's success and hidden key element shaping the course of cultural building projects. What really is leadership? What can it do and how does it function effectively to help an arts organization achieve its goals, particularly when it comes to construction?

In his landmark study of the most successful American companies, Jim Collins discovered that the great companies all had a leader with "Level 5 leadership" during their pivotal transition from being a good company to becoming a great one. He defines a Level 5 leader as "an individual who blends extreme personal humility with intense professional will" with the goal of "building enduring greatness."[9] The Level 5 executive is the final rung on a ladder of increasingly advanced leadership styles. Level 4 effective leaders catalyze commitment to a clear and compelling vision and stimulate higher performance standards. Level 3 competent managers find a way to get to predetermined goals, while Level 2 contributing team members find ways to work well with others and Level 1 capable individuals bring talent to the project at hand.

It is the Level 5 leader who makes the real difference and has the "ferocious resolve, an almost stoic determination to do whatever needs to be done to make the company great."[10] This leader moves beyond simply managing people and projects, and even beyond getting people behind a common vision, to ensuring that the group, organization, or company becomes exceptional.

But how does a leader make an organization great? Ronald Heifetz provides a framework for understanding what leadership is and how it can be practiced effectively to create successful change.[11] He defines leadership as "mobilizing people to tackle tough problems."[12] Leadership, as he defines it, is about getting a group of people to make the adaptations necessary in order to survive and thrive. Indeed, Heifetz argues that the "most valuable task of leadership may be advancing goals and designing strategy that promote adaptive work."[13] "Tackling tough problems—problems that often require an evolution of values—is the end of leadership; getting that work done is its essence."[14]

In understanding leadership and what makes it effective it is useful to make a distinction between two types of situations and their appropriate leadership responses. A technical situation is when the problem facing a group is recognizable and can be solved with a response that has worked in the past. In this case the leadership response should be authoritative. If the problem is recognizable, the leader simply demands that the group employ the solution that has worked before. For example, a theater leader may ask staff to cut back on expensive sets when the organization is facing tough times financially.

However, in an adaptive situation, progress on the problem requires changes in the group's values, attitudes, or habits. Therefore, the leadership response cannot be authoritative—a leader cannot simply tell people to change. Rather in the adaptive situation the leader must help the social system "learn its way forward."[15] The leader helps guide this new learning, and thus helps guide the group toward change. For example, a museum director facing declining attendance cannot simply demand that curators curate more effectively. Instead, a skilled director would analyze the problem and help the museum staff work together to create a new solution to the problem, which would, no doubt, involve changes in behaviors, attitudes, and habits. Adaptive problems are of course far more demanding than technical ones. To solve the complex challenges that arise during cultural building projects, building a team and then seeing to it that it moves cohesively in the right direction is the core of both the leadership and the organizational capacity question.

Breadth of Expertise

Given the prominent role we are claiming for breadth of expertise in ensuring project success, the question of which domains are useful for capital building in the cultural sector needs to be addressed. Though any building project will require a thousand small decisions, the large decisions that matter the most can be handled by people with knowledge of seven key areas of expertise: design and building project management, capital campaigns, financial structures like tax credits and bonds, public relations, financial planning, artistic facilities, and artistic programming. A leadership group with the broadest possible set of skills will include someone with knowledge of each of these domains. A strength in these areas will help move the project forward. Lack of any institutional capacity with these seven fields is likely to result in blindness to at least some risks and opportunities.

Four of the skills we have identified—artistic facilities, artistic programming, public relations, and business planning—are needed for normal operations outside of building projects as well. Yet some of these skills are routinely dismissed as irrelevant to facility planning.[16] The exclusion of people with these skills from decision making routinely results in blindness to some of the most important opportunities and risks—those most closely affecting the organization's ability to carry out its mission, interact with its community, and sustain itself financially. The same is true for the other three skills as well.

The first of these seven areas of expertise is the management of design and construction projects. Many of the trustees and arts executives we spoke to raved about the competence and the positive impact of their project managers. These specialists understand how design and construction proceed. From value engineering to change order handling, they help organize and direct the work of various consultants (like architects and cost consultants), contractors, and internal staff and trustees helming the effort. Ideally, these professionals will keep the process on track and on budget. They cannot, however, provide project vision or do much to contain design creep that emanates from the top ranks of organizations. Local governments sponsoring their own projects and a few of the largest organizations may keep a skilled design and construction manager permanently on staff. In other organizations, they are hired or, if independent consultants, retained for the duration of the project. Frequently, they work in concert with trustees and staff on a special committee dedicated to design and building issues. Failing to secure a person with expertise in this area for the project team is likely to make the process more chaotic and to add yet another burden on staff and trustees.

Aptitude for public relations within the leadership team helps to develop and oversee an execution of the strategy for when, how, and why the organization communicates with the external world about the building project. Which stakeholders will the organization engage and when? How much community input will the organization seek on its plans? How will it respond to criticism? To what standards of transparency and accountability does the organization want to adhere during the process?

Leadership teams that do not have active participants trained to ask these questions and knowledgeable about how to answer them may stumble blindly into public maelstroms. And since arts are a natural lightning rod for debates about issues like community politics and identity, many arts organizations that embark on building projects, especially those that seek public funds, may find themselves attracting controversy. This is why the leadership team will benefit from including someone with a proven track record of handling public relations.

Good financial plans are a stumbling block for many arts projects. Forecast inaccuracy is widespread, and the consequences are severe: curtailment of hours and programs, staff cuts, debt, deficits, and even bankruptcy. At least one root cause of the problem is the prevalence of incentive misalignment and the extent to which the quest to secure resources for building overshadows everything else. Incentive misalignment arises because the people who plan a building project are frequently not the people who have to run the organization after the doors open. Business plans are left to consultants. Though the majority of them are experts at the task, serious disincentives for providing pessimistic forecasts are the daily reality. When giving clients bad news, consultants are forced to work harder to justify their findings, and referrals, on which they depend for their livelihoods, become more difficult to secure.[17] While expert consultants may determine some of the capital project decisions, when it comes to the business model the organization will use in the new building, no substitute exists for engaging a financially knowledgeable and committed leader who will still be involved after opening.

Any building project that fails in its capital fundraising campaign risks bankruptcy. Fundraising is a key capacity for most nonprofits, and staff and trustees may already understand how to run campaigns for annual support. Yet capital campaigns—in which large amounts are sought and large gifts play a crucial role—differ in the skills required, and building capacity for capital campaigns specifically is a useful infrastructure investment. Staff and trustees need to understand how to structure a campaign, how to find potential donors, and how to persuade them to give. A building project begun without having at least one expert capital campaign leader within the organization risks trouble. Realistically, this leadership needs to come from the board. Staff can assist with structure, research, and organization, but the most effective appeals for funds will be made by people who themselves have the means to give and have already made a substantial commitment. Thus, an organization embarking on a building project needs a trustee or a group of trustees experienced in the art of the ask. A board connected to a wide network of philanthropists is helpful, but a compelling enough project and a skillfully executed cultivation effort can sometimes substitute for the power of preexisting personal acquaintances. With competent expert leadership at the head of the campaign, other trustees new to fundraising can be trained as the project develops. The complete absence of an experienced hand with large gifts on the leadership team may however be a shortcoming that cannot be overcome. And a capital campaign that fails to meet its targets can doom a project to failure.

Another method for funding capital projects in the arts is public funding. Such funding most frequently takes the shape of tax credits or municipal bonds. The financial and legal structures for these arrangements as well as the political process for putting them into place are complex, requiring that a knowledgeable individual be a part of any leadership team considering this path. Though many arts organizations are weary of the additional scrutiny to which they will need to subject themselves to get public funding, the truth is that governments frequently question proposals in constructive ways. Senior staff at municipal governments often have significant capital project experience and can suggest ways to make the project proposal more sound. Of course, one hazard of engaging in a political process is turning an arts project into a political issue.

Another useful area of financial expertise is debt. Most projects, even those that complete their capital fundraising before opening, end up requiring some debt to manage cash flows. For the best-managed projects, this debt takes the form of a revolving credit line that allows organizations to pay for expenses as they arise rather than as pledges come in. Such short-term debt should be used to smooth out expected lags between the time expenses are paid and revenues are received—not to deal with unanticipated expenses. Additionally, some arts facilities are made possible only by long-term loans, to be paid over decades after facility opening. We believe such long-term financing to be hazardous to organizational vitality since such debt reduces flexibility, adds to total project costs, and frequently causes annual deficits. Given the prevalence of debt financing, understanding the risks is critical. An individual who has a good grasp of debt financing options can help the leadership team evaluate all its options in an informed fashion.

Knowledge of artistic facilities, how they operate, and what physical characteristics are best suited to the organization's programming will be necessary to formulate a building program for architects and designers. This is likely to be a subject that the program staff knows well. However, knowledge of one's own current facility does not make someone an expert in all potential options. In the performing arts, an artistic director or a production manager who has worked on productions in different venues may be intimately familiar with exactly what is necessary, what is desirable, and what would be nice to have. Yet many organizations still turn to consultants to help them understand and evaluate the various dimensions of physical capacity. Care should be taken to make sure that the experts guiding the decisions do not have conflicting priorities. Architects and other design professionals may be more interested in project quality than in budgetary considerations. This is nothing more than another example of Maslow's Hammer Principle at play, and looking for a different kind of design team may not be the best answer to this dilemma. Becoming a better client—with a diverse leadership team that has a breadth as well as depth of expertise at its command—is usually a better strategy. Thus, it is important for the decision-making process to include someone who will understand how the organization's programs will operate in the new space, how artistic mission will be impacted by design decisions, and what is superfluous and what essential.

The planning of a cultural infrastructure project impacts artistic programs not only after opening, but also during the planning. In our discussion of the decision to build, we have seen how various powerful players within the community attempt to influence the organization's direction in exchange for providing resources. This pressure is not limited solely to how the building is designed and what is included. Sometimes, the pressure to change to better suit the goals of municipal leaders and donors is felt within ongoing programming as well. How will the organization's ability to take artistic risks be affected by a capital campaign, for example? How will the new programs or expansions in scope that are advocated by key resource gatekeepers affect the organization's mission? Most likely, a new building will demand an evolution. The vision for and organizational alignment behind the building cannot be separated from the vision for mission. Leaders in charge of artistic programs will need to be engaged in decision making. Besides, one of the difficulties organizations encounter after opening is caused by insufficient lead times for planning of programs. A performing arts center, planned largely by trustees and staff with expertise in areas other than the arts, may scramble in the last few months to come up with a slate of performances—and find that many potential star performers are already fully booked. Engaging artistic leaders in top-level decision making can help avert the situation in which a new facility struggles to offer compelling programs.

In summary, seven areas of capacity are particularly important during building projects: design and construction project management, capital fundraising, public finance structures, public relations, financial planning, artistic facilities, and artistic programming. With this many elements to balance, the task of building capacity for capital projects is not for the faint of heart. Yet cultural organizations tend to be resourceful in building the capacity scaffolds that support their programs and their other initiatives. Two tools are particularly relevant: use of people with varied relationships to the organization, including staff, trustees, volunteers, and contractors, and strategic timing of when they are brought on board.

Not all of the skills necessary must be contributed to the planning process by full-time employees.[18] Some expertise can be contributed by trustees and other volunteers.[19] In fact, because of the sheer amount of work, during building projects trustees commonly play an unusually active role in both making and implementing decisions.[20] At many organizations, the capital campaign and planning process become full-time unpaid jobs for several trustees. Some of the organizations undertaking capital projects are brand-new and have the luxury of focusing all their efforts on their planning. Others are planning new facilities in addition to overseeing their existing programs. Stress and exhaustion are common and may imperil an organization's ability to retain key trustees and staff.

The timing of when the organization acquires these skills is vitally important. Whether a building project signals the birth of a brand-new organization or the expansion of an existing one, additional staff will be necessary, both during the planning and after opening. Really, two separate capacity building projects are happening, one for the start-up staff that will lead planning, and one for the operational staff that will run the new or expanded operations after opening. The risks of overestimating how many people will be required—layoffs and budgetary stress—are well understood. The risks of underestimating staffing and trustee needs are less apparent but equally important to consider. First, the work will go undone and existing staff, trustees, and volunteers will be exhausted. Both of these consequences of understaffing can lead to an erosion in ability to deliver on mission. Second, a decision-making process that neglects people with key capabilities will result in organizational blindness to opportunities, risks, and potential solutions. Organizations solve problems with the tools at their disposal, and failure to include the right people on the leadership team leads to a situation in which decision makers do not have the right tools and are not even aware of the gaps in necessary expertise. The argument of this chapter is that the impact of this oversight on the end result can be profound.

Growing Capacity despite Resource Scarcity

When resources are scarce, capacity is difficult to grow. While efforts like the Art Institute of Chicago expansion and the building of the AT&T Performing Arts Center have sufficient funding and cultural capital to attract topflight candidates, other arts organizations may find expanding capacity in advance of planning a building project unfeasible. Rather than being a function of strategy and choice, the operational capacity at these organizations is seen as a function of necessity. Their boards, volunteers, and staff are composed of the best people that can be found. Slots on the board may go empty for months, vacancies may be difficult to fill, and budgets may not stretch far enough to allow for another expert's retainer. Yet recent history of the cultural sector in the United States is also filled with stories of organizations that manage to succeed despite these difficulties. They get the people they need to move forward through the power of vision, passion, and tenacity. The Long Center in Austin—which was the focus of the work by Cookie Ruiz and her instant messaging staff—was born out of the dogged efforts of three local women. Each a trustee of a local performing organization, none had the financial means or connections to give their dream of a new performing arts center credence. They found local professionals willing to do the early consulting work pro bono and kept inviting local business leaders out to lunch with them until they generated enough interest for a board. Though challenging, capacity building issues stemming from obscurity and lack of financial resources can be managed.[21]

In our fieldwork, we encountered two organizations that embarked on their capital projects at the same time they were undertaking major efforts to build or rebuild operational capacity: Portland Center Stage in Oregon and Workhouse Arts Center in Lorton, Virginia. Portland Center Stage (PCS) was still in the midst of an identity crisis precipitated by its divorce from long-term partner Oregon Shakespeare Festival. Without the aegis of this other, older organization, the board of PCS no longer had the same prestige and visibility, and many of their newer trustees had a lower profile than the older trustees, who were scaling down their commitment. A longtime artistic director was resigning, leaving the organization with both the opportunity and need to reshape its core. Meanwhile, Workhouse Arts Center in Lorton was a brand-new organization, started from a grassroots effort by community activists. Over the years of planning and then building the new arts center, the Workhouse had acquired and then shed many leaders. Two executive directors had come and gone, and the board of trustees had also been through three periods of turnover. In each iteration, some new skill was required, its lack thrown into sharp relief by the ongoing building project. The experiences of these two organizations show how capacity evolution for building and beyond works in the real world, and how the evolving capacity of an arts organization shapes the dimensions of the project strategy and future challenges. What is evident throughout these cases is that arts organizations' strategies for capital projects are shaped by their existing operational capacity. Though some capacity development during the course of the project is possible, realistically, strengths will compensate for weaknesses, with corresponding misalignments evident in the long term.

Portland Center Stage

In Portland, human capacity served as the impetus for the project. Portland Center Stage was created as a local arm of the nationally renowned Oregon Shakespeare Festival in Ashland. The city of Portland was in the final stages of construction on the municipally owned Portland Center for the Performing Arts, and the city aldermen were becoming increasingly fearful about this venue's success. They felt that leaving the programming of the new venue to the coterie of Portland's relatively obscure small theaters was risky. So they approached the Oregon Shakespeare Festival about producing programs for Portland. Many of these smaller theaters with deep community roots saw this move as a betrayal. The Oregon Shakespeare Festival came to Portland and produced theater there for six years. To the consternation of other theater companies, business leaders and philanthropic funds were drawn to the Festival like pins to a magnet. Still, the Shakespeare Festival lost about $300,000 on its Portland productions every year. When this organization decided to refocus all its energies on its core productions on stages at Ashland, Portland Center Stage was spun off into an independent entity. Now it struggled to define a vision. "It wasn't financially sustainable and it wasn't what people seemed to want here," said former board chair Julie Vigeland. "We weren't doing bad theater. We just weren't doing the kind that's needed here. There was no passion about what we were doing. We were losing subscribers."

In 2000, Portland Center Stage conducted a national search for a new artistic director. All the interviews were conducted in Vigeland's living room. She and her fellow trustees were looking for someone who could redefine the company's aesthetic and reinvigorate their productions. The candidate who impressed the trustees the most was a director named Chris Coleman. Coleman was young, warm, and charismatic. Previously, he directed works in a church basement in Atlanta, and yet he still managed to earn national and international recognition. He knew what kind of theater he wanted to make and he could speak eloquently about its relationship to the community. In other words, he could produce theater with a well-defined point of view, which was exactly what Portland Center Stage wanted. The board was elated by the prospect of his coming to Portland. "There wasn't anybody who wasn't excited about Chris," said Vigeland. "What we needed was not only a good artistic director, we needed a personality. There was just a magnetism about him."

There was one catch, however. Coleman was unenthusiastic about staging plays at the Portland Center for the Performing Arts. The house was too large, which meant that every production would struggle to find a sense of intimacy. Moreover, the scale of the stage was so big that it dictated the scale of the productions that had to happen there. Once he joined PCS, Coleman staged a production of *Uncle Vanya* there in which characters wandered on and off the stage. In the rehearsal space, this approach led to a feeling of a familial intimacy and chaos that Coleman strived for. Yet this sense was lost on stage because of the hall's scale. The stage Coleman wanted was smaller and more flexible. He knew this before he ever staged his first show at the Portland Center for the Performing Arts. In fact, when the board had offered him the job in 2000, he told them a new theater was one of his conditions.

The problem with the Center for the Performing Arts was that it no longer fit the changing artistic needs of its resident. The fact that this acted as an impetus for further building underscores the risks to community cultural vitality that attend to all cultural projects, as well as the hazards of following fashion in design features like stage types. The problem in Portland could be solved with either a different venue or with fundamental changes in the funding model. This was not an instance of facility operating expenses being passed on to the tenants and bringing them to the breaking point. In fact, the Center for the Performing Arts was a municipal facility and charged nonprofits heavily subsidized rents to help them prosper—$265 a day was the rate Portland Center Stage paid for the 900-seat theater.[22] Yet in Coleman's view, the venue was dictating an aesthetic. Large-scale productions were the only kind that seemed to succeed artistically at the Center for the Performing Arts because of the facility's design. For Portland Center Stage to produce only large-scale productions during the whole season, a much larger budget would be required. Moreover, Coleman thought that the quirky, countercultural community in Portland demanded a different kind of theater. He said: "Had we stayed in our existing facility, the only way that you could have made that successful, I believe, is if you had $10 to $20 million a year for your operating budget. There wasn't a way to configure the artistic programming with the budget, with the city, and with that space, and imagine a successful outcome."

When Coleman first raised the issue of a new venue during his job negotiations, the board was influenced by the fact that all the other finalists for the artistic director job were also convinced that a different theater was preferable. In the end, Bob Gerding, a real estate developer and the vice chairman of the board, promised Coleman that he would personally help find the resources needed to make the new venue a reality. Without the promise of this new theater, Coleman says he would not have accepted the job. Moreover, Coleman may not have been the only employee drawn to Portland Center Stage by an exciting new building. Years later, once the facility was finished, he credited the new theater with enabling him to hire a more capable staff, a change that happened gradually. "Once we moved into this building, some kind of magic sauce got poured on the group and I think it's because this is a fun place to walk into in the morning. So recruiting has been a lot easier." The experience at PCS points to the indirect ways in which facilities can enable excellence across an organization.

Between the point that Coleman joined the organization and the point when PCS moved into its new home, however, came a long stretch of time when its leaders were constantly playing catch-up to the things they needed to know. A resignation left the organization without a managing director just as the planning for the new theater got underway. The core group—Coleman, board chair Julie Vigeland, and Bob Gerding—kept a sense of humor about the process. "Back in grad school when I dreamed about running a theater, I never once saw a hearing before the Portland Development Commission in my future," Coleman wrote in his published reflections on the process. "As a small aside, I would note that my training is as an actor and director. As artistic director of a small theater company, I did draft the budgets . . . but anyone who works with me will tell you that understanding the complexities of finance is not my strongest suit. . . . To say that I was drinking from a fire hose would be no exaggeration."[23]

The way in which the project proceeded was through a sequence of openings of short windows of opportunity, followed by a breakneck scramble to push the organization through them. The general idea for the venue seemed to have been in place for years, having been under discussion since before Coleman's hiring in 2000. When he came to Portland for an interview, he was in fact shown the abandoned First Regiment Armory by another staff member, Creon Thorne, as a likely site for a new theater. The Armory was owned by Gerding Edlen, the development company where Bob Gerding, one of Portland Center Stage's most active trustees, was a partner. The company was in the midst of an ambitious urban reclamation of a former brewery that occupied five blocks around the Armory. Gerding Edlen bought the whole five blocks in 1999 for $19.5 million and planned upscale stores, apartments, condominiums, and office space for most of the site. But the Armory itself was a historic building, a nineteenth-century military base with a few narrow slit windows. This dampened its attractiveness for conversion into retail or office space, but Portland Center Stage did not need windows inside its theater. The downtown location inside the booming, gallery-filled Pearl District was attractive. The historic character of the building eventually became a point of pride. Yet even as Portland Center Stage staff like Coleman and Thorne quietly nursed the dream of adapting the building for a theater, Bob Gerding and his partner were entertaining commercial offers from candidates like a chain of fitness centers that was considering turning the building into a gym. Portland Center Stage did not have the funds to purchase the building from Gerding Edlen, much less undertake its rehabilitation, and though Gerding wanted the group to have the Armory, he was unable to gift a property that belonged to his company rather than to him personally. Yet in conversations with Portland Center Stage leaders like Coleman, Gerding also expressed a reluctance to see the building turned into a gym. That simply didn't seem like the best solution for the neighborhood, for Portland Center Stage, or for the character of the new development.

The situation remained in a holding pattern until Chris Coleman mentioned the idea of a new theater, potentially at the Armory, to the chief of staff for Mayor Vera Katz. When she heard of the proposal, Katz became its champion. She made a crucial introduction for Coleman and Portland Center Stage to the Portland Development Commission, a city agency for economic development. At this point in time, Portland Center Stage was still a fledgling organization, struggling to gain recognition as a community leader. "We would never have had that access," said Vigeland about their prospects to be taken seriously by the Portland Development Commission without Katz's endorsement. "We were too young, too green. We would not have that access, and without that, we wouldn't have done it."

Yet despite Katz's enthusiasm, the Portland Development Commission was skeptical about Portland Center Stage's capacity to undertake this project. PCS had never run a capital campaign. The people at PCS had never even managed their own facility—they rented from the city. The board of the Portland Development Commission wanted proof that Portland Center Stage was a credible partner. "So we went in there and they kind of gave us an impossible task. They listened to us and said well, you have to prove your worth to us. Six weeks to raise a million dollars," Vigeland said. "We had never raised a million dollars."

She and Coleman scrambled to find the money, calling all the people who came to mind first. Later, they attended a class about the most common mistakes made during the building process, and Vigeland jokes about how—even early on—the Portland Center Stage team had made most of them. One was allowing the availability of a piece of real estate, the Armory, to drive their decision making. Another was not conducting the campaign according to the traditional pyramid model, where the largest gifts are secured first. To raise that first million in six weeks, the Portland Center Stage simply could not proceed with deliberation.

"It was pivotal," she said. "But it was so emotional, and then Chris and I just went out and we just made it happen, and then we went back [to the commission], and that's when they connected us with Norris Lozano."

Lozano became a partner in the decision making about the project and brought a crucial skill with him to the leadership team. He was the head of the Portland Development Commission until 2004 and eventually became the CEO of Portland Family of Funds, a services firm that oversaw the specifics of the application and structured finance arrangements necessary to get Portland Center Stage federal New Markets Tax Credits. Lozano was a tax attorney by education and an expert in tax incentive funding and structured finance, both of which are fields that he knows leave lay people mystified. The diagram portraying the legal and financial apparatus necessary to get the funds from the tax credits to Portland Center Stage has twenty-two boxes, coded in three different colors. When asked to explain how this byzantine structure works, he jokes: "It's like asking a structural engineer why a bridge stays up."

This left the Portland Center Stage team with distinctive strengths in three of the eight capacity areas that can enable success in a cultural building project: artistic programming, artistic facilities, and financial structures. Lozano eventually secured $15 million in tax credits for the project, which ended up costing $38 million. The hiring of Coleman and a rebuilding effort that Vigeland had undertaken for the board had reinvigorated the company's capacity to execute its artistic mission. Moreover, Coleman was playing an unusually active role for an artistic director in every facet of the planning process for the building, bringing that focus on mission and knowledge of theater to every discussion. The presence of a person with expertise in the actual programming allowed the leadership team in Portland to stay focused on how every aspect of the plan would affect their organization after opening. They also had fewer issues than teams elsewhere coming up with the technical requirements for their performance space—Coleman knew exactly what he needed for precisely the kind of theater he wanted to make. The discussions about configuration and public space amenities on the other hand were more exhausting. The strength in artistic capacity eventually translated into strong programming during opening and beyond, leading the company into years of sold-out performances and audiences that keep getting younger—a sign of this theater company's continued relevance that many of its peers would envy.

Other facets of capacity for building were skills that the organization continuously worked to develop through training and experience throughout the campaign. Coleman and Vigeland were both learning how to get large gifts as they went along. They had brought in a fundraising consultant once, but found the experience useful only insofar as the consultant confirmed that their practices were in fact valid. Capacity for business plans and budgets was also developed during the project. During the time that the general manager position was vacant, Coleman had to oversee the financial aspects of both the project and the ongoing programs himself. In Vigeland's recollection, he was mentored by trustees with careers in finance and banking. See figure 5.1.

The organization's new home—the Gerding Theater at the Armory—opened in October 2006, just as the US economy was heading into a recession. There were two venues inside, a 599-seat theater and a 200-seat one. Of the $38 million they paid for the renovation of the Armory, about $30 million was covered as of December 2011: $15 million was funded by tax credits and another $14.8 million was funded through philanthropic giving. The capital campaign, which was put on pause during the recession, is still trying to raise the remaining $9.2 million to cover debt, with some of the money covering nonconstruction costs like interest expense. The city of Portland has committed to helping Portland Center Stage with its debt, though the theater notes that the city did not specify whether they would help with the repayment or with a long-term

5.1 First Regiment Armory in Portland. Copyright Art on File, Inc.

loan. US Bank, which is both a donor and a lender to the project, has also proved willing to assist the company. So as not to increase PCS's debt burden or the balance due, US Bank elected to forgo interest and finance fees that so far have totaled $1.5 million.[24] Still, the debt remains a threat to Portland Center Stage's long-term success.

What the Gerding Theater experience demonstrates is that organizational capacity that exists before serious work on a building project even begins may well determine the eventual outcome. Areas in which organizations have or develop capacity "spikes"—through hiring, training, or partnerships with other organizations that have those skills—result in victories. Meanwhile, capacity areas that are not distinctive strengths are put to the test and frequently produce results that are at best mixed or at worst disappointing.

In Portland, the leadership team was constantly forced to learn new skills to proceed. They had to formulate and kick off a capital campaign in a hurry, then run the gauntlet of tax credit financing applications, then manage a public relations crisis that ensued after a negative story in the paper. All of these challenges required Portland Center Stage to quickly acquire new skills or suffer setbacks. Their path toward a new building presented them with a broad array of problems, which they attempted to solve with a broad range of skills and solutions. Their project's completion was made possible by strengths in three key areas, but the Portland

Center Stage team also became better at the other four areas of building capacity as the project progressed. Their lack of expertise in certain areas did lead to shortcomings in execution in domains like the capital campaign. Still, other teams attempt to stick with what they know how to do well and avoid doing things in which they lack expertise. Sometimes, they even dismiss the extent to which those skills even *can* be helpful.

This is perhaps most pronounced in project teams that buy into the false dichotomy between business and art.[25] Within the world of arts leadership, there are people who believe that a career or an education in business is a better preparation for running a capital project than a career in art.[26] There are also individuals—particularly those who actually do the artistic work—who dismiss business concepts as useless to the work of an artistic, nonprofit organization. In our view, both paradigms are wrong. As evident from our list of the seven building blocks of capacity for cultural infrastructure projects, we believe that the best leadership team will engage people with financial, management, and artistic skills. Diversity of backgrounds within a decision-making body will strengthen the governance model by making the organization less blind to risks.

The Workhouse Arts Center in Lorton, Virginia

One of the projects that dealt with the business-art divide head on was also one of the least likely stories of cultural building of the past decade. Located in the suburbs of Northern Virginia, Lorton is a verdant community about nineteen miles south of downtown Washington, DC, in Virginia's Fairfax County, which has long been one of the wealthiest in the United States. Yet little development happened in Lorton until the early 2000s, because the community had long been the home of Fairfax County's locally undesirable land uses—LULUs for short—facilities like a DC prison and a landfill. The Fairfax County supervisor for the local district bemoaned the fact that the town was the "armpit of Fairfax County."

The prison in particular was a constant annoyance. The DC Correctional Complex at Lorton had capacity for 4,500 prisoners, but its actual population was 7,300 convicts, including some held under maximum security measures. Funds and staff were always short. In 1996, a court-appointed monitor told a federal court that the prison suffered from severe shortages of "food, cleaning supplies and heating oil."[27] Prison guards had been charged with drug smuggling and corruption. Riots and escapes were a regular occurrence. The escapes were so common that the prison instituted several different measures for notifying their neighbors in the surrounding suburban developments. At first, they had a siren, but community members complained that they still learned about escapes from the newspapers the next day. Sometimes the sound did not carry far enough. "Sometimes, would you believe, that they wouldn't turn on the siren because they were too embarrassed," said community activist and local housing association president Neal McBride. "They next came up with this call system." Each household that signed up for alerts would get a robocall with a curt, prerecorded message announcing the name of the escapee. Still, McBride said, sometimes the only way the locals knew someone else was on the lam was by hearing law enforcement helicopters circle. "It was rather frequent—though not as often as some of us thought it was—that you'd see a headline, 'Another escape from Lorton.' And the helicopters were going overhead."

McBride knew some of his neighbors feared for their safety, calling their kids home when they heard sirens, and one even kept a loaded shotgun by his front door. Far more pervasive, however, was the worry over the prison's depressive impact on home values. The Fairfax County Board of Supervisors had long advocated the closure of the prison complex, and in the late 1990s, the argument finally gained traction in the US Congress. As the closure became likely, the supervisors wanted to boost their case by proposing attractive uses for the large site. To this end, they appointed about fifty residents to an advisory task force to make recommendations.

McBride, now in his seventies, served as the cochairman of this first citizen committee. "We had a disparate group of people on that task force," said McBride. Some were experts on prisons or criminology. Other represented various housing associations throughout Fairfax County, both near and far from Lorton. Some were developers, others environmentalists, still others soccer moms. "Some of them were rabble-rouser types, like myself," said McBride. Another member was Irma Clifton, a round-faced gray-haired short woman. Clifton was a fifth generation Lortonite, a retired clerical worker at the prison, and a longtime history enthusiast.

The committee had three main concerns. The first was the supervisors' preference for a proposal that would not tax Fairfax County's coffers, a plan that would attract private money or produce revenue for the county. The second was the pervasive concern about the impact of the prison site's development on the quality of life for the rest of the town. "My god," said McBride. "We could end up with thousands of homes, with thousands more school kids, and many thousands of vehicles clogging up the old roads." Clifton served as an active voice for a third concern: the historical preservation of some of the buildings on the prison campus.

Clifton was one of the few who had seen the grounds behind the tall concrete walls and wire fencing. There, some of the first buildings, erected back in 1910, were built in the colonial revival style that she found "pleasing" and compared with the campus of the University of Virginia. In its first incarnation, the correctional complex had been the Occoquan Workhouse, a prison without walls built to embody Teddy Roosevelt's Progressive Party ideas about what incarceration should be like. During that era, sixty prisoners worked on the farm and in the hospital. The goal of this arrangement was to rehabilitate criminals into upstanding citizens through work.

The Progressive ideals about prisoner treatment did not always hold up, however. When protesters advocating for women's suffrage were imprisoned here in 1917 for demonstrating in front of the White House, some were beaten, and the public outrage over that mistreatment drew supporters to their cause. Clifton thought that both the architectural and historical legacy of the Workhouse and other historical sites on the grounds were worth preserving, and she intended to fight to make sure they were adaptively reused rather than razed. Still, after decades of pent-up anger over the presence of the prison, its continued existence in any form was going to be a tough sell. "Forty-eight people were deciding what to do with a property they've never been on," she said about the committee. Moreover, she knew the idea of historical preservation itself, though compelling for her personally, would attract few supporters or dollars needed for renovations. "People are not usually very interested in sending money just to save something to look at."

Because Clifton's main interest was preservation, she liked the idea of an on-site museum about the history of the Workhouse. In fact, she was for a few months employed and now volunteers as the manager of this historical museum's collections. She knew, however, that the 60-acre, 30-building campus had to have another purpose for the preservation project to be credible. "We can't just go in there without having a plan," was how McBride described Clifton's attitude about pitching her vision to his committee. To help her develop a plan that she could defend before the citizens' task force, she turned to her fellow trustees and members at the local historical society—fifteen people in all. Together, they came up with a few ideas for what the Lorton Workhouse could be turned into to save it from demolition. Chief among these ideas was a set of cultural or educational uses. Clifton's ad hoc focus group took inspiration from the nearby historical Occoquan village. "That may work here, some sort of upscale perpetual flea market. Something a little better than that," said

Clifton. Another idea was provided by The Barns at Wolf Trap, which was a performing arts venue at the national park. Yet another model was presented by the Torpedo Factory, a former manufacturing facility adaptively reused for artist studios in Alexandria, Virginia. "The more ideas that we fed into it, the more reality it had," said Clifton.

Clifton's proposal encountered only minimal dissent after she presented the little-known story of the Occoquan Historic District. Yet the proposal did not meet with much enthusiasm either. Once the prisoners started leaving, she took people on tours of the facilities, weaving her constituency's ideas about how the Workhouse could be used into her talk. "I never missed an opportunity to refer to the barn as the Wolf Trap of Lorton," she said. She spoke to everyone she could—fellow committee members, each of the county supervisors, Rotary Club, Lion's Club, business associations. "If three or more people get together, we'll come and talk to you," she said. One day, Clifton and McBride walked around the neighborhood and knocked on the door of every home in the Workhouse's neighborhood. Since road congestion is one of the top quality of life issues in the Northern Virginia suburbs, they told the residents about their proposal and the expected traffic and parking impacts. Their goal was to handle any and all opposition pre-emptively. "We didn't want anybody popping up at the last minute," said Clifton.

Clifton and McBride thus proved extremely effective at engaging stakeholders. But their project still lacked plausibility. Outside community engagement, their skills fell short. Their grassroots group needed people with expertise in other areas essential to planning a capital project, areas like design and construction management, fundraising, and even cultural programming. They also lacked funds to commission planning studies, which usually serve as the foundation of project credibility. They needed to convince the county's Board of Supervisors that the project was feasible, and, in the view of people who joined the project later, the supervisors' approval hinged on whether the gaps in the grassroots group's capacity could be filled. The supervisors wanted to see evidence that the stewards of this adaptive reuse project had the management skills to make the project a success. Clifton and McBride searched far and wide for resources, or at least people who knew how to find them, people who would give the proposal an aegis of plausibility.

As part of her efforts to educate and pre-empt community objections, Clifton met with Richard Hausler, a Lorton developer who was thinking about building a residential community near the Lorton prison complex. One day Clifton took him for a tour of the Workhouse. "We wanted to convince him that this would be a positive thing, that it would get people to buy his homes if we put this thing here," she said. It was 2001. The last busload of prisoners was leaving the correctional complex the day Clifton and Hausler came for a tour. The guard towers, the walls, the cramped cells, and the barbed wire fences were all still there. Yet Hausler felt taken with the proposal and the Workhouse campus, with its symmetrical arrangement of small red brick houses along a rectangular lawn, almost like a college quad. He started speaking to a few acquaintances who were familiar with these kinds of projects. One of them, Bern Ewert, was involved with the original Center in the Square project in Roanoke. Hausler was encouraged by what he learned and soon after, still in the fall of 2001, he incorporated the Lorton Arts Foundation and hired a consultant, Chad Floyd, an architect who examined the buildings and sketched a potential campus plan. Meanwhile, Hausler started putting together a board.

The first Lorton Arts Foundation board had 14 people, including Hausler, Clifton, McBride, and Ewert, as well as several other members of the citizen taskforce. Clifton was president, and Hausler became the vice chairman. He felt that the board needed another active member with business and administrative experience, someone who was more active in the business community. He wanted to offer that person the chairmanship, and in 2002 he recruited John Ariail, who owned several restaurants and stores in Northern Virginia and was a prominent leader in business associations. Ariail became extremely involved, sometimes in minute details that other board chairs leave to the staff. Over the course of our two-hour on-site interview with Sharon Mason, the second executive director of the Workhouse, Ariail called four times to check in.[28]

Ariail felt strongly that a business mindset was necessary to execute a project like the Workhouse, and he soon hired Tina Leone, initially as a consultant, to create a business plan. At the time, she was a 28-year-old CPA, who in her childhood and youth was involved with school activities focusing on music and theater. "I wanted to go to a performing arts school. My parents thought I was crazy," she said. "Ironically enough, without a CPA and a business background, there was no way for me to do the job." Eventually, she became the Workhouse Arts Center's first executive director.

Leone, Hausler, and Ariail were the main stewards of the project, a triumvirate that made most executive decisions. Hausler and Ariail enhanced the board's ability to oversee the adaptive reuse project in several ways. First, they added to the organization's credibility with the county government. Second, they both brought experience in real estate development, albeit in a for-profit context. Third, they had the means and the desire to get the organization's planning effort going in earnest. In 2002, the Lorton Arts Foundation spent $76,000, mostly on consultants, and all but $1,500 came as gifts from either Ariail or Hausler's development company. In the end, Richard Hausler together with his company, KSI, was one of three donors who gave over $500,000. Joining him in that category was another, later recruit to the board, a local developer named Tim Rizer. John and Leslie Ariail were one of the five parties making gifts between $100,000 and $499,999. Over the first five years of the project, before construction began, Ariail and Hausler/KSI provided over half the funds needed to pay staff and consultants. "Rick and John pretty much funded the early operation of the organization," Leone said.

At this point in the planning, the Lorton group was converging on the idea of an artist village and performance venue concept for the Workhouse, a hybrid of the two other successful adaptive reuse facilities in the DC metropolitan area, the Torpedo Factory and the Wolf Trap barns. Seven of the Workhouse's dormitories would be transformed into studios for visual artists working in a variety of media, about 76,000 gross square feet in all. The rental rates would be below the market price, and artists would submit portfolios to be reviewed by a jury, which would make recommendations about their acceptance.

Each building would also house a gallery where the resident artists could sell their pieces. A main campus gallery would host exhibits from both tenants and outside parties. A proscenium stage theater with seating for 300 would be built in another existing building. A three-story barn would be converted into a music shed for summer performances. The former gym, dormitory, and rehabilitation complex would be converted into a 35,000 square foot performing arts center with reconfigurable stage and seating arrangements. The cafeteria would be turned into special events space that could also host festivals and popular acts. Other buildings were contemplated for restaurants, office space, artist residences. The historical museum would be built too. With about thirty buildings to contemplate a new use for, the Lorton Arts Foundation had plenty of space to fill and few compromises were necessary.

What bedeviled decision making in Lorton was a disagreement of a more fundamental and subdued sort—a disagreement about principles, values, and precepts for making decisions. From the start, leaders in Lorton worked to refine and expand their human capacity, struggling at all times with attracting the most desirable candidates and avoiding cultural and personality clashes. Board building was one of their primary challenges. By the end of 2002, the board expanded to eighteen people. These eighteen people included a district manager for Congressman Tom Davis, who had been crucial in getting the prison closed in 2001 and now was pushing Fairfax County to limit private development of the land, preserving some of it as parkland for public use. The other members of the board fell into one of three groups: historical preservationists, local visual and performing artists, and business people, many of whom worked in real estate development. The trustees' main task was refining the concept for the site, developing a business plan, raising money, and getting the approval of the Board of Supervisors.

The three camps on the board each approached these tasks from very different perspectives. Business people focused on scrutinizing the business case and finding revenue sources to sustain the fledgling nonprofit organization. Historical preservationists cared about preserving the buildings first and foremost. What programs took place there was a secondary concern, though Clifton and McBride both pushed for their vision of an on-site museum dedicated to the reformist and suffragist history of the prison. Clifton had long been collecting potential exhibits. One of the items was an electric chair nicknamed Old Sparky, though she wasn't entirely convinced the museum should include it—the historical case for the chair was dubious, since the Lorton prison was not a facility for the death row. Meanwhile, the artists cared greatly about the types and characteristics of the spaces dedicated to artistic programs.

In some ways, the ideal board member for such a project is someone who can easily switch between idioms and paradigms of each of these domains, someone who is conversant with the basic concepts of business, historical preservation, community, and culture. In Lorton, however, some of the trustees were prone to value their fields of expertise above others—the artists thought that artistic values and programs were of chief importance, while business people wanted to make decisions on the basis of the business case.

The importance of the business case for each potential use was paramount in the minds of Hausler, Ariail, and Leone, and they were at times frustrated with others' lack of familiarity with tools used for decision making in business. Over the years, the board membership underwent several rounds of cuts, intended at least in part to address this perceived problem. "We already had a lot of artists, and we spent a lot of time trying to winnow them out, because they weren't very helpful," said Ariail.

The executive committee in Lorton did seek the help of two local artists—Sharon Mason, a gallery owner, and Linda Evans, a theater professional. Together, these two women studied the issues, consulted their artistic communities, and provided advice that amounted to market intelligence about competition and likely demand for the Workhouse Arts Center's product offerings. To the surprise of some board members, especially the theater artists, Sharon Mason found that the demand for studio and gallery space was stronger than the demand for performance venues. The studio buildings would thus constitute the bulk of the immediate construction.

When other arts people finally saw the strategic plan written by the executive committee, they found details they deemed the most important were missing. "They thought about the first year of programming in general concepts, rather than, okay, where do you want your theater to be five years from now? What is the identity of your theater? You will start to develop a reputation, and what is that reputation, what do you want it to be? Because if you don't start to develop it, a reputation will happen," said Joseph Wallen. In the end, he and other programming staff wanted to see an artistic vision in addition to all the operational details.

After these beginnings, several rounds of radical changes in organization and leadership at the Workhouse followed. In 2003, five trustees left and six new ones joined, expanding the total size to nineteen. The board would be transformed again in 2005, with seven of the nineteen trustees departing and only one new trustee joining, for a total of thirteen trustees during the construction phase of the project. The group has kept its size smaller ever since. In 2008–9, the board underwent another transformation, with six members, Clifton and McBride among them, leaving, and five joining.

What prompted all these changes was an attempt to get the mix of people right. "Cultural fit" was an issue mentioned frequently in interviews, but one about which leaders were reluctant to supply specific details on the record. The first major reshaping of the board, in 2002, was meant to address the issue of balance, both in skills and geographic distribution. "It was time for more business people to come on the board and spread out the reach," said Leone. "Instead of people from the Lorton area, we needed to spread it around the Beltway, or at least get more people from Fairfax County."

The mix of areas of competency counted too. Ariail was discouraged by what he saw as artists' inability to contribute productively to the decision making and wanted to see fewer of them as members. Hausler offered a slightly different interpretation. "You have to be grounded in the work that you're doing," said Hausler. "If you're not doing that, you can have all the business people you want, but that's not good enough." Eventually, the governing group saw that they needed more diverse skills and perspectives. "What really needed to happen was a more balanced mix of expertise. You need to have a certain number of artists on your board. You need to have financially experienced people on your board," said Leone. The question of how to balance these two groups persisted.

In the end, the question of the artist presence on the board pointed to the larger issue of what kind of leadership qualities were really needed in a complex arts building project. Not only did the Workhouse need artists, but it needed artists with leadership and management experience, as well as time and interest. These people had to be able to advocate for the interests of the arts community actively, with arguments that could bridge the divide between arts and business and appeal to all the constituencies on the board. The organization was able to find a few such trustees, but not everyone who joined had the desired combination of qualities.[29]

"It's not easy to find good people," observed Ariail.

"You got to have some critical mass," said Hausler. "You're not going to get—again that's a chicken and egg thing, but you're not going to get a lot of business people to put a lot of their time into something that doesn't exist."

Even as they struggled to recruit board members, Ariail and Hausler were also trying to shed others. Over time, the trustee departures happened in one of several ways. Some trustees resigned. Others were not re-elected by their peers. A third group was asked to step aside by Ariail. "A lot of these people were glad," said Leone. "They really didn't realize what they were getting into being on the board like that. We were moving from a loose-based community group to a full-fledged organization with a real set of rules, business rules. They were really relieved that they had done their part and that someone else was ready to take it to the next level."

Last but not least, some of the artists on the board transitioned from board roles to staff roles. For this purpose, a board bylaw preventing anyone receiving a salary from the Foundation from serving as a trustee was enacted. Because some of the artists involved with the project early on hoped to eventually transition to staff roles, many opted to serve as consultants or volunteers rather than trustees.

In the midst of all this turbulence, the project continued to be managed largely by the triumvirate of Ariail, Hausler, and Leone. "We ran pretty much everything by executive committee," said Leone.

In retrospect, Leone wishes there had been a greater diversity in the decision-making body. "I had an executive committee that all thought the same way. That's not always a good thing. You need somebody that is appointed that has a different perspective and is willing to take on your chair or your vice-chair and say, Mmmhm, that's probably not the best use of your money, or maybe we shouldn't try and pursue that now." She wanted someone to point out her and her colleagues' blind spots. The three of them thought similarly enough that in hindsight she wished there had been more disagreement.

A parallel process was the reshuffling of duties among volunteers and staff. The staffing plan for the Foundation had called for several employees who found that changes in anticipated programs left them without responsibilities. Simultaneously, the Workhouse Arts Center discovered an unanticipated demand for arts courses. From pottery to glass blowing, in the first year, the Workhouse Arts Center ran over 70 courses in the arts, all with sufficient enrollment to justify the costs. (The Workhouse had proposed over 130 courses to the community, and then went ahead with those classes that attracted a sufficient number of paying students.) Area schools also became interested not only in scheduling fieldtrips, but also in having Workhouse staff and artists teach courses and lead after-school programs. This initiative the Workhouse funded itself, with schools paying no fees for the service. However, the staff believed that the educational component would generate additional grant-maker interest in their organization over time. After the theater was cut from the Phase I building program for reasons of financial sustainability, the two employees hired to manage the performing arts program refocused on the educational programs instead. "We were brought on to get the theater rolling, to get the performing arts center programs going, and because we like this place, and because we want to be here when the theater's ready to go, we adapted," said Joseph Wallen. "We thrust ourselves into the educational effort to keep ourselves employed," he said half-jokingly.

Yet even with these kinds of adaptations to changes, the composition of the staff still shifted radically. More than fifteen employees were laid off because of the disappointing financial performance of the Workhouse shortly after opening in 2008, and Leone resigned shortly thereafter. She was replaced as CEO by Sharon Mason, who herself resigned in April 2011. Her replacement was John Mason, a former mayor of the city of Fairfax, who was appointed as president and CEO.

The plan to cut positions encountered little opposition. "This is what has to happen for us to survive," said Leone. Positions handling sales transactions in the studio buildings were first handled by volunteers, but their attendance proved unreliable.[30] The Workhouse looked to its tenant artists to take on the role instead, training them on cash registers. Some embraced the opportunity to interact with buyers, while others resisted this reduction in services, for which they were paying, even if the fees were below the market. In these ways, the organizational structure—and capacity—of the Lorton Arts Foundation was constantly changing.

The organizational structure that evolved in this fashion had acquired several specific traits that contributed to both specific successes and specific oversights, as well as to the departures of the first two CEOs. As with many teams, the Lorton Arts Foundation board relied heavily on its strengths to solve problems as they arose. Yet other methods for resolving issues went unexplored because no one close to the decision making was an expert in the specific field. This shaped the project in significant ways.

Given the presence of successful real estate developers on the board, instead of turning to fundraising to fund the cost of construction, trustees focused on financing instead, as is often done in private development projects. The Workhouse board had the expertise to put together a bond package for $25 million. These bonds, issued by Wachovia, took two years to arrange. The business case showing the revenues that would be generated by studio leases was crucial to convincing Wachovia that the bond made sense. In addition, the Lorton Arts Foundation came up with a creative arrangement for the county to provide a kind of a guarantee. Though Fairfax County would not underwrite the debt, the supervisors did guarantee rental income—if Lorton Arts Foundation was unable to find tenants, the county would take over the buildings and use them for office space. If the business model proved to be unsustainable, the Lorton Arts Foundation thus had a Plan B, albeit one that did not entail the Workhouse functioning as an arts facility. Throughout the process of physical design, the potential use of the buildings as government office space was a consideration. This concern contributed in part to the need to postpone the building of the theater, which would be difficult to adapt for county use. As a financing structure, this arrangement was hailed for its creativity. *Bond Buyer* magazine even gave the deal an award.

Yet as planning progressed, Leone increasingly felt that fundraising needed to be a larger part of the financial plan. Between 2002 and 2007 the Lorton Arts Foundation raised $5 million for construction and planning, which was about the amount they promised the county they would raise when the cost of the project was estimated at $12 million. Leone thought this a great achievement for a fledgling organization without a track record of success, but she wanted more. However, the trustees were resistant to setting their goals higher.

5.2 Lorton Workhouse Arts Center, courtyard. Photo by Norma L. Burton.

"Who were we going to get $26 million from?" said Ariail. "We couldn't run a fundraising campaign. We didn't have a constituency. Once you got something, it's a lot easier."

"Nobody on the board was serious about fundraising," said Leone. Soliciting philanthropic donations was not how her trustees solved the problems they encountered in their professional lives. "You get too many people that are business."

The issue became acute after opening, when the organization found itself under an immense amount of financial stress. The recession made 2008 a difficult time to open an arts facility, and operational costs were exceeding revenues. The layoffs hammered the point home for Leone. Then she left herself. "Tina had no social life, she was working 18 hours a day, and we decided she was perhaps better in an entrepreneurial phase than she was in the management phase," observed Ariail. "And Tina was a big salary." See figure 5.2.

Another effect of the organizational structure was how closely the trustees on the executive committee were involved in the daily operations.[31] Leone's replacement, Sharon Mason, pointed to this: "The executive committee has been really, really involved in the day-to-day in the way they shouldn't have been and should not be now, but what is happening is they are recognizing that. They don't like it, and it's painful. It's like, they don't need me anymore. I've given my heart and soul to this place, and nobody needs me. They're throwing me out."

During her tenure, Sharon Mason attempted to transition the responsibilities formerly belonging to the executive committee to the staff. "This board does not understand what a nonprofit is supposed to be about," she said. "They have not ever worked for a nonprofit or ever had that experience." Then she continued on to the issue of the board's diversity and its consequent ability to guide the organization. Again, the issue was balance, six years after the first board was rearranged. "Only a couple of people on the board are artists," she said. In the end, Sharon Mason was the one who left the organization.

"For whatever reasons, the relationships did not evolve in a way that left her vested with the responsibilities of a CEO," said her successor, John Mason. "When I came on board, I was clearly invested with total management responsibilities. As frankly it should be."

Financial problems persisted. In 2009, its first full year of operations, the Workhouse Arts Center incurred expenses of $5.2 million to run its programming and took in $4.4 million, incurring an $800,000 deficit. As the county Board of Supervisors considered the organization's request for funding, they asked their auditing office to review the Lorton Arts Foundation programs and performance. The audit lauded the Workhouse Arts Center for its diverse range of programs, then noted that its financial sustainability was threatened by "poor operational revenues and the lack of success in developing large scale donor programs." According to the auditor's report, the organization itself was in agreement with this assessment. Fairfax County government was eager to help and promised support of $1 million a year for the first five years, in addition to $750,000 to close prior year deficits in 2011. The county executive's staff was also going to "increase the level of expertise being shared with the LAF" during quarterly meetings to review financials.[32]

"The simplest way of describing our financial concern is that servicing the debt on the bonds was predicated in the pro formas far too optimistically. For various reasons, the revenue projections that were anticipated are not possible to achieve . . . yet," said John Mason. "I've been quite clear that the execution of the business plan for the Workhouse has not worked. Fundraising here has been insufficient. Fortunately key individuals on the board have been generous in their personal contributions." The process of capacity building for the Lorton Arts Foundation marches on, and the organization continues its ever-ongoing process of evolution, board building, as well as the planning for the next phases of construction.

* * *

The first salient observation from the Workhouse Arts Center case is how difficult it is to find capable leaders who bring the necessary skills to the organization. Whereas in Portland, leaders attracted one key member of its leadership team by partnering with another organization, in Lorton, board leaders struggled to find the right candidates for positions at all levels. The Lorton Arts Foundation has gone through several iterations of its board and executive directors and as of 2011 was still looking for the right combination of skills, experience, resources, and cultural fit. Yet engaging the right people in decision making is what enables project success. So many planning efforts take for granted that the right people will be found to fill new and vacated trustee, staff, and volunteer positions. In reality, building capacity is a difficult and nuanced process aimed at an ever-shifting target.

The governance and human capacity model at the Lorton Arts Foundation was thus forced to rely on a small, committed group of trustees and staff to accomplish all the necessary tasks of planning. This organizational blueprint gave rise to a culture of daily involvement of trustees in operations that has been difficult to discard. The group shared a business approach to problem solving, which became a foundational element of the decision-making culture. At times, this created tension between those trustees with business experience who found the approach natural and trustees from other fields who did not. The business experience of the leadership enabled the project to proceed and secure critical debt financing. Yet other financial skills essential to nonprofits—like fundraising and understanding of operating models employed within the arts specifically—were not as developed in this organization during the planning process. This capacity configuration resulted in a project that was funded largely through debt, after an intentional omission of a capital campaign that was dismissed as infeasible.

Now in Phase II of its building project and working on the adaptive reuse of more buildings, the organization is intent on developing better operating plans, building its fundraising capacity, and refining its mission. To achieve these goals, the Workhouse will need to develop its capacity. In this way, the Workhouse Arts Center is an example of a project that finds itself in misalignment in considerable measure due to a lack of diversity within its governance group during project planning. Yet it is also an example of an organization that managed to bootstrap its way from one phase of capacity building to another, relying on its strengths to advance the creation of a new arts center and attract financial resources, staff, trustees, and volunteers to develop and grow. In each phase, its capacity needs have shifted.

In the end, board and staff composition as well as culture are pivotal in the decision making about building projects in the arts. In devising a human capacity strategy, arts organizations should consider how to best handle the extraordinary amount of additional tasks that the organization will need to accomplish along the long journey from planning to reality. If building capacity is not done carefully, staff and trustee burnout may become a serious issue.

Equally important is an honest analysis of whether the organization is up to the task of a capital project in terms of its overall capacity and skill set. The seven specific skills outlined earlier—design and building project management, capital campaigns, financial structures like tax credits and bonds, public relations, financial planning, artistic facilities, and artistic programming—are essential in undertaking a capital project. Governance teams best able to succeed in these tasks under the pressure of a capital project will balance the needs to stay cohesive, remain flexible, maintain reserves, and generate creative solutions.

6 | *Refining Mission*

Any organization that embarks on a capital project is beginning a process of accelerated evolution. Both during and after, organizations' missions change. Some organizations change in ways they anticipated and prepared for, while others scramble to alter their goals to respond to internal or external stressors. Though many individuals in the nonprofit world and especially the cultural sector want to believe that mission is inviolable, the reality is that mission is and must be contingent on other factors. The choice arts leaders have in the matter is whether they plan for and embrace this evolution, struggle against the changes in a state of stress and misalignment, or forgo a capital project altogether.[1] Of course, a change in mission can and sometimes does result in stronger cultural organizations and community cultural vitality.

The timing of the decision to make adjustments in mission can explain some of the differences in impact. Some changes in mission are anticipated before projects begin. Many organizations embark on capital projects with the explicit goal of altering either their mission or their ability to achieve the desired impact.[2] For reasons from size to acoustics, buildings do start because groups need different physical facilities to better deliver on their artistic and social commitments. The Dallas Opera was driven by a desire for a venue better suited to its artists. Portland Center Stage wanted a setting that fit its definitive style of making theater. Projects like these are conceived and their operational plans are prepared with an eye toward these changes. Yet these preparations can fall short for reasons of misalignment between the desired mission and the other foundation blocks of strategy. The sources of this misalignment and the adjustments they force are the first topic of our discussion here.

Other changes in mission arise out of the bargains leaders make while trying to bring their project to reality. Few arts organizations start these projects with all the resources they need. The natural consequence of this fact is that arts organizations must expand their reach to attract new resources, and one of the levers they have at their disposal for accomplishing this is the mission platform.[3] From promises made to donors to deals with community stakeholders, many compromises steer the project away from its original course, sometimes toward greater engagement and impact and at other times away from it.[4] To get the Taubman Museum built, leaders in Roanoke had to accept the stewardship of an IMAX theater, which represented a definitive expansion in a fine art museum's mission. To get the Fishers' art collection and an extraordinarily generous monetary gift, the SFMOMA had to make a commitment to a permanent display of Donald Fisher's paintings, thus restricting to some extent future curatorial decisions. Whether and how the many promises made are kept, and how the group's DNA is altered in order to incorporate the necessary changes, can lead an organization to a state of either alignment or misalignment.

Yet more mission adjustments are begun as the facility opens and over the following few years. Some of these are forced by deficits, with organizations becoming unwilling to take artistic risks or overly enthusiastic about any program with even the slightest chance to turn a profit and bring in needed earned income.[5] Other adjustments grow out of changes in leadership, which, according to the findings of a survey of managers by our colleagues, are extremely likely over the course of a capital building project.[6] Yet another coterie of mission changes grows out of the same ambition that got the project started in the first place. With a decade and tens, if not hundreds, of millions of dollars invested in a new facility, some organizations find that the original goals no longer seem grandiose enough. They start to think of what else they can accomplish, and sometimes new programs are born as the result.

Regardless of when and with whom the process of mission evolution begins, its core question is, How do we maximize the return on investment we ourselves and our community have made in the new facility? This question is closely related to the cultural sector's legitimacy and involves to some extent making a claim about the purpose the arts serve in our society. Of course, this issue is at the center of a long-standing passionate debate, and the answer is not easily provided. Yet a simple taxonomy of potential purposes is useful to our discussion of mission alignment. Broadly speaking, we can divide the goals that arts leaders and community stakeholders articulate for the cultural sector into two buckets: transcendent and worldly.[7]

Transcendent goals involve presenting art for art's sake. The end goal is the artistic experience itself and not any of the potentially positive externalities that accrue to the community because of an individual audience member's aesthetic experience. Naturally, a broad range of possible emphases, subjects, aesthetics, and perspectives can be selected as components of a transcendent mission to distinguish each organization's individual goal.

Worldly goals treat art as a resource to be deployed in a struggle for a different public good. These can have social and political goals as their main objectives, striving for equity, diversity, civic education, formation of civic identity, ideological education, and ecologic conservation. Alternatively, organizations can choose to espouse a philosophy that posits art as an economic resource in increasing cultural tourism, economic development, as well as job and revenue creation. Also, occasionally organizations behave and organize themselves as if their art is a tool for securing benefits for individuals, benefits like memorialization of donors, advertising opportunities for corporations, unsustainably high standards of living for employees, and prestige by association for a select group of stakeholders. The pursuit and prioritization of all of these goals can be both explicit and implicit, and can manifest as superficial pandering or as profound, integral values that inform every decision.

Recent research, like George Yúdice's *The Expediency of Culture,* has traced the increase in the justification of public arts institutions in worldly terms. Yúdice argues that emphasizing art's utility in achieving other public goals, especially economic ones, has become a way of legitimizing the existence of public arts institutions in an era of increasing cynicism about their purposefulness. "The arts and culture sector is now claiming that it can solve the United States' problems: enhance education, salve racial strife, help reverse urban blight through cultural tourism, create jobs, reduce crime, and perhaps even make a profit," Yúdice writes. "Because almost all actors in the cultural sphere have latched onto this strategy, culture is no longer experienced, valued, or understood as transcendent."[8]

Yet transcendent and worldly objectives are not mutually exclusive. As evident in the cases we present, worldly arguments and claims about the transcendent values and power of art are made by the supporters of the same projects. For example, in Virginia Beach, some proponents of the Sandler Center made claims about worldly benefits like educational opportunities and economic development. Yet others made emotional appeals, rooted in the joy they derived from performances and anecdotes about family outings to theaters. Though worldly goals can legitimize an arts building project in the eyes of some, others will continue to use and be convinced by arguments focusing on transcendent goals. In their quest for resources to build, arts institutions increasingly base their appeals on a broad range of benefits they may provide to their community.

Keeping in mind these theoretical sketches of the points at which missions are altered and the two domains into which mission can be expanded, let us consider the stories of four projects—two we have discussed before, and two others that we have not. At Harman Center for the Arts in Washington, DC, a new building poses a question as to whether its owner genuinely wanted to expand its mission to become a performing arts center in the first place. While the opening of the new facility prompted a reconsideration of a previous commitment at Harman, the museum at the Spertus Institute in Chicago goes in the opposite direction. Once their new building opens to acclaim, the leaders search for ways to expand their reach and programs—sometimes to their old constituents' displeasure. While the leaders at Harman resist change, the leaders at Spertus change at full throttle. Their experiences suggest that the best path lies perhaps somewhere in the middle.

In the next two cases, the leaders of both the AT&T Performing Arts Center and Portland Center Stage try to embrace their organizations' evolution. Disagreements about values and goals either stymie their efforts or push them forward. Yet in the end the outcome seems determined by the timing of when the question of mission change was first contemplated, underscoring the need to consider the issue from the earliest stages of planning.

Harman Center for the Performing Arts

When in 2003 the Shakespeare Theatre Company (STC) decided to embark on a $78 million project to build a new theater in Washington, DC's Penn Landing district, the case for building was compelling. After 17 years of leadership by artistic director Michael Kahn, STC was acknowledged as one of the world's best classical theater companies by news outlets like the *Economist* and the *Wall Street Journal*. The company's resident actors appeared on stage along with stars like Patrick Stewart and Avery

Brooks. (In the *Washington Post,* the STC artistic director quipped: "I don't believe in discriminating against an actor just because he's well known."[9]) The company's focus on classical theater—which included plays by Sophocles, Marlowe, Jonson, Shaw, and other canonical playwrights in addition to Shakespeare—found a receptive audience in DC, so much that the company's home, the Lansburgh Theatre, was filled by paying ticket buyers to 90 percent capacity. The company's productions occupied fifty weeks a year on the Lansburgh calendar, and after necessary maintenance and other tasks were completed, no free nights were available to expand a production's run or the company's season. The company had no room to grow its audience, and few seats left to offer young audiences at reduced prices.

Meanwhile, the management considered flat ticket sales a harbinger of doom. "It still takes the same number of actors to do Hamlet as it did when Shakespeare wrote it. Beethoven's symphonies still require the same number of musicians," said head of development Ed Zakreski. "Price of labor continues to go up, price of materials goes up." As the result of a phenomenon known in scholarship as Baumol's cost disease, the costs of producing classical theater would continue to rise.[10] Therefore, revenues had to grow. Shakespeare Theatre staff regarded this growth as a matter of survival—survival that seemed increasingly predicated on a new building.

Then, in the very first stages of the exploratory planning for a new downtown theater, a trustee made a generous and unexpected offer. Dr. Sidney Harman had been an audio equipment magnate and pioneer, as well as a trustee of the STC board. "This is a guy who can quote Shakespeare, by memory, at 90 years old," said Zakreski. "Multiple soliloquies." Harman offered STC $20 million as a naming gift for the new theater. He was not, however, content with the project brief as presented. In keeping with his past as an audio technology innovator, a man who introduced American consumers to stereo receivers, Harman wanted the center that bore his name to set the standard for what a performing arts space could be acoustically. His company, Harman/Kardon, would donate state-of-the-art acoustical systems. The Harman Center for the Arts—as the new building would be called—would become a world-class stage for the performance of not only classical theater, but also opera, and symphony, and jazz, and ballet. See figure 6.1.

But this was not what the STC had in mind. They were the owner, operator, and exclusive performer at the Lansburgh. Now Harman was asking the organization to change this model and become a landlord to

6.1 Harman Center for the Arts, home of the Shakespeare Theatre Company, Washington, DC. Photo by Sarah Stierch. Creative Commons Attribution-Share Alike 3.0 license.

companies performing in entirely different forms. In essence, Harman was asking the organization to expand its mission from being a theater organization to becoming a performing arts center, with a new responsibility for finding and promoting programs outside its own medium, produced outside the organization. The director and president of the STC were facing a crucial and difficult decision: given Harman's conditions, should they accept this extremely generous gift?

Along with a $20 million grant from the city of Washington, DC, and $3 million in early gifts from other trustees, Harman's $20 million contribution would permit the STC to start on the first $67 million phase of construction immediately. Moreover, the prospect of another gift of similar generosity was uncertain. The Shakespeare Theatre Company accepted.

This decision had a profound effect on the organization. Ironically, at opening time the new hall's acoustics were stellar for every artistic form with the exception of theater. And compared with opera and symphony requirements, theater acoustics are a simple and inexpensive task. After some small renovations, the Harman Hall has become a great theatrical venue too, but other issues persisted. The way in which the organization presented itself to the outside world became confusing. "There was a difference in vision of the funder from the organization, and I think it caused us to talk out of the two sides of our mouth," said STC's new director, Chris Jennings. After the new building was complete, another new hire, Stacey Shaw, took charge of its marketing. She discovered that though the organization now had other performers' productions in its home, she did not have the staff necessary for their promotion. Her budget did not foresee her needing to spend money to promote other people's events at the Harman Center—only productions of the STC. At some point a Harman Center budget category had been included in the forecasts, Shaw thought, but the money was cut at the first projection of a deficit. Within her department, everything from the organization's website to staff priorities is affected by the STC's now dual and uncertainly divided emphasis.

Moreover, as the new building opened, staff and board burnout became a problem. A board survey found frustration with the change in the organization's identity as an issue second only to extreme fatigue in contributing to employee dissatisfaction. "Suddenly, there was this entity named the Harman Center, and people here had signed up to work for a theater company. There was an emotional issue at stake," said Shaw. Jennings said he found the same sentiment common among trustees when he joined STC. "There was a lot of concern about, Who are we now? Are we a performing arts center? That was scaring the core people." Ever since, in addition to all its other challenges, STC has been trying to strike the delicate balance between reaffirming its traditional commitment to classical theater and grappling with how to get comfortable in its expanded role.

The organization thus found itself in a state of misalignment after opening, with funding and human capacity out of sync with commitments about mission made during fundraising. One way to look at the causes of this misalignment would be to say that fundraising pressures and donor demands had resulted in a distortion of STC's true mission.

But another way to look at STC's situation is to say that the misalignment stemmed from the organization's slowness to plan for and accept its necessary evolution. Instead of begrudging the need to act like a performing arts center in order to get a new building, could STC have articulated a compelling unified vision for its new mission that would have won the support of key stakeholders like the trustees, community, and staff? Probably. After opening, the STC moved back toward strategic alignment by reorganizing and changing its funding allocations. They also found tenants, community arts organizations with artistic values that are similar to theirs and of interest to their audiences. Yet learning how to allocate time and resources between competing mission objectives and how to represent the organization to the community has been a struggle.

Spertus Institute

At other organizations, capital projects have arisen out of ambitions to expand mission and programming, or because the new expanded building increases pressure to change and grow, to reach broader segments of the community and offer diverse programs. A capital project can enhance an organization's status within its community or it can lead to trouble. Consider the "Imaginary Coordinates" exhibit hosted by the museum at the Spertus Institute for Judaica in Chicago. The goal of the exhibit was to explore how various cartographers' personal viewpoints and beliefs were reflected in the maps and other geographic objects they produced. A seventeenth century Amsterdam Haggadah map traced the Biblical wanderings of the Jews through the desert. Other historical maps of Biblical events and Old Testament borders between countries, as reconstructed by Europeans during the early Modern period, were displayed. A woodcut print of Daniel's prophetic vision of the four kingdoms looked borderline hallucinatory. A 1940s British survey of the Palestinian territory—marked "Not to be published" by its creators—charted demographic statistics, perhaps in the hopes of arriving at a satisfactory land settlement between Palestinians and Jews. More contemporary maps charted house demolitions in Palestine by Israel, and artistic installations explored themes of dispossession and restrictions from the Palestinian perspective.

To some, the exhibit was an exploration of different viewpoints, a provocative collection that could serve as fodder for a discussion about geographic paradigms. To others, the exhibit was an attack on the legitimacy of the state of Israel. A rabbi writing for the *Jewish Daily Forward* saw the maps as "seeming to question the Jewish people's territorial claims in the

Middle East" and thought some of the artwork "wouldn't have been out of place in a show mounted by an anti-Israeli group." He also saw some of the art as uncharacteristically prurient for a formerly traditional institution. He wrote: "A glass case containing a 'Paligirl' T-shirt and black shorts with 'Palestine' emblazoned on the back greeted visitors at the entrance. A continuous-loop video showed a woman, displayed in full-frontal nudity, spinning a barbed-wire hula-hoop around her waist against a peaceful backdrop of a Tel Aviv beach."[11]

The exhibit opened in May 2008, six months after the Spertus Institute moved to an acclaimed new $55 million building. This new facility both precipitated and enabled the exhibit. The new home was twice the size of the institute's old facility and was the first home purpose-built for the Spertus museum, library, and educational programs. Before, all of these programs operated from an office building formerly belonging to IBM on the same block, where deficiencies like lack of temperature and humidity controls hampered collection and preservation efforts, and the floor plan isolated the institute's three operational units from each other. During the architect search, the frontrunner for the commission suggested the capital budget needed to be increased by 40 percent. In June 2003, the board instead chose the Chicago firm of Krueck and Sexton.[12] See figure 6.2.

At the start of the construction in the summer of 2005, the Spertus Institute reported its financial situation to the Chicago City Council as follows. In fiscal year 2005, their annual budget was $5.9 million, with a deficit of $300,000. The budget included $1.9 million for academic programs, $1.9 million for the museum, and $1.1 million for the library, with the balance allocated to administrative and fundraising expenses. Its endowment was $18.3 million. Investments valued at $11 million—proceeds from the capital campaign pledges already paid in cash—were held by the Jewish Federation on Spertus Institute's behalf. The institute also owned its old building, which it sold in November 2005 for $8 million.[13] The city of Chicago offered Spertus $3 million in funding. Spertus Institute's presentation to the city said the rest of the construction cost would be paid for with loans—$40.7 million in bonds and $8 million in bank loans. No concrete plans for repaying these loans or any plans for funding the increased costs of operating in a larger building were detailed.[14]

Indeed, Spertus Institute's postopening performance suggests no rigorous financial plan for these costs existed. After opening, operating expenses increased precipitously, to about $10 million a year. Interest on the newly incurred debt accounted for $1 million of the difference, deprecia-

6.2 Spertus Institute. Photo by Yk Yk Yk/Wikimedia. Creative Commons Attribution-Share-Alike License.

tion for $800,000, and the increased costs of staffing and occupancy for the rest. The beginning of the worldwide financial crisis exacerbated the situation. The Spertus Institute found itself under tremendous financial strain. The new building opened in November 2007, and by the end of June 2008, the organization's annual deficit was $760,000. This increased the financial pressure on the organization and raised the stakes for achieving programmatic and mission success.[15]

From the point of view of construction management and architecture, the building was an enormous hit. The design and construction were completed on schedule and within budget, with the new facility opening in November 2007. Krueck and Sexton's angular glass façade for a building that had to fit into a lot just 80 feet wide was highly acclaimed by the architectural critics. They lauded the building for how well it managed to fit within its historic block while still adhering to a contemporary aesthetic.[16] The *New York Times* and the *Wall Street Journal* both published articles praising the architects for achieving so much with limited funds. The new facility included 8,000 square feet of galleries on its top floors, a roof garden, a 400-seat theater, a floor for the library, a children's center, a gift store, and a kosher café overseen by Wolfgang Puck Catering.[17] The view of Chicago from the new classrooms was said to be so spectacular that the dean of Spertus College joked that only the most engaging of the professors would be assigned to teach there, lest the students become too distracted.[18]

As the facility neared opening, the Spertus Institute reconsidered its mission. Its new facility would increase its visibility. Also, having chosen to stay in downtown Chicago instead of moving to the suburbs where the Jewish population of Chicago was now concentrated, the institute wanted to embrace a broader range of constituents. This recalibration of mission manifested itself most prominently in programming that courted controversy—an exhibit on circumcision, an installation of moldings of stereotypical Jewish noses, a comedy tour by Israeli and Palestinian comics making fun of the crisis in the Middle East.[19] The most traditional members of the Jewish community were increasingly discomfited by the new approach, which no longer focused on educating visitors about Jewish traditions and life. The approach to the display of religious objects had changed too. These were now shown without any signs offering context (though there was an audio guide) and seemed to be offered more for their artistic merit than their sacred content. The mistrust inspired by these changes was only exacerbated by the opening of the "Imaginary Coordinates" exhibit.

When a significant number of these religiously conservative, affiliated Jews expressed outrage over the exhibit—complaining that Spertus failed to present Israel's perspective fairly—the management of the museum and the institute as a whole found themselves in a tough position. They certainly anticipated that their exhibit would provoke their base, but they seem to have underestimated the size of this reaction. Their dire financial straits made alienating donors dangerous. The leaders of the Jewish Federation saw the exhibit and cancelled a fundraising event scheduled there for mid-May. This organization provided over 10 percent of Spertus funding and was receiving complaints from its constituents. By the end of the month, the exhibit was closed for "unanticipated maintenance." A few days later, the exhibit returned, albeit slightly edited. Patrons were now required to be chaperoned through the exhibit by guides, who would provide context for each piece.[20] Despite these measures, the outcry from patrons and supporters continued. The trustees began to fear that funding from a major foundation would be pulled imminently. One member of the board threatened to resign.[21] Over the objections of the head of the Spertus Institute and the museum, the board closed the exhibit early.

Just as the exhibition's opening damaged the standing of the Spertus Institute with one constituency, the closing damaged the organization's standing with others. This closing came three months before the scheduled end, prompting accusations of censorship. A plethora of voices, both from within the Jewish community and from without, criticized the decision, accusing the Spertus Institute of letting financial considerations trump an artistic vision. Now a wide array of community members, critics, academics, and other commentators were all paying attention to an institution they had not noticed before, all because of concerns over curtailments of freedom of speech and expression. Both the opening and the closing of the exhibit had damaged the Spertus Institute's ties, weakening the organization at a crucial moment.[22]

Over the course of the next year, the deficit rose to $4.4 million.[23] The capital campaign struggled to raise funds and Spertus was able to repay just $9 million of the $52 million in construction loans. The endowment dropped by 25 percent. Gifts to Spertus declined as well, by 30 percent. As the fiscal year came to the close, longtime leader Howard Sulkin was relieved of his executive responsibilities (though retained as the chancellor). The measures taken by his replacement were dire. Sixteen of 60 full-time employees lost their jobs, including senior curators and other key programming personnel. Hours were curtailed severely—for a while, the museum at the Spertus Institute was open just three days a month.[24]

Part of the fault with this outcome can be located in poor planning. No rigorous plan was in place to fund either the expanded budget necessary to operate in an expanded new space or the construction itself, which was largely financed through loans. This precarious financial footing made the Spertus Institute more vulnerable to negative community response, curtailing the independence of its mission-related programming. All of this again suggests that strategic alignment is a crucial factor in project success. The Spertus Institute needed to have the financial resources to pursue a broader mission, not just a new building. Its stakeholders needed to be better prepared for the changes. Indeed, after the fact, both the director and the head curator admitted they could have done more to communicate their aims more clearly and to prepare their base for the exhibit and the evolving mission of the organization. Because of failures of planning and mission management, the Spertus is less able to achieve its goals than it was before the building process began.

AT&T Performing Arts Center in Dallas

One project that built a broad mission platform and accumulated a great deal of funding as the result was the AT&T Performing Arts Center (PAC) in Dallas. The leaders of this project raised over $300 million, much of it from people who had never before supported the arts. Both at the newly created PAC and at the artistic groups who would perform there, hopes were high that these new-to-the-arts philanthropists would like AT&T PAC's programs enough to continue supporting them after opening.

In securing funding for the project, its inaugural president and CEO Bill Lively scouted far and wide in search of sources of support. One of the accomplishments that Lively was most proud of was securing gifts from donors who had never given to the arts before—103 of Lively's 133 donors with gifts of $1 million or more, by Lively's accounting. "We tried to find all of the messages and all of the reasons that someone would support this thing, and we found a lot of them," Lively said, describing his strategy. Some of these reasons for giving focused on how the new performing arts center would complete the vision for the Dallas Arts District, how the new complex would make Dallas a better place to live. There was not one vision and one goal, but many overlapping claims and promises that appealed to a range of donors.

After Lively left, the person charged with bringing this tangle of visions to reality was Mark Nerenhausen. Before coming to Dallas, Nerenhausen helmed the Broward Center for the Performing Arts for over a decade. In Florida, he oversaw increasing revenues and programming attended by 600,000 people a year in Fort Lauderdale. He'd studied Russian history as an undergraduate and was inspired to go into a career in the arts by the stadium-sized crowds that turned up for poetry readings in the 1960s in the USSR. One of the realizations that he took away from watching that era was "that art could and did change people's thinking." He had a business degree and a provocative, intelligent way of speaking about the expansive role that arts could play in their communities. However, he thought that to achieve this, the assumptions for how a performing arts center related to its community had to change.

"We have underperformed relative to our investment in buildings," Nerenhausen said about the arts. Capital and publicity campaigns for new facilities touted their worldly benefits to communities, like economic development, broad community impact, and attraction of businesses. The capital campaign for the AT&T PAC had made such promises in Dallas. Yet after the facility opened, these goals were usually pushed to the background, so that arts programmers could continue as before, only in different buildings. "If we're making the argument to the philanthropic community or the governmental community that we deserve funding because of these benefits, that implies that we have to ask ourselves, what are we doing to actively manage towards those metrics?"[25] In Dallas, over $350 million was invested in the new buildings. What social returns and community building benefits would this large expenditure produce?

Another way in which Nerenhausen challenged assumptions concerned his center's artistic mission. Nerenhausen thought that having the AT&T PAC serve only as a home for a few artistic organizations was an insufficiently ambitious objective for an institution of its size. The new PAC would help the opera and the Theater Center attain greater aesthetic excellence by providing them both with better performance venues. Yet the PAC had to accomplish other goals too, nurture other companies. "The opera has to perform there. The theater has to perform there. That's not success, that's a given."

Nerenhausen wanted to focus on achieving broad impact outside the arts as well. With a broad enough reach, a performing arts center could also serve as a catalyst for civic engagement, bringing citizens of all backgrounds together around a shared experience, facilitating conversations about social issues. But first these goals had to be considered during decisions on programming. "Arts are a means, not an end," Nerenhausen said. One of Nerenhausen's most ambitious goals was ensuring that even people who never attended a single cultural event appreciated the role that the performing arts center played in their lives.

The way to achieve this ambitious goal, he thought, was by leveraging his performing arts center's sheer scale. First, his organization would begin actively tracking externalities of cultural events like rising real estate prices, business relocations, increased economic activity and travel, as well as improvements in the quality of life. Nerenhausen believed most of these to be a natural consequence of increased attendance, so what he wanted to know most was: Was the new space alive? Was it popular with people who had never attended the opera or the Theater Center productions before? How many people came in any given year? If the center drew large audiences, then quality of life improvements, like shops, restaurants, and increased economic activity would follow. Second, a performing arts center would monitor and analyze what kind of programming worked to achieve these goals. Then the PAC could manage these programs within the cultural ecosystem as a whole, thus ensuring that the promises of social impacts that garnered the AT&T PAC so much support would become reality. In Dallas, Nerenhausen thought, the size of the new performing arts center would make the new institution the perfect lever for affecting this magnitude of change. "Major performing arts centers are unique among arts organizations because they are capable of looking at the larger balance sheet of the cultural economy, the cultural ecology," he said.

What Nerenhausen wanted to achieve, in other words, was measurable, demonstrable excellence in both the worldly and the transcendental aspects of the performing arts center's mission.[26] Yet in growing more specific and less ambiguous, the organization's mission also lost the vaulting ambition of its old pitch: to transform the very face and fabric of Dallas. This pitch had been essential to getting people of means to make large gifts to the capital campaign. Now the value proposition was becoming more actionable and less idealized. Whereas before, the nonexistent PAC could be a blank screen for projecting many dreams, now the PAC was a building and an organization that had to ground its ambitions in hard facts and reality. Would this real enterprise meet with the same enthusiastic level of support as the ideal?

Three initiatives illustrate how the PAC struggled to balance these various visions of excellence and overcome the obstacles to achieving them. The first is a program Nerenhausen attempted to build support for during his first year: a free ticket distribution system. Most arts organizations who used his building wanted to reach underserved populations and enable them to attend their performances in the name of greater equity. To that end, they donated or provided at low cost tickets to young people. Nerenhausen wanted to centralize the distribution program at the PAC and build partnerships with social service organizations like Big Brothers, Big Sisters. Those organizations, he thought, could help the artistic organizations reach the truly underserved clientele. Having the PAC distribute the tickets for five or six performing arts groups through partnerships with these other nonprofits would increase the program's scale, thus helping to draw the right partners and to decrease total costs of the program for the cultural ecosystem as a whole. Yet it would require the PAC's tenants to allow their own ticket distribution systems to be supplanted by the PAC's. The undertaking required trust, trust that could not be created by the existence of a new building alone. The same issue of trust had surfaced during the planning stages too, when the decision to build two separate halls was made at least in part because of the lack of trust between the organizations that would use them. "There's a lot of novelty we have to overcome," said Nerenhausen. "We're at the stage of building those alliances."

A second example of how the AT&T PAC has tried to leverage its scale and centrality to achieve its mission objectives was the performance by the internationally acclaimed Soweto Gospel Choir from South Africa. The AT&T PAC, which acted as the presenter, made this performance the focal point of a collaboration with other cultural institutions in Dallas to create programming meant to facilitate community conversations about heritage and strengthen economic ties to South Africa. Nerenhausen was particularly proud of bringing the Deputy Chief of the South African Embassy to the United States to Dallas for one of the related events. While in Dallas, he met with the mayor and leaders from the chamber of commerce and economic development department. As a whole, the series was bringing exactly the kind of attention, civic engagement, prestige, and exposure that arts facilities promise to their cities, Nerenhausen thought.

A third example of a specific program was the partnership with TITAS, or the Texas International Theatrical Arts Society. TITAS was a presenter of dance productions from around the United States and the world with an annual audience of twenty-five thousand to thirty-five thousand. As a relatively small organization for Dallas, TITAS found its annual fundraising difficult to continue when the economy headed into a tailspin in 2007. "The past few years have been incredibly brutal," said executive director Charles Santos. In fact, the matter had become dire enough that his organization was considering closing. "It was an issue of cash flow. Donors who would normally give a $30,000 check in September were postponing until March."

All of this meant that TITAS was willing to attempt the risky plan for broad-based collaboration with the performing arts center that Nerenhausen was proposing. TITAS could shed most of its staff and operating costs and count on AT&T PAC to perform activities like ticket sales and marketing. From a staff of around 10 people, they changed into an organization with 3 employees, all of them focused on programming. TITAS lost some control, but they gained financial breathing room. In exchange,

AT&T benefited from a series designed by expert programming staff with a proven record of success in drawing diverse audiences and performers. AT&T and TITAS also agreed to split the costs of underwriting and marketing the events equally. "We are equal partners in this collaboration, but we're not of equal capacity," said Santos. "The center is much more capable from the fiscal point of view. We have the reputation, the history, the skill in a certain kind of fundraising."

Overall, Santos speaks highly of the partnership. "It provided tremendous financial relief. I'm of the opinion that we're in the era right now that you either collaborate or close." Because of its scale, AT&T PAC is also able to spend less than TITAS on the same tasks. "Their dollar buys a lot more marketing real estate than my dollars do," said Santos. Now, TITAS is in a position to commission new works and host residencies for choreographers and dancers. In this way, the PAC was able to advance one of its visions for artistic growth. In its collaboration with TITAS, the PAC could go beyond its role as the landlord to the Dallas Opera and the Dallas Theater Center. Yet this collaboration was born out of exigent circumstances, and few other collaborations of this sort have been tried since.

On the way to a fruitful collaboration, TITAS and the AT&T PAC had to face the challenge of silo thinking. TITAS needed to feel confident that the PAC actually would embrace a much smaller organization and prioritize the fulfillment of its goals. TITAS was, after all, only one of a dozen producers whose programming the PAC was hosting. As usual, good dates for TITAS performances were difficult to find on the PAC's busy schedule, and overcoming inefficiencies in ticketing required trust between the organizations. This mutual trust had to be based on confidence in the willingness of both organizations to look out for each other's interests. Building this relationship over time required a leap of faith and effort. "There's a learning curve to learning how to work together," said Santos. "The biggest hurdle has been developing open lines of communication and transparency. We've made huge strides in that."

On the basis of these programs, we can conclude that two factors have been crucial determinants of the PAC's degree of success in achieving its postopening mission, neither related to the physical aspects of the PAC's sumptuous new buildings. The first was the strength of partnerships. In places where the PAC was able to strengthen its collaborative relationships, the PAC has been able to achieve some of its ambitious goals. Yet in areas where its partnerships were weak, gains were more difficult. The other groups performing at the AT&T PAC have varied in their enthusiasm about the operational changes Nerenhausen has advocated. Some have been wary of letting the PAC take over tasks like marketing because this required sharing mailing lists and subscriber databases. Arts organizations tended to be concerned that the move would cost them a competitive advantage. After all, the PAC intended to consolidate the lists and then cross-promote events produced by other organizations performing there, thus exposing each organization to the risk that its patrons would come to prefer another company's productions instead. Arts groups may deny that competition is a concern, but at the end of the day, they are protective of their customers and subscribers.

Some groups can also become territorial in protecting their claims to the best dates on the venue calendar. A few simply do not see a reason to change how they have always operated. They neither seek nor respond enthusiastically to overtures about partnerships, whether artistic or operational. For example, multiple off-the-record interviews and confidential survey responses mentioned that the Dallas Opera pursued a policy of extreme isolationism in its dealings with the PAC and other groups performing there. Some referred to the Dallas Opera's attitude to the new Winspear Opera house as "feudal." The AT&T PAC's road to a collaborative relationship with all its constituent arts groups will thus be difficult.

To some extent, perhaps, the collaboration challenge could have been made easier if a stronger partnership had been emphasized when the groups had to come together during facility planning. Yet the exigencies of the capital campaign had prevented this from happening. In a few ways, the interests of artistic groups—which after all compete for audiences and resources, sometimes even performers—inevitably conflict. The last distraction Lively wanted during the capital campaign was to have the various camps on the board and within the donor community work on resolving their conflicting priorities. Nerenhausen declined to comment on conversations with specific groups, but said that in general, the idea of the PAC serving any role other than simply functioning as a facility was new to the resident groups and difficult to sell.

The change to a collaborative model throughout the Dallas cultural ecosystem has been slow. "From Day One, the mentality is, I'm a tenant in a piece of real estate," said Nerenhausen. This mindset is difficult to change, especially until a trusting relationship between all the groups develops. Moreover, the performance seasons were planned years ahead of time, and these plans did not anticipate the PAC being able to contribute in any substantial way to the marketing or community events. Nerenhausen wasn't hired until a few months before opening. "I do think we could make a little more headway had these discussions taken place earlier," said Nerenhausen. Of course, for these conversations to have taken place earlier, the AT&T PAC would have had to be less single-minded about fundraising during its construction stage. A change in focus would have been difficult while the organization was in the throes of attempting to raise $350 million.

In addition to collaborations, a second factor in determining the success of various PAC programs and attainment of the four mission objectives is funding. During our survey of the local arts community, leaders of local cultural groups shared their concerns about the deleterious effect the PAC's scale and budget has had on its eventual impact. The PAC's annual budget is $30 million. For many small and medium-sized groups, the rents are unaffordable, even after subsidies. Moreover, the large budget, unfinished capital campaign, and economic recession have been exerting pressure on the PAC to earn as much operating income as possible. To that end, the PAC has been charging high fees on services like parking and concessions. The groups who use the spaces do not have a choice to provide lower-cost amenities, despite concerns about affordability and patron complaints. Just like the issue of collaborations, the issue of funding is largely independent of the physical characteristics of the building. Both are, however, outcomes of the same decision-making process as the physical design.

The inaugural season of the AT&T PAC ended with the organization running a $3 million deficit. The broad worldly mission that had been promised to the community from the beginning was not garnering enough financial support. Attendance for many events was below expectations. Whereas the capital campaign for the buildings promised a wholesale transformation of the fabric of Dallas, the goals and accomplishments of the actual center have differed from that ambitious vision. In other concrete ways, the AT&T PAC is changing aspects of the cultural life in Dallas. Yet many donors who supported the construction of two architectural landmark buildings downtown chose not to support the PAC in operating the buildings. According to Nerenhausen's successor, Mark Weinstein, many of these donors had not historically been supporters of the arts, and are not planning to support them in the future. Their interest was in facilities, not in the mission. Yet their support for new facilities enabled a growth in scope for both the capital project and the operational budget that has been difficult to fund now that the facility is open.

To what extent these financial difficulties can be attributed to the economic climate the AT&T PAC has faced in its first few years of operations is unknown. Little progress was made during this first year on the

$40 million that remained to be raised to meet the $350 million capital campaign goal. This financial situation seems to have made AT&T PAC a challenging organization to lead. In July 2010, just as the first fiscal year after opening was wrapping up, Mark Nerenhausen abruptly resigned. His replacement was hired in May 2011 and resigned abruptly again less than a year later, in March. Such instability suggests that recruiting and retaining staff is becoming a challenge for the AT&T PAC. When added to the PAC's financial challenges, this means that ambitious programs to deliver social returns worth the $350 million investment in infrastructure—social returns beyond providing space—will have to wait until more prosperous times. The process of finding a mission that the organization can fulfill and the community can sufficiently support continues.

Portland Center Stage and the Gerding Theater

Portland Center Stage differed from the AT&T PAC and Shakespeare Theatre Company in its approach to adjusting to both the capital campaign pressures on mission and the calibration of the mission to available resources after opening. They had embarked on a capital project because they believed that a different theater would enable them to reach a greater level of artistic excellence in their productions. The promise to build a new theater was crucial in attracting a talented artistic director, Chris Coleman, to Portland Center Stage.

Much like Sidney Harman's gift shaped the vision for the new venue for Shakespeare Theatre Company, funders in Portland shaped the direction taken by Portland Center Stage. The Gerding Theater was built using both private and public money. Almost half of the $38 million in project costs came from the sale of tax credits. The rest came from philanthropic and corporate gifts, with $4.5 million still needed to pay off bonds and credit lines taken out for the construction.

Portland Center Stage's relationship to the funders of its new theater was shaped by two public controversies. The first was an edgy staging of a Shakespeare play. At the end of January 2004, as the Gerding Theater project was finally getting traction, Portland Center Stage opened a production of *The Merchant of Venice* directed by Robert Alföldi. The sets and clothing were contemporary. The production opened with the actors playing Antonio and Bassanio—whose relationship's homoerotic subtext in Shakespeare's work has long been a topic of academic studies— embracing naked. Jessica and Lorenzo also shared an explicit scene on stage. Many graphic portrayals of groping and violence followed, and the character of Shylock was greeted with the Hitler hail gesture by the other characters, bringing to the foreground the anti-Semitism within the play. Justin Wescoat Sanders, a critic for the *Portland Mercury*, wrote that this adaptation was "the vilest, rudest, ugliest, crassest, most offensive project you will ever witness on a well-funded regional stage." This review was not a criticism; on the contrary, Sanders gave the show an emphatic endorsement: "Some of it is entirely unnecessary, but never is it boring to watch. This play filled me with a loathing and discomfort so acute I can only recommend it. Rarely in this city is theater so affecting."[27]

The production was a sensation in Portland. "Everybody in the city was talking about it, for good or for bad," wrote Coleman in *Voices of the Armory*. "We, of course, sold a ton of single tickets and had a fantastic run. But we also lost at least 500 subscribers as a result of the production, we lost a few major donors, and at least one major foundation chose not to participate in the Capital Campaign because of the show."[28] This and other productions taken on under Coleman's direction were rejuvenating the Portland Center Stage audience, bringing more young people than ever into its subscriber and ticket buyer base. Yet the new vision for programming was also alienating the older, more conservative, and potentially more affluent segments of the base right in the middle of a large capital campaign. The new theater had not even gotten off the drawing board, and yet, already, the problem of funding was exerting pressure on the organization's mission and mission-related programming.

The impact of *The Merchant of Venice* was an important touchstone in how the company continued to evolve. "Had I known that *Merchant* was going to light the fire it did, would I have chosen to produce it in the middle of a capital campaign?" wrote Coleman. "Who knows? Hindsight is 20/20."[29] Vigeland thought the uproar influenced Coleman's programming choices from then onward. She described his approach to adjusting his programming in response to audience feedback as "creative" but "pragmatic." "Whereas it might tear him apart inside, he can look with his brain and say, 'If I don't do this, we won't have this theater.' And he wanted to make this theater."

Simultaneously, an entirely separate controversy was shaping Portland Center Stage's relationship to another key partner in funding the project, the Portland Development Commission. Portland Center Stage's partnership with this public agency was pivotal in enabling them to secure the tax credits that paid for more than half of the project costs. The Portland Development Commission (PDC) works on urban renewal, frequently by helping investors navigate applications and complex legal structures for tax increment financing. Many of their projects focus on housing and attracting businesses. The nonprofit theater company's new home did not seem like a natural fit for their program, and the PDC's involvement with the Gerding Theater only came about because of the enthusiasm of Vera Katz, Portland's mayor. The fit between the two organizations was at times awkward, especially at first.

In March 2003, Coleman and board chair Julie Vigeland first argued their case in front of the PDC board of commissioners. At the meeting, they tried to convince the PDC to purchase the historic Armory building for them from a local developer. The hitch was that the developer in question was Bob Gerding, a longtime trustee on Portland Center Stage's board. He was redeveloping several blocks around the Pearl, and finding a tenant for the windowless Armory was proving to be a difficult final piece of his five-block development's puzzle. The most enthusiastic of all potential tenants had been his beloved Portland Center Stage.

Some PDC commissioners were uncomfortable with the appearance of a conflict of interest in this real estate deal. Coleman recalls a vocal opponent of the project on the board saying, "I am not comfortable using public dollars to buy out a private investor's building." The money from PDC was a loan meant to secure the building for Portland Center Stage as they sought philanthropic funding in a capital campaign. Yet the purchase of the Armory from Gerding's development company using public funds still gave rise to controversy. Nine months after this first meeting, the local alternative weekly put the Armory on the cover, with a story under the title of "The Great White Hoax." The principal accusation in the story was that Bob Gerding got a sweetheart deal and was being overpaid from the public purse for a real estate investment gone sour.

A few factors complicate this picture. First, the *Willamette Weekly* article relied on interviews with other developers—some Gerding's business rivals. Second, two other potential plans for the Armory were on the table for Gerding's company—one to convert the Armory into a gym, with lease contracts he claimed were finalized but not yet signed, and another to demolish the building and build offices or a hotel. The demolition permits were already secured. Coleman said that Gerding didn't like these plans. Gerding wanted an exciting locus of activity to help his development succeed, and he knew that Portland Center Stage, an organization he had been serving for years, needed a theater. Third, the size of Gerding's personal gift to the theater exceeded the purchase price Portland Center Stage paid the development company where Gerding was one of the partners. He was investing enough personal funds to buy the property his business owned for PCS. But at the time he was opposed to making the size of his gift public. This was necessary to maintain his credibility as a developer, perhaps, but hurt Portland Center Stage.

The controversy was a challenge for the budding relationship between Portland Center Stage and the Portland Development Commission, which as a public agency was sensitive to fluctuation in public perceptions. Moreover, the Gerding Theater became one of the first projects for which PDC sought funding through the newly designed federal New Markets Tax Credits. In light of that, the project's visibility and the stakes for ensuring the project was a success raised the stakes for the PDC.

Even before the controversy, the PDC staff member responsible for steering the project through the tax credit process, Norris Lozano, aggressively pushed for changes to the new theater's building program. Portland Development Corporation needed to be able to prove that their support for the Gerding Theater was in line with their mission. Public scrutiny was increasing, not only over the Armory purchase but also over the use of public funds for a theater project. The PDC needed the new building to accomplish other public goals as well, not merely provide a performance venue for Portland Center Stage. Their goals for the project were worldly rather than transcendent. All of this put pressure on PCS as it sought to define its mission, its artistic values, and its place in the community.

"That was a total battle, a turf war," remembered Coleman.

Two issues became topics of spirited debates between Norris Lozano of the Portland Development Commission and the leaders of the Portland Center Stage project. The first was the building's public amenities. Here, the question centered on how to make the new building of greater use to more segments of the community. What kinds of spaces and programs would turn the building into a busy hub of activity for the neighborhood? For ideas on how to answer these questions, Lozano was looking far outside the usual programs undertaken by theaters. At one point, to the consternation of his partners at the theater, he brought up the idea to incorporate a daycare center somewhere in the lobby. Whereas in other cities, much debate about building programs centered on negotiating conflicts over the size and qualities of performance spaces, in Portland, the program for the public spaces was proving to be the most contentious.

In theory, the leaders at Portland Center Stage also wanted their new space to be a community hub. They liked the idea of a theater lobby always humming with activity. Sometimes, they differed with Lozano on which amenities would make the most sense and realize the greatest payoffs from the synergy of a community meeting place and a theater. Eventually, however, Coleman and Lozano arrived at a compromise, with a café, open community spaces, and interactive exhibits filling the lobby.

The initial separation of viewpoints on green building practices was far greater between Coleman and Lozano. Lozano wanted the project to adhere to the highest environmental sustainability standards—an expensive proposition that Coleman doubted was highly germane to a theater project. Tim DuRoche, Portland Center Stage's head of community outreach from 2006 to 2010, summarized the situation: "From a ledger standpoint, it would be much cheaper to tear this building down and have us find a building for ourselves that would work. Instead, we decided we would change a fair amount of our mission, refocus our energies around a building like this, and engage in what is seen as separate polarities of sustainability and the arts." Thus, the decision-making process that was ostensibly about the shape of the new building was pushing the organization to reevaluate its goals.

Coleman described his hesitations in *Voices of the Armory* as follows: "I kept seeing images of salmon runs in the lobby. I remember saying, 'I don't want someone walking into the building five years from now to see a play, and say, 'What the heck is all this environmental stuff doing here?'" Yet Lozano was adamant. "He was really trying to get the PDC commissioners and the city council to buy into investing into this thing and support us going for the New Markets Tax Credits," Coleman said. "That was a hard sell. The bigger sell for him was, This is going to be a showcase for sustainability. And that was PDC's mandate—every building they invest in had to be a LEED building." Environmental sustainability is valued by the civic community in Portland and the hope was that sustainability would attract support. "He got the politics of it much better than I did," said Coleman. PCS would become an environmentally sensitive theater company as a result of the project, something Coleman usually thought little about while making theater.

These disagreements between Lozano and Coleman were at their core about mission. First, they were disagreeing about the mission for the building and that mission's embodiment in the architectural design. Lozano and the Portland Development Commission had a commitment to public purposes like sustainability and urban development that were orthogonal to Portland Center Stage's mission to tell stories on stage. Lozano wanted the project to win broad-based support within the community and, to that end, was pushing for the project to embrace as its purpose not only greater artistic excellence, but also community values with broader appeal, like environmental sustainability and civic community building. Second, this disagreement about the building's form was also about function, since these concepts are deeply interconnected. The building would be the home for Coleman's organization. If expensive, prominent components of the design were entirely irrelevant to Portland Center Stage's mission, Coleman did not want to include them. He feared that they would burden the organization unnecessarily long after the building was complete.

The difficult and contentious process of settling on what the public spaces included and whether their design emphasized environmental sustainability thus involved finding compromises. Coleman and Lozano needed to find public, community-building uses for the Armory that both the Portland Development Commission and Portland Center Stage could live with. And they needed to resolve their differences about sustainability. In the end, having two strongly opinionated voices on these topics helped the team find solutions germane to the missions of both organizations. Between Lozano's mastery of community politics and Coleman's commitment to ensuring that every aspect of the building program could be incorporated into the long-term artistic mission, they arrived at a compelling compromise.

The turning point for Coleman was his realization that sustainability could become part of the Armory's story as well as influence what stories were told there and how. A transplant from Atlanta, Coleman came to accept that environmental sustainability was a core value for his new community in Portland. Once he felt that he could embrace this facet of the mission that Lozano was advocating within Portland Center Stage's programming, Coleman became enthusiastic about attempting to achieve LEED certification for the project. "Ultimately, once we figured out how to do that in our own voice, it became a huge win for the organization," he said.

As the planning proceeded, Coleman and other Portland Center Stage leaders incorporated the ideas of sustainability and community building into the organization's thinking. If they were going to spend funds and place emphasis on sustainability and community-building aspects of the building program while securing support and community approval, they were going to find a way to make use of these in their mission. One result of this process was a programming philosophy that covered the central goals of the Armory: community, sustainability, history, and the arts. These four goals were embodied by the approach to the building's design, with its emphasis on place making, green building, historic preservation, and artistic excellence in theater. Once the theater opened, Portland Center Stage meant to integrate these principles into their programming too. DuRoche described the approach as follows:

> We're in a very new urbanist setting. All of a sudden the ideas on stage have a grounding for community conversations. We started using more of idea-driven, conversation-based public programs, which is, Can we do a lecture or a panel that spirals out into a wider conversation that allows people to feel more invited into the life of the organization? It creates a level of access and participation that ordinarily you wouldn't have. It grounds the work that we do more firmly in the community. It broadens the kind of conversation we can have with people about the metaphor of theater and the delivery mechanism of theater. It brings people together around ideas.

The approach Portland Center Stage took to integrating all four of these concepts into programming was to add an overlay of other types of events to its theater calendar. One of these overlays is a series of lectures and brown bag lunches with speakers or panels on themes relevant to the plays. In addition to these talks, Portland Center Stage looks to partner with other organizations, like architectural societies and the public library, on events that touch on the same topic there too. When Portland Center Stage mounted a production of *R. Buckminster Fuller: the History (and Mystery) of the Universe*, this series of events centered on design thinking. When they staged *Ragtime*, an exhibition by the American Institute of Architects looked at the history of Portland and Portland's architecture during the play's period. Recently, Portland Center Stage staged a play about Janis Joplin at the same time they hosted a forum on affordable housing. Through programs like these, they have managed to keep ideas about urbanism, design, and sustainability an active part of the organization's life, even years after the end of construction. Moreover, these events allow Portland Center Stage to reach segments of the community that would not have otherwise come to the theater or learned much about the play.

"Our mission has shifted and shifted in a really positive way," said Coleman. "It's not just about theater anymore. The mission statement is inspiring our community by bringing stories to life in unexpected ways." The process of shaping a building while simultaneously paying attention to alignment has allowed Portland Center Stage to become comfortable speaking in new languages to new audiences. "Where we're located with the building, the way in which we've utilized the design of it, and the stories that we're telling on the stage are giving us multiple layers of strategies for talking to different audiences," said DuRoche.

In keeping with the commitment to provide open community space, Portland Center Stage's new Gerding Theater at the Armory also opened its doors to a wide range of events, from lunchtime tai chi classes to weddings. The relationship these events have to theater or even the new programming principles sometimes seems dubious. Events like weddings provide earned income, of course, yet they also fit in other ways. Coleman was surprised by how unexpectedly well classes like tai chi fit at the theater. "It's beautiful, surprising, alive," said Coleman about the martial art. Many of these events came to the Armory because of the attention that the LEED certification and the building's adaptive reuse attracted. "It was actually a wonderful opportunity to connect things that ordinarily might not be connected."

Most of all, Portland Center Stage has benefited from these programs through its enhanced ability to publicize core programs. In the first year, the Armory's two theaters were home to 455 performances and 300 other events, and these 300 other events were attended by forty thousand people, some learning about PCS and its programming for the first time by entering the theater lobby. Portland Center Stage estimates that a third of its first-time ticket buyers initially learned of their programs by coming to the Armory for an unrelated event. A full calendar with a wide variety of multiform programming is one of the tactics that has yielded sold-out houses and an audience with a significant portion of young people. The percentage of audience members under the age of 35 has risen from 2 percent to 17 percent since Coleman joined Portland Center Stage in 2000, a major accomplishment that other arts groups can only envy.[30] See figure 6.3.

Mission growth is not a panacea. Despite its continued success with the audiences, Portland Center Stage has struggled to complete its capital campaign and has incurred operating deficits. The Gerding Theater opened with $4.5 million of the $35 million in construction costs still left to raise, with the recession putting a hold on these capital fundraising efforts. The construction deficit could be attributed to the initially unanticipated high costs of adaptive reuse and "green" construction. Yet these also made much of the funding possible, and the extent to which the sustainability emphasis has both hurt and helped the finances of the Gerding would be difficult to estimate with any accuracy. Since opening, the annual budget for Portland Center Stage has been $8 million (up from $4 million before the relocation). According to Form 990 filings, PCS had

6.3 Gerding Theater, interior. Copyright Art on File, Inc.

an operating loss of $256,000 in fiscal year 2008, loss of $1 million in 2009, a surplus of $567,000 in 2010, followed by another loss of $495,000 in 2011.[31] The company's programming continues to meet with popular and critical success and its leaders are hopeful that their financial situation will improve once the recession ends. Their successes and challenges highlight how difficult the process of calibrating mission scope to resources is, and how crucial a role it plays in reaching strategic alignment.[32]

One challenge that is close to universal comes down to striking a balance between mission and money in terms of where to focus attention. In the arts sector, it is far easier to determine whether a project is a financial success or failure than it is to arbitrate mission advancement or artistic quality. This asymmetry between financial metrics and artistic or mission metrics introduces across almost all the projects we have studied a strange tension. The leaders behind these projects want to do what is best for the organizations they support. They want to see the mission fulfilled and the community benefit from increasing artistic quality, and they are often willing to make changes in programs and mission to achieve these objectives. But the leaders also know that the public will be able to assess far more precisely the financial consequences of the choices they make as cultural building projects evolve. An operating deficit is an operating deficit. A construction cost overrun is a construction cost overrun.

However, when it comes to assessing at the end of the day whether the mission of the organization was enhanced or not, the tools at the disposal of the organization's stakeholders are much more blunt and imprecise. This tends to push many leaders to focus on managing the financial side of the project far more closely than the mission side, even if the mission is shifting during the project. After all, it is natural to focus on what can be measured and observed.

In undertaking capital campaigns, organizations like Portland Center Stage, AT&T Performing Arts Center, and the Shakespeare Theatre Company begin a process of evolution. The tremendous pressures of planning and finding resources will frequently lead to changes in mission scope. Yet instead of meeting this prospect with apprehension and resistance, arts leaders should embrace the possibility of repositioning and renewal. Many visions for mission are in fact old and tired and in need of refreshing. Thoughtful changes can help an organization secure the resources needed for its evolving goals. These changes may necessitate a difference in emphasis or an expansion in scope of programs, perhaps even a change in aesthetic. If such changes drive great community acceptance and support, building projects may well help an organization move to the next level. In the end, the success of the organization will depend on how quickly its leaders are able to find that place of equilibrium where mission scope and resources fall into balance, when the dreams of the organization match up with the support available in the community. When this happens, the result is not only artistic value, but sustainable organizations as well.

7 | *Seeking Strategic Alignment*

A critical factor in the success and failure of building projects is the relative level of alignment achieved among mission, funding, community, and capacity. By alignment we mean the fit among the strategic choices in each of the four domains, and how well they reinforce one another. Good alignment means that the mission of the organization, the people inside who constitute the core capacity of the group, the stakeholders in the community around the project, and the underlying finances all can and do fit coherently with one another into something representing strategic design. This state of alignment is elusive, given that all four underlying elements shift over time as projects are conceived, built, and then operated. Many projects start out in a state of fundamental misalignment and then struggle desperately to get to a greater level of coherence over time. Other projects begin with all the elements fitting well with one another but then stumble out of alignment and into incoherence and conflict. The capacity of the organization to move toward or maintain alignment over time turns out to be a good predictor of overall success and failure.[1]

In Austin, two projects illustrate well the stakes involved in the search for alignment, fit, and coherence in the name of the strategic design of cultural facilities. The Austin Museum of Art (AMOA) made three distinct moves to build a home for itself over two decades with no success, despite having substantial real estate holdings. AMOA "failures to launch" are instructive because they illustrate the nuanced challenge of actually getting a building erected.[2] The story of the Long Center for the Performing Arts, a large multiuse facility that was completed in 2008 in Austin as a new home for the opera, symphony, and ballet, is one that points to the importance of adaptation and compromise in the search for strategic alignment. Taken together, the two projects provide a comparative perspective on the dynamics of success and failure in cultural building.

While many factors determine how cultural building projects turn out, here we focus on the issue of flexibility and nimbleness, as well as their relationship to alignment. When obstacles arise—whether they take the form of financial stress, community opposition, or something else—project leaders face a moment when change and recalibration are needed. How soon can the challenge be identified, acknowledged, and addressed? In the two Austin projects, the capacity for creative adaptation in the name of strategic alignment helps to understand the radical difference in outcomes.

Three Strikes at the Austin Museum of Art

In its first iteration, the plan to build a new downtown art museum in Austin was a partnership between the city and a small museum housed in a donated private home in an area formerly considered a suburb. The Laguna Gloria Museum was located in a Renaissance mansion near the shore of the Lady Bird Lake in West Austin. Peacocks—which wandered in from the neighboring nature preserve—strolled the lush grounds. Laguna Gloria focused on hosting traveling exhibits and a few home-grown shows of contemporary local artists, as well as popular instructional programs for adults and children. The museum did not have a collection. Though many institutions are noncollecting as a matter of philosophy, the Austin museum was noncollecting as a matter of strategy; they explicitly wanted to focus their energies on building a new home first, with larger galleries. They were also attempting to boost their relevance to greater numbers of Austin residents. They had a reputation as a place for the well-heeled and hoped that the move from West Austin to downtown would help the museum seem accessible, broadening the museum's geographic and demographic reach. See figure 7.1.

They began searching for an appropriate site in 1981, and soon, one of the museum's trustees, a local developer named John Watson, convinced his business partner that their firm should donate a piece of land at a prominent location downtown. In the deal with the city, the property was valued at $3 million. In addition, Watson-Casey pledged $1.7 million toward construction. To secure additional funding, Laguna Gloria approached the city council.[3]

7.1 Laguna Gloria. Photo by Mathew Fuller. Creative Commons Attribution-Share Alike 3.0 License.

The city of Austin was in the midst of a growth spurt and had major redevelopment projects planned for its Warehouse District. The Laguna Gloria proposal was greeted with enthusiasm by the mayor and the city council and placed on a January 1985 ballot, bundled with another bond package for building a theater. By this point, Laguna Gloria had already hired an architect, Robert Venturi. In 1991, Venturi would win a Pritzker Prize in architecture, but when he was hired in 1984, the Austin facility was still his first museum commission. Only later would he become one of the architects of choice for the art world. His drawings of the new museum tackled Austin's identity conflict, trying to reconcile both its Texas roots and prevailing countercultural norms and nascent urbanity in its iconography. The facility's program called for four stories and 25,000 square feet of galleries, as well as an auditorium and a restaurant and other public spaces. Venturi's concept for the building imagined a museum built of gray limestone and pink granite, a building intended to fit with the midcentury aesthetic of the surrounding blocks while striking a contemporary note.

The Venturi renderings of what the museum would look like are still fondly remembered by some in Austin. The architect himself called the design one of his favorites. When $14.7 million in bond funding was approved by the voters in January 1985, many thought that the Venturi design helped convince Austinites that the new museum was worthwhile.[4]

Also playing a role in finding public support was the financial agreement the museum reached with the city council. The museum was going to raise private funds to pay for 25 percent of the costs of building. In fact, with the land then valued at $3 million and the Watson-Casey pledge of $1.7 million, Laguna Gloria seemed to have the resources to pay for their share of the $20 million project. Then the economic situation in the region changed. Watson-Casey filed for bankruptcy, with most of the firm's pledge to Laguna Gloria still unpaid. Moreover, at the time of the original gift of land, Watson had made the gift conditional on the museum's construction and existence. The conditions placed on the gift set a deadline for construction to start and stipulated that the building was to function as an art museum for at least twenty-five years. If these conditions were not met, the land would revert to Watson-Casey. These reversion rights now belonged to the bank that had foreclosed on a Watson-Casey property. While the gift conditions were not seen as a problem before, now that the reversion rights belonged to someone other than a longtime museum supporter, the same conditions were making project leaders anxious—especially at city hall.

In the time since the contract with the museum had been signed, the city leadership and financial situation had changed too. The economic situation was reducing tax proceeds, and the new mayor called the museum project extravagant. City leaders were now also nervous about investing $15 million of public funds into a museum that could not be closed for twenty-five years, regardless of its financial solvency. Previous contracts required the city to contribute 20 percent of the new museum's operating costs, but the council now worried that the museum would need even greater support. They were not prepared to guarantee sufficient public funding to keep the museum afloat. The museum leaders were struggling to furnish evidence that they could in fact afford the new annual budget—projected at $3 million a year, a $2 million increase for Laguna Gloria—without requiring any additional funds. They promised to make a fundraising push after construction started. The economic climate was already making fundraising difficult, and the project's delays exacerbated the situation by prompting donors to hold back payments on pledges because of the museum's credibility loss. The museum could not raise money to assuage the council's concerns before the construction began. Meanwhile, though the bank was willing to extend construction deadlines, giving up all claims to reversion rights was not an option the bank would accept. The city refused to start the project before the issue with reversion rights was worked out. The council members could not accept the possibility that if Laguna Gloria went bankrupt, the ownership of a completed, city-funded museum would pass to a private, for-profit bank. The project was at an impasse.

As the city, bank, and museum negotiated the museum's financial future, the community consensus about building the museum crumbled. Several other cultural organizations began to protest what they perceived as Laguna Gloria's privileged access to public funds. The city funded arts organizations through hotel and motel taxes, and if the new museum would receive city funding in amounts even greater than those previously discussed from this limited pool, smaller organizations feared for their survival. Local artists filed a lawsuit. They cast aspersions at Laguna Gloria over its perceived elitism. Competing proposals making claims to municipal bond money surfaced, from the Carver Museum and the proponents of a new Mexican American cultural center. These institutions focused on topics related to the history and culture of minority ethnic groups within the city, and their competition with Laguna Gloria for support further made that institution's plan vulnerable to accusations of elitism.

Not only was Laguna Gloria facing competition from its peers, but its own longtime supporters were beginning to rebel. At the end of 1989, forty-eight of Laguna Gloria's former trustees, including its founder, wrote a public letter to the city council asking to cut Laguna Gloria out of the plans to build a new museum. The planning and design were consuming all of the Laguna Gloria staff's efforts, the letter claimed, to the noticeable detriment of the quality of existing programs. Active trustees and staff protested in a separate letter, for which they took out a full-page ad in the local daily paper, but the struggling project was already crippled. To exacerbate the matters, Robert Venturi, the architect, asked to be relieved of his responsibility to oversee the project, though he stayed on as a consultant.[5]

With such a preponderance of problems, the project was scrapped in 1989 by a vote of the city council. Laguna Gloria was paid roughly $800,000 by the city to sever the contract. The site was bought from the bank by the state, which planned to build a government office there. By this point, of the $14.75 million allocated for the new museum's construction through the bond election, $3 million had been spent on planning efforts and fees for the architect and other professional consultants.[6]

In the aftermath, the executive director of Laguna Gloria, who had led the organization for sixteen years, resigned.[7] The arts community in Austin was splintered, its turf war of the previous few years leaving behind many rifts. Even years later, a former Laguna Gloria staffer described the public battle as "a Texas shootout" that had "all the dignity of Saturday night mud wrestling."[8] The credibility of the entire Austin cultural sector was damaged. Other requests for public bond funds to pay for capital projects in the cultural sector for the Carver Museum and the Mexican American cultural center failed too.[9]

This first failure to build a museum in Austin allows us to focus on several characteristics of misalignment. First, in this case as in many others, the strategic misalignment was a preexisting condition. Laguna Gloria began this project aware of its aura of elitism and its shortcomings in reaching across all demographics to engage all constituencies in Austin. In other words, the museum existed in a state of misalignment, where community engagement practices did not fit with the museum's mission or its aspirations for public funding. In fact, the new downtown location was in part intended to fix this problem. Yet buildings rarely if ever solve problems with strategic alignment. Instead buildings frequently exacerbate preexisting misalignments, as was the case here with Laguna Gloria, when community sentiment eventually derailed the project.

Second, this case also points to the importance of alignment above all else—including individual alignment components, like funding. Coherence and fit of all the elements together are vital for strategic alignment. Change in any one of the elements requires recalibration of the others. Leaning too far in one direction—for example, toward funding—risks throwing the entire organization off balance. At Laguna Gloria, single-minded pursuit of funding wreaked havoc on the organization's human capacity, distracting it from its ongoing programs and current efforts to fulfill mission. This tension between funding, capacity, and mission further added to the controversy when the debate spilled over into the media. Yet the organization's overriding belief that funding the construction of the new building would solve all its problems did not stop here.

Laguna Gloria did not give up. In 1992, after their own efforts to secure public funds for capital projects failed, the Carver Museum and the supporters of the proposal for a new Mexican American cultural center joined Laguna Gloria trustees on the board of a new entity called the Austin Museum of Art. Their goal was the resurrection of the Venturi design for a new art museum as well as the advancement of the Carver and Mexican American cultural center projects. They agreed that the new downtown facility would be managed by the team behind Laguna Gloria, with some programs contributed by the Carver Museum and the Mexican American cultural center. These two institutions were still proceeding with capital projects of their own, but came to see the advantages of a downtown space where they could occasionally present exhibitions. As part of the reconciliation between city's factions, ethnic diversity of the staff and board was written into the operating guidelines of the new organization. In the following year, the old Laguna Gloria museum was subsumed into this new organization, and its West Austin location came to bear the Austin Museum of Art name.[10]

The museum's next shock came in 1996, when a sudden vacuum at the top formed by the resignation of two senior staff members, the senior curator and the executive director, caught the Austin arts world completely by surprise. The executive director soon found a position elsewhere, but his resignation was described in the newspapers as prompted by the organization's increasing need to raise large amounts in anticipation of the capital campaign. The city's opinion-makers held that the executive director had been a capable leader who was adept at raising moderate amounts of funds needed to support operations—but not the large amounts necessary for a new building. His resignation came as the board moved to redefine leadership roles. Two months later, the board appointed his replacement, a businessman with experience raising money for a foundation. A few weeks later, the city council gave its unanimous approval for the new AMOA to resume the task of planning for "the Venturi," as the museum project had come to be known locally.[11]

AMOA also wanted to demonstrate its ability to program and fund a larger space, as well as to convey the positive impact a downtown location would have on its accessibility and programs. To that end, in 1996, they leased a first floor in a downtown high-rise. The new galleries opened to great fanfare in November, with exhibitions that put the spotlight on works by or about minority women. The space was a former bank lobby, with an imposing receptionist desk greeting visitors at the door. The décor was dated, inconsistent with the programs that focused mostly on contemporary art. The cigar shop next door meant that sharp odors sometimes wafted through the small galleries. At the reception desk, staff and volunteers kept getting questions about the location of expected museum amenities like the Egyptian floor and gift shop—neither of which existed in Austin. This was why the museum's next step was continuing its quest for a new downtown purpose-built museum.[12]

Because the site donated by Watson-Casey was now gone, AMOA's first order of business was securing a new piece of downtown real estate, and the museum purchased a lot in 1995 for $800,000. The change in site required updates in the design, with foundation plans altered to conform to the new site's requirements. The back of the building needed a complete redesign, since in the original location the wall was not supposed to be visible. The balance of the bond money left from the 1985 election would be insufficient to fund construction, so the museum also had to raise funds.

The attempt to adjust the original Venturi design to the new era and new setting came to naught. When the museum planning first started, the Austin Museum of Art decided that at some point in the future, they would begin collecting art. Therefore, preservation and storage facilities were now required. The museum's leadership claimed that Venturi's design could not be updated to reflect new practices in exhibit design and conservation, and in 1998, they scuttled the Venturi design and announced they were searching for a new architect. After reviewing two hundred proposals, they settled on Richard Gluckman.

The new site was larger, and Gluckman's proposal for the building was even more spacious than Venturi's. Instead of 86,000 square feet, now there were 141,000, distributed between three—rather than four—stories. Two of the floors would be occupied by galleries and public spaces, and the third by the museum's administration. The initial unveiling of the design claimed the building could be built for $60 million, though over the years, this budget was increased in small increments, eventually reaching $65 million in 2001.[13]

Battle-hardened, this time around the leadership of the Austin Museum of Art kept their plans to themselves until the first phase of the capital campaign was complete. They unveiled their new plans for a building by Gluckman along with an announcement that $30 million had already been found, including about $11 million in remaining municipal bonds and $13 million in pledges from several newly minted millionaires working for Dell. Laura Bush, then First Lady of Texas, was appointed as the honorary chair of the capital campaign. The other cochairs of the capital campaign included some of the most notable and generous philanthropists in Austin. In addition to raising the $60 million initially budgeted for the new museum, this illustrious group would also look to secure a

$10 million endowment as well as $12 million for renovations at Laguna Gloria. The campaign proceeded apace, reaching $44 million in pledges within another year.

All signs seemed to point to success, and at this point in time, the museum decided to forgo public funding in hopes of avoiding another period of public deliberations and scrutiny that had proved so catastrophic for the previous effort. The refusal to take money from the city meant the capital campaign was set back to $33 million. But the campaign was garnering enough pledges to inspire confidence, and museum leaders thought that a new building could be built without city funds. Just as they reached and announced this decision, the economic situation worsened. The high-tech bubble deflated, and the capital campaign stalled.[14]

Citing their loss of faith in the museum's leadership, major donors were postponing scheduled payments until they saw signs of progress. Another AMOA executive director resigned in July 2001 amidst layoffs and severe budget cuts meant to bring the museum's operations within a more stringent budget. To respond to these problems, in 2002 the new executive director trimmed the plans for the building. A floor was cut from the design, and this along with smaller changes brought the budget down from $65 million to $43 million. Yet even this large cut in the budget failed to restore the philanthropies' faith in AMOA, and fundraising never again showed any signs of vigor. In 2004, the plans to build the Gluckman iteration of the museum were officially tabled. The museum's new leadership stated that the building no longer seemed like a financially feasible proposition, either to erect or to operate.

By the time the cancelation was announced, $14.25 million in pledges toward the new museum had been collected in cash. Some of the $35 million in pledges had been held in abeyance by donors. Some had also been paid to AMOA and spent, with donor permission, on renovations at Laguna Gloria. Of the $14.25 million actually collected for the Gluckman project, $5 million was spent on architectural fees, $3 million funded the purchase of a city block to locate the new museum, $2.7 million had gone toward fundraising costs, and another $3.5 million was spent on other miscellanea (including the renovations at Laguna Gloria). Only $860,000 remained. The museum would be unable to return any of the pledges. A second attempt to build was dead in the water, and the damage inflicted on the museum's credibility this time was arguably even worse than the first.[15]

This second attempt to build saw AMOA try to readjust its strategy. This time, efforts to demonstrate capacity to succeed with downtown programming and goodwill toward Austin's minority communities were an integral part of the attempt to raise money. Still, one thing remained unchanged: AMOA was planning a building for the museum it aspired to be, rather than for the museum it already was. Without a doubt, some changes in the facility were necessary, but AMOA's ambition outstripped a few updates in décor and layout changes. The museum had set its sights on a palatial 141,000 square foot home, designed by a marquee architect. Furthermore, its leaders aspired to get this building done without meddling—and thus without financial support—from the city council, thus ensuring their independence. Yet nothing about the museum's performance or leadership so far indicated that the museum was capable of such an undertaking. Indeed, the support for this undertaking proved to be insufficient. In other words, though the museum had taken a few small steps toward alignment, its aspirational plan was far out of alignment with its existing financial and leadership capabilities. Funding requirements were once again disconnected from human capacity, mission, and community support.

Nevertheless, AMOA's resolve to build survived intact. They still owned a block of downtown real estate, and as Austin kept growing, the land's value increased. For its third attempt, AMOA decided to create a smaller building that would cost less to build and less to maintain. The entire block would not be needed. In fact, the rest of the site could be occupied by a partner who could build in concert. In October 2005, just a year after the Gluckman plan was officially scrapped, Austin Museum of Art invited a select group of developers to discuss prospects for a partnership to erect a new landmark at a prime central location.

By August 2006, AMOA was in negotiations with a local developer, Tom Stacy, whose firm also happened to be AMOA's landlord for its leased space downtown. Stacy was working on another high-profile project at the time—a high-rise designed by Pelli Clarke Pelli, where famous architect César Pelli was a senior principal. The idea bandied about in Stacy's discussions with AMOA was to have Pelli design a condominium tower with an integrated art museum for Austin as well, for construction on the AMOA lot. Yet Stacy and AMOA were unable to agree on the terms for the arrangement.[16]

Eventually, another private developer for the partnership was found. In February 2008, just four years after its second attempt to build was officially scrapped, AMOA announced that they had found a new partner in Hines Interests, a Houston-based developer that wanted to build a thirty-story, LEED-certified office tower in Austin. The Hines Interests project was named Museum Tower, after a three-story building for the museum that would be located at its foot. The new museum would have a total of 16,000 square feet of space—far below the once-contemplated 100,000 but also twice the space the museum occupied at its rented bank lobby. The museum estimated its new building—designed by Pelli Clarke Pelli— would cost $23 million. A $3 million lead gift by board chairwoman, Bettye Nowlin, and her spouse was announced when the project was first taken public. Overall, between the gifts from the Nowlins and anonymous donors, the real estate deal with Hines, and the remainder of the capital campaign contributions toward the Gluckman building, the museum had $14 million in cash and promised funds to put toward the construction costs. Nine million dollars remained to be raised.[17]

Yet over the next nine months the real estate market soured, and the commitment of Hines Interests waned. The developer pulled out of the project, and because their financial contribution was absolutely critical to the plan, the project was scrapped yet again. For the museum, this was strike three, a third embarrassing, high-profile failure to get a project off the drawing board after drumming up great fanfare. Millions were invested in a project that was never going to become reality. For nearly three decades, the museum existed like a nomad, waiting for a new facility to start working on exhibitions and collections in earnest. Now, no one in Austin was likely to believe again that they would really build a new museum. The obstacle that cynicism and incredulity presented for a fourth attempt seemed insurmountable. In 2010, AMOA put its downtown lot up for sale so that it could settle debts, admitting defeat.[18]

To exacerbate matters, as the economy worsened yet again after the fiscal crisis, AMOA's downtown pied-á-terre in the old bank lobby became prohibitively expensive for the museum to sustain. In 2011, they pulled out, retreating to their old galleries at Laguna Gloria. The space was smaller and farther from the city center. Other cost-cutting measures became necessary too, and another round of layoffs—as well as another executive director's resignation—followed.[19]

AMOA's repeated failures to build and the damage these inflicted on the organization's reputation can be attributed to a strategic misalignment. This was certainly not due to a lack of effort. Time and again, the organization found its proposal could not win the necessary support, and time and again, they adjusted and readjusted their plans. When community debates became heated and focused on questions of racial and social justice, AMOA leaders reached an understanding with key community groups and made commitments about diversity to prove their seriousness. When city funding was rescinded and a key donor went bankrupt, AMOA found other funders. Every time another hole in the plan became apparent, they changed their tactics. Their principal recalibrations—like the reconciliation with smaller arts groups—were shrewd and well executed. Yet while the tactics changed, the strategy did not. The mission for the new facility—its vision, scope, and intent—changed relatively little, even after the problematic prospects for funding capital and operating costs became apparent early on. Even though some cuts in size were made, the museum project always kept a forbidding price tag. Simultaneously, few changes were made in AMOA's ongoing or future mission to attempt to gain broader support. Last but not least, the construction project put a strain on AMOA's human capacity through multiple director resignations that deprived the organization of continuous leadership. Multiple rounds of layoffs exacerbated the situation, though to a large extent these were attributed to general economic conditions rather than difficulties with the capital campaigns. Over the course of its three decades, the project lurched from one state of misalignment to another.

Amazingly, the story of the AMOA quest for a downtown location does not end here. Another effort for a downtown exhibition space proceeded simultaneously with AMOA's efforts, right across the street from the bank lobby AMOA used to occupy. This effort was spearheaded by the Texas Fine Arts Association, which later renamed itself Arthouse. Arthouse and Laguna Gloria had once been one organization, and before its move downtown, Arthouse rented a building on the Laguna Gloria campus. Then in 1995, just as AMOA was looking to lease a downtown space, Arthouse bought a vacant three-story department store for $375,000, largely financed through debt. At first, the only space they renovated to make fit for use was the first floor, where the galleries opened to the public in 1998. The space was dedicated to exhibiting contemporary artists. The remaining floors as well as the façade were renovated and expanded in a project planned by the Lewis.Tsurumaki.Lewis architectural firm and opened in 2010 as the Arthouse at the Jones Center.

The next year brought two crises. The first was debt. Unlike AMOA, Arthouse chose to build despite not having all the money for construction at hand, and the arts center was now struggling financially. By 2011, they had accumulated $3.2 million in debt and the interest payments were pushing the arts center toward insolvency. To exacerbate matters, a public controversy ensued in 2011 after Arthouse granted permission to the hosts of a corporate event to alter an art work on display to suit their needs. This mistake by the cash-strapped institution seemed in direct

7.2 Arthouse at the Jones Center. Photo by Larry D. Moore. Creative Commons Attribution-Share Alike License.

violation of the Visual Artists Rights Act, and both artists and members of the community were outraged, precipitating the resignation of both the executive director and the curator.

Two cultural organizations in Austin, Arthouse and AMOA, found themselves looking for new leaders at the same time. AMOA had just abandoned a long-cherished dream of a downtown home, but had a large cash reserve after sale of its downtown land for $21.75 million. Meanwhile, Arthouse was in possession of a new building but was struggling to pay for it. It was only a matter of a few months before the organizations began to discuss a merger. See figure 7.2.

In November 2011, the two organizations officially merged, and AMOA was finally part of an organization that owned its downtown building. The Jones Center has about 21,000 square feet of usable space, and that includes 5,000 square feet of event space on the rooftop, where a projection screen for films is installed. In size, the Jones Center is smaller than any of the facilities the Austin Museum of Art had long strived to build. Its architectural team is less known than either Venturi's or Gluck-man's firms, but they have managed to produce a building that has earned Arthouse both community interest and approval. How the joint programs will make use of both the Jones Center and Laguna Gloria remains to be seen, since the two organizations' programs remain separate for now, as the search for a new leader continues.[20] What is clear is that AMOA finally owns an exhibit space downtown—far smaller than its leaders had hoped for, but, judging from both financial and mission standpoints, far more suitable nonetheless.

Another Austin project—the Long Center for the Performing Arts—also failed on first attempt. But the leaders of the Long Center were able to regroup from the same economic turbulence that stymied AMOA and instead of abandoning their proposal wholly, they were able to under-stand the points of misalignment, re-envision their project, and address the core problems. Their experience demonstrates how alignment and misalignment are not fixed states, but rather phases that building projects shift into and out of during their evolution depending on the managerial insight and talent of boards and staff leaders.[21]

Problems and Solutions at the Long Center

In the early 1990s, a small group of civic leaders and arts patrons in Aus-tin, Texas, began discussing the construction of a major new performing arts center. A city that prides itself on its counter-culture ways, liberal politics, and educated population, Austin is filled with bumper stickers calling on the locals to "Keep Austin Weird." With the University of Texas, the state capitol, the second largest high-tech concentration after Silicon Valley, a relaxed social culture, and a reputation for being a live music mecca, civic pride runs deep in Austin. Yet tailoring a performing arts center size, budget, scope, and programming to local audience tastes, donor preferences, and local culture was a difficult task.[22]

In the summer of 2003, two trustees of the planned but still unbuilt Long Center for the Performing Arts came to convince their largest donor, Joe Long, to become the board's chairman. The chair was vacant after the resignation of the center's second chairman in four years. The most recent board meeting had been a turbulent discussion of the dwin-dling options for how to make a new performing arts center in Austin a reality. The Long Center needed money—over $140 million to start ex-ecuting its ambitious plan—but only $60 million had been raised and the campaign had stopped generating new pledges. Several of the trustees, including the chairman, had left the board. The existence of an independent performing arts center in Austin seemed more in doubt than ever, and the remaining trustees thought Joe Long was the one person who could save the project.

The two trustees who came to propose the chairmanship to Long were Marvin Womack and Steve Davis. They thought that the project could be salvaged if scaled down in ambition and budget. This change in scale would require a drastic and difficult shift in paradigm. The board, staff, and leaders of the three founding companies of Austin Symphony, Austin Lyric Opera, and Ballet Austin would have to start the design and planning process almost entirely from the beginning and reevaluate many strategic choices, from the question of adaptive reuse to the operating model for the future and the number of stages and seats. They would have to weigh many strategic priorities, including artistic excellence, community support, and the financial sustainability of the future center and its founding companies, as well as carefully assess their existing capabilities and resources. Promises made during the first design process—promises like the one to build a rehearsal hall and to deliver world-class acoustics—would have to be reconsidered. The Long Center was a decade-old dream for many of its constituents, including donors and artistic companies who would perform there. All of them would have to be persuaded to make significant compromises in how they saw the future home of the performing arts groups in Austin. Davis and Womack thought that Joe Long was the person capable of succeeding in this difficult job.

Long is a tall, gray-haired man who speaks with a slight Texan accent. He came from a small town, went to the University of Texas at Austin on a ROTC scholarship, and made a large fortune in banking after serving in the army, working as a teacher, running a dairy farm, and studying law. He had a reputation as a shrewd and tough businessman, a calm, confident man who valued structure and data over emotions and instincts in decision making. Even in Austin's informal culture, he is called "Mr." by his peers out of respect and deference. He had been a Long Center trustee for several years, but according to Davis, at the most recent meeting Long had told him "he was not prepared to waste any more time on this."

In order to convince Joe Long to assume the chairmanship of the Long Center Board, Womack and Davis arrived with back-of-the-envelope calculations of how much could be cut from the construction budget and how much more could be raised. Joe Long listened but gave them no immediate answer, taking the evening to think about the matter further and to consult his wife, Teresa Lozano Long. He realized that the decision he was making was about the Long Center project continuing at all. "I felt like if it was going to get done, I was going to have to do it," he said.

* * *

The idea for the Long Center was born because the ballet, symphony, and opera were afraid of becoming homeless. A hall of the right seating capacity is important to all performing companies, who depend on earned income from ticket sales to sustain their operations. A hall that is too large for a given company's audience leads to loss of intimacy and has a pronounced psychological effect on both the performers on stage and the audience members sitting in a half-empty theater. A hall that is too small necessitates longer runs of each production in order to collect sufficient revenues. These longer runs may not be possible owing to scheduling conflicts at the venue. In Austin, the only venue of sufficient size for the opera, ballet, and symphony was the Bass Concert Hall on the campus of the University of Texas at Austin.

When Bass Concert Hall first opened, the university courted the symphony and the ballet to become resident companies there and thereby increase Bass's cultural cachet. When Austin Lyric Opera was founded, Bass became its home too. Now, however, the companies found themselves being crowded out of the schedule by university performances and touring, national, lucrative acts like Broadway shows. The dates the companies could now secure frequently fell on the days of the football games at the stadium about 200 yards away, when parking was scarce and rivers of orange-clad Longhorn fans streamed down the streets either to the game itself or to one of the hundreds of tailgating parties in the surrounding area where beer flowed freely and clouds of smoke from the cooking of brisket filled the air. The patrons of the opera, ballet, and symphony found getting to Bass under those conditions difficult. Moreover, with Bass in increasingly high demand, rental fees suddenly doubled, with university officials suggesting that Bass could not continue being the home for these independent classical companies much longer. In the short term, the companies faced the prospect of being without a home for two seasons as Bass planned to close for mandatory fire safety renovations and lobby expansion. The companies dreamed of a home of their own, where they could have first priority in reserving dates and where they, rather than the university or the city, could be in charge of their destinies.

Three trustees of these companies known as the three Js —Jo Anne Christian, Jare Smith, and Jane Sibley—saw a new performing arts center not affiliated with a university as crucial to the groups' survival in Austin.

At some point, all three served as chairwomen or presidents of the boards of their artistic companies. Jo Anne Christian, whose husband had been the White House Press Secretary during Lyndon B. Johnson's presidency, is a lawyer with a memory her friends describe as a steel trap. Jare Smith is the youngest of the three as well as a trustee of Ballet Austin and the cochair of the capital campaign beginning with the summer of 2003. Jane Sibley is legendary in Austin not only for her leadership at the Long Center and the symphony, but also for her historic home with a heart-shaped pool in central Austin and her custom of wearing a feather in her hair.

To make their dream a reality, the three Js started small, by inviting a few business leaders to have lunch with them. They continued this lunch campaign until they had stirred up enough interest to incorporate a nonprofit, which after several name changes would become known as the Joe R. and Teresa Lozano Long Center for the Performing Arts. A board of trustees was recruited. Several professionals, including a local architecture firm, TeamHaas, offered their services pro bono.

By 1998, the proposal took a concrete shape. The Long Center asked the city for the Palmer Auditorium, which occupied a large lot overlooking Lady Bird Lake in Central Austin. Palmer had hosted performing arts events before, but was now used mostly for charity events and smaller conventions like the city's summer camp expo. The building's green dome, a familiar Austin landmark since 1958, seemed as beloved by some city residents as it was hated by others. The Long Center proposed to gut and renovate Palmer as a new performing arts center using private funds that would be raised in a $40 million capital campaign. After opening, the Long Center would operate the building under a 50-year, $1-a-year lease arrangement, but the city would still be the legal owner. The city council was concerned about the size of the Long Center's future operational deficits, and the Long Center proposed to raise a $10 million endowment as well. The council reasoned that at a 5 percent annual draw rate, a $10 million endowment would be sufficient to cover the projected operating deficit of $500,000. This city estimate was not based on any operational forecasts, but on the benchmark of the existing Palmer Auditorium's annual deficit of $500,000. Furthermore, the city asked the Long Center to build a smaller venue for use by Austin's smaller performance groups. For its part, the city council agreed to spend $46 million of municipal bond money to build a new events center nearby as a replacement for Palmer and a parking garage that could be shared by both facilities. Cliff Redd, the current executive director at the Long Center, described this deal as the city giving the Long Center "the most important piece of dirt in the city," but attaching not just strings to their gift, but "ropes enough to lift the Titanic." This proposal was approved by Austin voters in a 1998 referendum.

Initial rounds of fundraising went well. Joe and Teresa Long pledged $20 million to the effort in 1999, thus giving the project an air of credibility. Over $25 million came from "Dellionaires," including Michael and Susan Dell as well as other present and former Dell employees. By 2000, $40 million had been pledged.

Meanwhile, a board owners' representative committee was working with the professional consultants on a building program—the list of required features for the building—and a design. The consultants included a top-tier theater consultant named Fischer Dachs and Associates, acousticians, cost consultants, and two teams of architects—Skidmore, Owings, and Merrill (SOM), a national, award-winning firm, and the local TeamHaas.

The scope of the venture expanded as more ideas for improving the project were generated. "You get people's vision machines going. Everybody who was in that room was in the 'yes' mood," said Cookie Ruiz, the executive director of Ballet Austin. With fundraising going well, at the architect's request, the board approved an increase of the construction budget to approximately $80 million, though a lack of clarity about whether the $80 million was supposed to cover hard construction costs alone or the total costs of the project persists among project leaders. In addition to a large, 2,000-seat hall for the symphony, opera, and ballet and the 250-seat black box theater for the smaller groups, the Long Center trustees now planned to build a third theater of 750 seats. The main hall would have a crystal chandelier and world-class acoustics. A rehearsal hall would be included in the facility. The architectural concept by SOM also retained Palmer's distinctive architectural features like its dome at significant cost. "They [SOM] did what we asked them to do," said Joe Long. "They designed a world-class facility. I think like a lot of architects they were just accustomed to designing, and cost wasn't a factor."

Cliff Redd was less charitable. Redd was a lifelong Texan and fast-talking arts impresario fond of colorful language and funny metaphors. He said that the first design suffered from "overdesigning" and "overreaching." He said: "You're dealing with the symphony, opera, and ballet who are coming out of the situation where they feel like they have been maligned, where they didn't have the tools they needed to do what they needed to do, and so they want everything."

This design was approved by the board in 2001 and SOM was paid

$8 million for their work. The other consultants were paid another $4 million. Eleven hundred pages of blueprints were printed and sent out for contractor bids, the lowest of which came back with the construction price tag of $115 million in 2002. An additional $25 million would be necessary to cover consultants, financing costs, capital campaign costs, and the $10 million endowment promised to the city. Donors not involved with the board were "furious." To the trustees themselves, the new price tag felt like a "train hitting the wall" and the project was beginning to look like "a Rubik's cube that may not have a solution," said Redd. After paying the architects, the Long Center had $12 million remaining in cash and $35 million in outstanding pledges. The board faced the prospect of raising another $90 million in order to cover its ambitious plan.

Setbacks, Solutions, and Trade-offs

At this point, external conditions and community sentiment toward the project worsened. Just like AMOA, the Long Center experienced the impact of the 9/11 attacks and the dot com crash, which sent the national economy into a recession that heavily affected Austin, with its significant concentration of high-tech companies and jobs. Moreover, the community was becoming increasingly skeptical about the project. Austin is the self-titled "Live Music Capital of the World" because its blend of hippie and hipster culture have supported a thriving country and rock music scene for decades. But the symphony, opera, and ballet were perceived by some as art forms that belonged to the "establishment." As Redd pointed out, "Austin's core value is, we have this adversity about 'The Man.' Our parents and grandparents were Man-averse. That's why Austin is so quirky. Anything that represents a lot of authority, they are just not about it." David Fleming, the CEO of the Long Center from 2000 to 2003, described this sentiment as follows: "Many people in town scratched their heads and said, 'I don't have any interest in symphony, opera, and ballet. Why is this center being built for them?'" The plan for the Long Center included smaller venues for the more avant-garde groups that were in keeping with Austin's countercultural bent, but the perception of elitism still proved difficult to combat. Moreover, raising $90 million looked like an impossible task, and the community began to doubt the Long Center would ever be built.

The trustees and staff pressed ahead. For a while, the board counted on construction bonds pitched to them by Bank One. The bonds would cost $6 million but, Bank One salespeople suggested, not only would ensure a timely groundbreaking but also would provide an arbitrage opportunity. The bonds would bear a low, tax-exempt interest rate, costing the Long Center a mere 4.5 percent. Surely, Long Center could get a higher rate of return on past and future donations in the stock and bond market. The difference between the investment income and debt payments would boost the Long Center's budget. The conditions of the pledges received in the past posed an obstacle, however, and before the deal could be completed, the stock and credit markets contracted. The bond financing proved unworkable.

At the time, the failure to secure bond financing was seen by many trustees as an aggravating setback. Yet with the benefit of hindsight, the failure of the bond deal is now regarded by some as a tremendous stroke of luck that freed the Long Center from making large, annual debt payments out of its operational funds. The director of finance, Dwayne Cooper, joined the Long Center after an accounting career in the private sector once the bond discussions with Bank One were already underway. He thought that the promise of bonds had enabled the costs of the first design to go unexamined. Joe Long said he had always thought the bonds a "harebrained idea."

Once the fact that no loans would be forthcoming became clear, the Long Center trustees and staff tried other strategies. In the early part of 2003, they tried to reboot the capital campaign. They hired consultants to train trustees and staff in fundraising and held several special events, one to raffle off a donated Porsche. But an aura of failure had already attached itself to the project. The new campaign was not any more successful than the old.

In Austin in particular, this aura of failure was a kiss of death because the city had seen several high-profile constructions stall. The concrete shell of the building that Intel had abandoned after beginning construction in 2001 took up the entire block a short walk from the downtown offices of the Long Center. Even two and a half years after Intel first stopped construction, the naked cement rib cage was still an eyesore in the middle of downtown. A few blocks northeast was the Austin Museum of Art, which had experienced its own setbacks. Though the museum had failed to execute its plans more than once, Austin philanthropists, both large and small, never received refunds. These experiences made the Long Center's potential donors and community stakeholders jittery. Not only was little additional money forthcoming, but some donors refused to make further payments on pledges before ground was broken.

By spring, starting over and formulating a different building program and developing a different design started to look like the only option for ever making the Long Center a reality. This was the undertaking that Steve Davis and Marvin Womack were now asking Joe Long to lead.

Long weighed several arguments as he considered the matter the evening of Davis and Womack's visit. First, they had convinced him that his assuming the chairmanship was the only way the Long Center would become a reality. His primary concern was the risk that sufficient funds could not be raised and that debt would need to be assumed. "I wasn't going to be a part of a project that borrowed money. That didn't interest me at all," Long said. Another issue was his personal interest in not seeing any more of his philanthropic funds go to waste if the Long Center building effort failed. "Let me just say that it would have saved me a hell of a lot of money if we hadn't gone forward," Long said. "It would have saved me $7 or $8 million." The Longs' $20 million pledge was conditional on progress toward the Long Center completion, and if the project stalled now, only the $12 million they had already given in cash would be lost. A net of $15 million had been spent by the Long Center so far on operational costs and fees of architects and other consultants.

The strongest argument for taking the chairmanship and making sure that the project continued was the likelihood that if the Long Center failed, then all cultural capital projects would fail in Austin for the foreseeable future, just as several had already in the recent past. The community faith in the cultural sector's competency needed to be restored. Long was also concerned about seeing other donors' money go to waste. "I wasn't concerned so much about the large contributors, I was concerned about the small ones. Of course, we spent a lot of the money, so it wasn't there to refund. I knew that was going to leave a real dirty taste in a lot of people's mouths." Finally, he was confident in his own abilities. "I wasn't accustomed to failing at anything," he said. "I wasn't about to fail at this."

The next day, Joe Long announced he'd accept the chairmanship, with one condition: Steve Davis was to head the owners' representative committee in addition to staying on as treasurer. Davis had just retired from an engineering career and was looking forward to free time, but he agreed. "I thought he'd be able to prevent what happened the first time," said Long. He thought that Davis and the other members of the committee "could watch the architect and the engineers and ride herd over them and keep them within the budget because that had to be done."

The owners' representative committee was expanded from three board volunteers and two staff members to a committee of twelve—six trustees, three staff members, and the three directors of the Big Three classical art groups. Jo Anne Christian, one of the project's original Three Js, became a member. (Her fellow Js—Jane Sibley and Jare Smith—continued serving on the board.)

From August through December 2003, the committee met weekly to work on the new program and design. Many of the negotiations over the new hall's features could not be resolved in the meetings, and discussions continued during phone calls and electronically through email and instant messages. Cookie Ruiz of Ballet Austin remembers one exhausting, four-hour-long conference call between the consultants and the executive directors of the classical companies. The goal was to cut half a million so that another half-million feature could be added. Many decisions were just as grueling.

* * *

The redesign process started with Davis and two other trustees as well as key Long Center staff like David Fleming, the CEO who resigned in September of 2003, and Dwayne Cooper, the director of finance, asking all of their consultants to fly to Austin for a meeting on June 9, 2003. The Long Center representatives informed them that the design on which the consultants had worked for three years was being abandoned. The Long Center also sought opinions on how to get the project quickly back on track. Could the design and construction process be expedited? What could be built for a construction-cost-only budget of $33.5 million, which was what the Long Center could afford with the $47 million it already had?

The main hall that the Long Center could afford to build for $33.5 million seemed dire. This building program became known by the owners' representative committee as Program Zero. The meeting's minutes described the resulting building: "All of the 2,100 seats would be on one level, which would make it harder to see the stage from the back of the hall. The audience chamber would be sized wide and low. This would produce a chamber with a low volume ratio that would result in poor acoustics, particularly when the symphony performs." The space would have acoustics comparable with a high school auditorium, albeit one of the very best ones. The seats would be made of plastic and not metal or wood. The hall would have a tiny lobby, if any, and an insufficient number of restrooms for all of the patrons. Only limited performance equipment like lights and rigging would be available, and much of the mechanical equipment needed by production staff of resident and touring companies would have to be stored off-site.

This program satisfied none of the trustees or founding companies. This left the owners' representative committee with two questions:

1. What are the minimum requirements for a performing arts center that is worth building?
2. Is this building program financially feasible? Can the additional money to improve on Program Zero be raised?

The committee proceeded by debating every issue long enough to reach a consensus. At the beginning of the committee's work, Davis and the other members reviewed the Three Js' original vision: to provide an artistic home, primarily for the three founding companies. Over time, the committee developed three guiding principles to refer to as they considered what the new hall should look like: fiscal responsibility, universal support, and essential need. The members also weighed the possibility of postponing each design element until a future, more prosperous time.

On occasion, emotional attachments to design features already promised during the previous process came up in the committee or board meetings. These were the moments when Joe Long's presence and leadership—and the deference he inspired among his peers—were crucial to keep the design on track. If a nonessential feature was requested, he would challenge the trustee to find the money. "You want that chandelier, you pay for it," Ruiz remembers Long saying. "I'll take your check right now." Since he had recently suffered a hip injury, he had in his possession a walking cane which he sometimes thumped against the floor to emphasize his point. Objections tended to be withdrawn quickly.

The project cost was driven by four decisions that the owners' representative committee needed to reconsider: the number of venues within the center, the architectural aesthetics, the quality of acoustics in the main hall, and the extent of adaptive reuse. All were considered important to project success, and the committee's goal was to find an optimal compromise between them that would permit the center to be built within budget.

Number of Venues. The first decision made by the trustees was which of the four venues included in the 2001 SOM design should now be retained. Program Zero—the building program that could be executed using only the $47 million the Long Center already had—allowed for the construction of the largest main hall only, significantly lower in quality than desired by the founding companies. All of the other venues would require funds beyond the $47 million. However, the $47 million included the money from the sale of the naming rights for three of the four venues.

The rationales for the venues' existence varied. The 2,300-seat main theater was primarily intended for use by the three founding companies. The naming rights were given to Michael and Susan Dell in exchange for their $10 million gift. The founding companies would have priority scheduling here, thus limiting the hall's potential as a rental for the lucrative performances like Broadway tours. Between the three of them, Opera, Symphony, and Ballet planned to use the hall for 89 performances a year as well as rehearsals and load-ins. The three classical companies would pay some of the highest rental rates in the nation among nonprofit artistic groups, most of whom benefit from subsidized rents. The Long Center planning documents also anticipated 55 days every year when Dell Hall would be rented for performances and commercial events by outside groups. Additionally, the Long Center planned to program its own presented series of performances in the main hall, with 38 performance days. Dell Hall was the venue that would cost the most and, in the trustees' opinion, had the largest claim to existence. Most of the donors who had given thus far were trustees of the three classical companies and intended for their money to go toward building a new home for them.

The 750-seat Topfer Theater was to be named for the Topfer family in exchange for their $5 million gift as well as advocacy of the Long Center to the community of the newly wealthy Dell executives. The Topfer Theater was intended to meet the need for medium-sized performance spaces in Austin both for groups that already needed them and for smaller groups that would not otherwise have an opportunity to grow in the future. No other theaters of Topfer's size existed in Austin. "That's a reason to do it," said Davis. "But it's also a good reason not to do it, because there's usually a good reason there aren't any around. That's a strange theater size for a proscenium theater with a fly tower." The Topfer would be used by Ballet Austin fourteen days a year for productions of contemporary pieces, for which the group expected smaller audiences than for its classical fare. Youth theater would have a home at the Topfer Theater too. "It was a tar baby," said Ruiz. "If we didn't know where else to put something, we stuck it in there." Topfer was a place of possibility, a place for artistic growth, where cultural experiences that did not yet have a home in Austin could be offered.

During the 2001 design process, the Topfer was also projected to produce an operating surplus for the Long Center according to the planning documents, which projected the theater would be in use 300 days of the year. Ruiz questioned this assumption. "I remember one particularly snarky call where one of the consultants called and said, 'I hope you know there are 45 groups that are ready to book out the entire calendar.' And I said, 'Really?'" Ruiz asked for the list of the prospective bookers, noting that unlike the consultants, she was from Austin. She found that many of the groups who promised to rent Topfer were struggling to draw audiences and pay for space. Some used the Ballet Austin building rent-free on the weekends.

The 225-seat Rollins Theater was meant for the smaller community performing groups, of which Austin had over 200. The black box format was conducive to intimate, small-scale storytelling. On the basis of conversations with leaders of the community groups, Long Center staff and consultants estimated this theater would be rented 42 weeks and 5 days of an average year by 39 external groups. This was the community theater that the Long Center promised to the city council, and the council expected the rental fees for half the events here to be either waived or significantly subsidized by the Long Center. Ruiz questioned whether this theater was financially sustainable. "I was keenly interested in the business model behind everything. And I clearly understood the cause and effect between my rental rates and what else was happening there," she said. She was afraid that the Rollins Theater would result in operating deficits that her group would be expected to cover with higher rents. "I took a lot of abuse for that," she said.

The owners' representative committee discussed the possibility of finding a partner to build and operate this theater as well as the potential of building it off-site or postponing its construction to a later phase. Joe Long intervened in these discussions early to say that both the promise made to the city and space for community groups were crucial, worthwhile objectives. The project cost of building the Rollins Theater was $6.4 million. The theater built for this money would be the best theater of its size in Austin, but far from a world-class theater. The Long Center had a naming gift of $5 million for this space from Debra and Kevin Rollins, another Dellionaire family.

The rehearsal hall was envisioned as a space that would make the Long Center more flexible, permitting more simultaneous performances. The hall would also boost the operating budget of the Long Center by providing rental and catering income from private events. Depending on the desired equipment and acoustics, this hall could be added to Program Zero for $2 million–$4 million.

Architectural Aesthetics. Few vocal proponents of architectural aesthetics remained on the board. One of Davis's first acts as the head of the owners' representative committee was to study the cost of architecture at a typical performing arts center by looking at recently completed projects with the help of the Donnel Consultants. "One of the things we discovered was that in a typical performing arts facility, 'architecture' represented 40 percent of the costs of the project," said Davis. "It's what I'd describe as something without particular function but principally designed to improve the visual appeal of the facility."

The need to be budget conscious eliminated the possibility of a large architectural statement. However, the Program Zero building would be a rectangular box, and several of the trustees wanted a place where artistic performances happened to look more appealing than a warehouse. The question of whether the Long Center could afford to spend anything at all on aesthetics remained.

Dell Hall Acoustics. Most of the trustees and members of the owners' representative committee thought that superior acoustics were an essential need for the main hall where the symphony, opera, and ballet would perform. "We all agreed that for the large hall we wanted the best acoustics we could possibly afford and we were willing to trade off many things in order to realize that," said Steve Davis. Joe Long said he "insisted we have world-class acoustics." "The place we did not skimp on is the place where art is created," said Ruiz.

Acoustics for unamplified musical forms like symphony and opera are considered black magic by people who work in the performing arts. Acoustics are usually designed by highly paid specialized consultants, and even these experts are frequently uncertain as to the exact level of acoustic excellence the building will achieve until they hear the first performance. Despite some unpredictability in the final result, many leaders in performing arts swear by the benefits of an acoustically superior building, where the audience experiences the sound as clear, warm, and enveloping and musicians perform better because they can hear one another on opposite ends of the stage. One performing arts center director who was a retired singer mentioned that an acoustically perfect hall felt as if it were lifting him up as he sang. These experiences lead many such directors to hope that superior acoustics will boost their halls' competitiveness.

However, some doubt the value of capital expenses on acoustics. David Fleming, the former Long Center CEO, had in the previous seven years become one of the skeptics. "I've had battles with acousticians who have argued with me that this [the acoustical level] needs to be an 8 and not a 7. Millions of dollars ride on this decision, and that's hogwash. It's not a question to be asked. It's a question that justifies the existence of acousticians. It's not a question that makes a difference in the operations of a performing arts center."

To some extent, Davis sees Fleming's point. He thinks that 90 percent of the people are incapable of hearing the difference between good and great in acoustics. He said many of the audience members will be persuaded by what others tell them about the quality of a given theater. Nonetheless, professional musicians are likely to fall in the 10 percent who know the difference and perhaps perform better because of it. Thus, Davis was a stalwart supporter of acoustical excellence during the committee discussions.

Program Zero provided for a hall with acoustics of a high school auditorium, and many trustees did not consider such a space worth building. The acoustician suggested multiple improvements. Going from a noise criteria (NC) rating of 30 to 20 would bring Long Center in line with many of its peers in how far distracting noise like coughing and candy wrapper crinkling carry within the audience chamber. Going further, from NC 20 to NC 15, would put Long Center in the 80th to 85th percentile for noise attenuation in performance halls. Concrete shielding for the roof and grout filling for walls would protect the audience chamber from external noises like thunder and traffic. A Shaper orchestra shell, though more expensive, would have a significant effect on how far sound would carry and how enveloping it would feel to both musicians and audience members during symphony performances. Without a Shaper shell, Jaffe Holden Acoustics believed that Dell Hall's potential for acoustical quality would be limited to a maximum grade of 8 on a scale from 1 to 10. Tiered seating—like parterre, boxes, and balconies—would help the space feel more immediate by minimizing the distance between the stage and the farthest row of seats. Tiered seating, just like higher-quality wooden seats, would also provide reflective surfaces for sound, thus allowing it to travel further and to feel warmer to a greater portion of the audience. Acoustical banners and moveable forestage pieces would enable some acoustical tuning of the building between events to improve the sound of each individual discipline. All together, these improvements to Program Zero would cost $16.7 million.

Adaptive Reuse vs. New Construction. Another major decision for the owners' representative committee was whether to reuse some of the existing Palmer Auditorium or to raze this building and start anew. DCI said that an adaptive reuse would cost $1.4 million less than a new construction, but another source estimated the cost of reuse could exceed the cost of new construction by $2.5 million. This kind of uncertainty about costs is endemic to adaptive use projects, since the exact condition of the existing building is never completely certain. Both the schedule and the cost of a new construction can be more reliably predicted.

Another argument for complete demolition of Palmer was that the master plan of the site would then have more flexibility for future additions of more venues and other spaces. The backstage spaces would have a more efficient layout in a new construction. A deeper stage to accommodate larger sets would also be possible.

On the other hand, the adaptive reuse option also presented several advantages. First, "recycling" a building was likely to be seen in a positive light by Austin's environmentally conscious population. Everyone involved with the fundraising effort agreed. "We had a shot at telling a rejuvenated story," said David Fleming. "The worst thing would be to tell the public, 'We really failed on the first go around. Everything's trashed, we have to start from scratch.' We'd rather be saying, 'You know what, we want to be true to our values, our core values, from the artistic standpoint. And we have to do this on a more economical basis and in keeping with a recycling ethic that is valuable to us.'" Second, the reuse of Palmer would result in a larger building, with a covered "porch" about 30 thousand square feet in size where the audience could go on a nice day to enjoy a view of the lake and Austin downtown. Additionally, the reused building would contain another eight thousand square feet in reserved, unfinished space that could be easily renovated into classrooms or office space later. These additional spaces were valued by the owners' representative committee at about $1.7 million. Last but not least, working with the existing structure could potentially result in a more aesthetically pleasing building for the same price if existing elements were imaginatively used.

* * *

Building a new performing arts center requires compromises. An abundance of funds can obviate these compromises and require fewer difficult decisions about trade-offs. In the case of the Long Center for the Performing Arts, however, financial restriction and the necessity of concessions factored in the project's eventual success. They required the board to achieve clarity about the new organization's priorities. The mistakes of the first design made the trustees more knowledgeable and capable of

7.3 Long Center for the Performing Arts. Photo by LoneStarMike/Wikimedia. Creative Commons Attribution-Share Alike 3.0 License.

undertaking the second. Yet, the protracted, iterative process required absolute doggedness. Few of the project's leaders had anticipated the scope of the responsibilities they eventually accepted. Many paid a large personal cost—Cliff Redd, for example, attributes his recent heart attack to the stress. See figure 7.3.

By the end of 2003, the Long Center owners' representative committee produced a building program that would cost $50 million to build and $10 million to design. An additional $17 million would be needed for the endowment, staff salaries, consultants, and other soft costs. The Long Center still had $12 million remaining in cash and $35 million in outstanding pledges, most of which would need to be re-earned. The board set out to raise an additional $30 million for a total of $77 million. Donors had to be convinced the new plan was feasible and right for Austin.

Only two venues were included in the final building program: Dell Hall and Rollins Theater. The medium-sized theater that was supposed to be named after the Topfer family was omitted. The Long Center relationship with these major Austin donors was difficult to rebuild.

Other features of the building program recommended by Davis and the committee included the decision to reuse parts of Palmer, inclusion of many though not all of the acoustical improvements recommended by Jaffee Holden Acoustics, and some enhancements of the lobby finishes. Joe Long added $2 million to his gift to pay for the latter, for a total gift of $22 million. Skidmore, Owings, and Merrill were not rehired. The new design was largely completed by Zeidler Partnership Architects and Austin's TeamHaas, which was bought by Nelsen Architects during the construction.[23]

Joe Long handpicked a new executive director, Cliff Redd, to replace David Fleming, who had resigned in 2003 so that he could return to his core specialization of running existing performing arts centers. Redd proved to be an effective spokesman during the capital campaign. Together, Long and Redd hosted dinners at Long's home, where prospective donors were invited for presentations. Long addressed allegations of wastefulness during the first design campaign by saying that the $12 million spent on the first, abandoned design was covered by his and his wife's gift. A native Austinite, Redd was finely attuned to the local attitudes and chose to stress civic pride and the building's environmentally friendly adaptive reuse during his pitches. Overall, $82 million was raised. The $5 million surplus was used by Redd for a reserve fund to cover future deficits and to renovate some of the unfinished empty space that resulted from Palmer's reuse into on-site administrative offices. Otherwise, he and most of his staff would have had to commute to the building.

After the long journey that the Long Center had taken to completion, widespread community support—as shown in our community survey— has been one of the most surprising results. Many of the project's leaders are satisfied with the center's new design as well. Cookie Ruiz calls it "a monument to what the city has created in a post-9/11 world," noting that the lavish SOM plan would have felt out of step with cultural changes. Joe Long felt the 2003 crisis and the need to start over improved the project. "In retrospect, that [cutting the midsized theater and the rehearsal hall] was a wise thing to have done because I'm not sure the city could have supported four venues." Overall, he is happy with the result. "I never go over there that I don't have three or four people that I don't know tell me how grateful they are that we got this done and built the center. I get people stopping me on Congress Avenue."

Like many projects, the Long Center plan stalled when funding could not be found. Yet unlike so many projects that either never got built or resulted in disaster, the Long Center had leaders who were able to bring the project into a greater state of alignment. What was clear to them was the need for a complete project overhaul. Indeed, the people in the top leadership positions—from executive director to board chair—changed. The new leaders were better suited to take the project forward, better adapted to the project's changing conditions. The approach to the Long Center mission—what the building would do once built—changed as well. The process of rewriting the building specifications forced the group to focus on a few needs that had to be met, rather than on all things that seemed desirable. Thus, the midsized hall—which had a less compelling use case than the small and the large halls—had to be cut, even though the decision was an emotional one. Many of the luxurious concert hall trappings had to go as well. As the new leadership contemplated how to present itself following a high-profile setback, the approach to the community changed as well. The new building was re-envisioned as a facility that was more in touch with Austin culture and values.

One reason that the Long Center got built is that its leaders were willing to face the facts and make difficult trade-offs. The need for strategic abandonment—the willingness to adjust the overarching vision or concept in the name of financial feasibility and community support—should not be dismissed as unprincipled capitulation. By giving up two performance spaces out of four and by changing the design to something more modest and less sleek, the Long Center team actually stumbled upon something important. Austinites responded positively to the green building approach, to the creative reuse of the old building, and to the more modest scale of the project. While AMOA sought over and over to make a grand architectural statement that would attract patrons and donors, the Long Center project recycled old aluminum roof tiles and gravitated toward a design that embraced the city's motto ("Keep Austin Weird") and appeared to fit right into the local scene.

Both AMOA and the Long Center experienced the ups and downs of major capital project planning and execution. How they dealt with these swings in fortune varied greatly. Critical to achieving fit alignment and coherence across the four areas of funding, capacity, mission, and community is the ability to first spot tensions and then resolve them. While both groups were able to spot the problems that arose with the community and with funders, only Long found a way to change gears, placate community leaders by building the small performance space, get the lead donor engaged, and forge support for a scaled-back vision that was in keeping with local sentiments.

Cultural building would be a lot easier if all projects marched slowly but steadily toward alignment through trade-offs, compromises, and deals. Unfortunately, this is not the case. All too often projects either fail to launch or launch only to crash back to earth after opening.

8 | *Better Building for the Arts*

As cultural building projects unfold, they follow four main narratives or master scripts that reflect the starting and ending conditions of arts organizations.[1] When arts organizations ponder major cultural building projects, they inevitably start in one of two places. One possibility is that they enter the cultural planning process in a position of good strategic alignment or fit, with a clear and powerful artistic vision guiding the enterprise, with their financial house in order, with the community behind the project, and with capable staff, board, and volunteers ready and committed. Across the core managerial challenges, the organization performs well. The building project thus comes at a time when the organization is poised for growth and ready to take the next step toward greater artistic achievement.

The second possibility is that the organization begins a building project in a state of misalignment and chaos. Misalignment can be a function of one, two, three, or all four strategic elements—funding, capacity, community relations, and mission—being absent or out of alignment with the others. The vision might not be aligned with the financial realities. Or the community support may be present, but the internal capacity is in a state of flux. Sometimes, an arts organization may have a compelling vision, but no support, no money, and no capacity. Whatever the nature of the misalignment and whatever its relative level of severity, some arts organizations embark on projects at a time when their strategic positions are shaky. The building project is the event that the organization hopes will drive organizational growth and improvement.

Table 8.1. The Four Narratives of Cultural Building Projects

		Starting Point before Building Project	
		Alignment	Misalignment
Ending Point When Project Is Complete	Alignment	Going from Good to Great	Turning Things Around
	Misalignment	Moving Backward	Still Searching for Solutions

Building projects inevitably lead organizations toward two very different outcomes as well. Some projects will result in an organization "finding itself," bringing community, staff, funders, and vision into tight alignment and fit. In these cases the project is in fact the great unifier. In other cases, the outcome is just the opposite. The building project results in greater financial and mission stress than what existed before the entire initiative was undertaken. These are the cases in which the project throws the organization into cultural and fiscal chaos, unearthing different visions and exposing conflicts over control of the new facility. From these two starting points and with these two termini in mind, four narratives or pathways can be defined, as shown in table 8.1.

Each of the case studies we discussed has followed one of these paths in one way or another. Of course, alignment is a continuum rather than a binary variable, and the classification here is presented with that caveat. Also, each decision has the power to alter an organization's strategic alignment, and as such, the actual trajectories of projects can be circular and curvilinear, with organizations reaching and losing alignment now and in the future. Still, some broad conclusions about the pathways of projects can be reached. See table 8.2.

A few projects started in the state of alignment and ended there, one building project later. We consider the Art Institute of Chicago and the Shakespeare Theatre Company two such organizations. Though both went through their moments of misalignment, overall, their funding, capacity, mission, and community are all mutually supportive of each other. Both organizations are suffering the effects of the recession. The Art Institute of Chicago needs to resolve a lawsuit against an engineering

Table 8.2. Categorization of Case Study Narratives

		Ending Point Once the Project Is Complete	
		Alignment	Misalignment
Starting Point before Building Project	Alignment	• Art Institute of Chicago • Shakespeare Theatre Company	• The Sandler Center for the Performing Arts • Taubman Museum of Art • Spertus Institute
	Misalignment	• Dallas Theater Center • Long Center for the Performing Arts • Atlanta Opera	• Portland Center Stage • Workhouse Arts Center • Dallas Opera • AT&T Performing Arts Center

firm that had been involved with the expansion. Shakespeare Theatre Company is working on recalibrating its mission. Yet both organizations find themselves strengthened artistically and benefiting from an increase in their public profiles as the result of their buildings.

The second group is arguably even more successful than the first, since this group includes projects that were able to transition from a state of misalignment before building projects to a state of alignment after. The Dallas Theater Center was a principal partner in the foundation of the AT&T Performing Arts Center. When that project began, Dallas Theater Center was languishing artistically. Resources were short and audiences were declining. Then the impending and enormously risky move to the expensive new venue galvanized the organization into action, leading them to hire a new artistic director and embark on a $12 million campaign to build an operational reserve. Together, the new artistic vision and additional financial resources have permitted the Dallas Theater Center to use its new landmark theater as a platform for community outreach and artistic success. Its audiences have been increasing, and it remains in a state of financial health.

The Long Center for the Performing Arts in Austin, Texas, is included in the misalignment-to-alignment narrative for different reasons. The Long Center came to the brink of defeat when design creep had put the project of building a new performing arts center far out of its sponsors'

BETTER BUILDING FOR THE ARTS | 227

financial reach. Moreover, the overly ambitious proposal was out of community reach. Yet changes in leadership brought with them a change in approach, and the project was trimmed until it became financially feasible and gained wide community support. We attribute this radical change in the project's feasibility to greater alignment.

The last organization in this category, the Atlanta Opera, went from a state of misalignment at the Civic Center, where its audiences and revenues were steadily dropping, to a state of alignment at the Cobb Centre. They achieved this by moving from a technically subpar venue in downtown Atlanta to the suburbs. The Atlanta Opera also decided to forgo pursuing a building project of its own. Its financial situation and audiences now improve with every year.

In the next category, the Dallas Opera, the AT&T Performing Arts Center in Dallas, Workhouse Arts Center in Lorton, and Portland Center Stage all went from dealing with one set of misalignment challenges to dealing with another set in a different venue. The Dallas Opera moved because it wanted to expand its season as well as enjoy greater artistic choices offered by a purpose-built opera hall. The expenses of operating in the new venue have caused mounting deficits, however, and instead of expanding its season, Dallas Opera was forced to cut a production. Its landlord, the AT&T Performing Arts Center, has a costly, ambitious new campus of buildings and yet is struggling financially as well as struggling to deliver on its ambitious transformational goals. This organization is new, so its starting state is difficult to determine. Yet we have decided the organization started in a state of misalignment because the community responses during our survey made it clear the organization overlooked community engagement from the first.

In Lorton, Virginia, attendance and demand for studios at the Workhouse Arts Center demonstrated the local community's demand for local arts organizations, especially for the Workhouse's unorthodox model. This suggests that before the center's existence, community needs had gone unmet. The Workhouse Arts Center took a community with a fundamental misalignment between community desires and arts organizations presence and created a functioning arts center, overcoming the initial scarcity of resources. Yet though the Workhouse is an improvement for the cultural vitality of its community, the project is not perfect and challenges for the leadership team remain. The high turnover of executive directors suggests instability, though the recent appointment of former Fairfax mayor John Mason is a hopeful sign. In addition to these leadership challenges, the project is still searching for a sustainable business model. So far, Fairfax County has helped the organization with deficits by providing as much as $3 million a year, but this support seems intended as a temporary measure. To reach alignment, the Workhouse must find a pathway to financial independence and sustainability.[2]

Meanwhile, Portland Center Stage traded one type of misalignment for another. At its old location in the city-owned performing arts center, Portland Center Stage could not produce the kind of theater it wanted owing to the characteristics of performance venue like stage dimensions and seating capacity. The company's mission was out of alignment with the other elements. The new Gerding Theater has led to dramatic successes in the domains of mission, community relations, and capacity. This may be a better state of affairs than the company's condition before its construction project. Yet balancing the annual budget and paying off the last loans for the construction have replaced mission as the company's main strategic challenge. To reach alignment, the organization must resolve its financial difficulties.

The last category includes organizations that have fared the worst, by going from a state of alignment to a state of misalignment. The Spertus Institute strived to expand its profile and reach by moving to a new building. Yet its attempts to alter its programming and expand its audiences were stymied by the increase in its sensitivity to financial pressures after the completion of the new building. Sandler Center for the Performing Arts grew out of the Pavilion Theatre. The Pavilion was a community theater. Its funding, community relationships, and capacity were all aligned with its mission of providing affordable performance and rehearsal space to local groups. During the planning effort to build a replacement for the Pavilion, this mission was brought into question. Other goals for the replacement theater were set. These conflicting goals led to compromises in physical design that make success in accomplishing any specific goal difficult. The Sandler Center functions from the standpoint of a basic misalignment of capacity and mission. Taubman Museum of Art went from being a financially sustainable, affordable museum with a budding collection of American painters, to existing in a state of a constant financial crisis. This state of affairs was brought about by a project that was over budget, and a capital campaign that could not garner enough funds, as well as operational forecasts that severely underestimated the organization's annual deficit. Both organizations face large obstacles in regaining strategic alignment.[3]

Conclusions about Cultural Building

What have we learned from these and other projects we studied? In each of the four main constituent elements that surround the core concept of strategic design—funding, community, mission, and capacity—we believe there are some critical rules that all leaders should follow when planning and managing cultural building projects. Some are common sense and readily adoptable, while others are more complex and harder to put into practice. Still, we have looked across the cases explored here, and over fifty others that were the subject of less intensive case analysis but for which ample data were collected, and tried to focus on fifteen rules for the cultural builder to live by.[4]

Funding

1. Fund Operations and Endowment as You Go. One of the most important conclusions of our study of major building projects relates to the way funds are raised and spent. Too many projects postpone raising operational funds or endowments until the last minute, or until after opening, with the predictable outcome that these funds are never raised. From Miami to Madison, the number of venues that have opened only to confront operating deficits and broader financial crises is disappointingly large. This single mistake seems to occur with mind-numbing regularity. And it is made by some of the most sophisticated and intelligent leaders and organizations.

How is this mistake made with regularity? One contributing factor is a lack of discipline in sticking to a budget. The design for the building keeps getting more expensive, and a bigger capital campaign becomes necessary. Raising money for the additional construction expenses becomes a priority. Endowment and operating fund campaigns are postponed. Meanwhile, donors who would give toward operations are cannibalized for building campaigns.

Another factor is forecast inaccuracy. If construction costs and feasible capital campaign targets are never estimated accurately in the first place, planning to raise an endowment in the last phase of the capital campaign is unlikely to result in success. Yet forecast inaccuracy is common. Forecast inaccuracy can cause arts leaders to be too optimistic about not needing operational and endowment funds as well. Many arts leaders believe that operating costs can always be covered by increased revenues from ticket sales, and hence choose not to divert funds away from capital costs to future operations during the construction phase of a project.

A third factor comes down to a misalignment of incentives for project leaders. More often than not, the construction phase leader of a large arts organization is not the person who will actually manage the organization over the long term. In fact, the exhausted entrepreneurial leaders who oversaw the construction will move on once the final touches are put on the project at hand. With this transfer of responsibility comes a problem. The person raising the money for the project has no ownership of the operational needs. Ultimately, leadership turnover presents challenges for endowment and operational campaigns.

The inclination to put all fundraising efforts into securing funds necessary for construction is natural. Bills from contractors flow in and payment must be made to keep the project on track. Nevertheless, a single-minded focus on capital expense and a neglect of future operating expenses is a very dangerous road to follow. A lack of operational funding can lead to financial problems after opening. It also represents a failure to fully capitalize on the fundraising opportunities opened by a building project.

The best way to prevent this scenario is to partition funds as they are raised between building costs and future operating costs. An even better idea is to raise the endowment first and construction money second. This means requiring donors to a building campaign to pay not just for the bricks and mortar but also for the staff, utilities, and maintenance costs associated with new or enlarged facilities.[5]

2. Start Project When All the Money Is in Hand. "If we start building it, they will give." It is hard to imagine a worst mantra to live by—and very possible die by. In almost all fundraising campaigns, pledges are made at the outset and fulfilled over time. It is extremely tempting to begin the building process once the pledges have been received and partially paid. After all, some of the money is in the pocket and burning a hole. Why wait?

The most powerful reason that waiting is wise comes down to the psychology of donors. When ground is broken, there is an immediate sense that the project is headed for completion. Why else would ground have been broken? Thus, the onset of construction can destroy the sizzle or promise of a project and replace it with mundane reality. Moreover, many donors like the idea of being catalysts and seeing the gift close out a campaign and open the way for construction to start. Once ground is broken, the donor is no longer making possible a dream, but picking up a tab.

In addition, once construction begins and a completion date is projected, the deadline for finishing the capital campaign becomes firm. If the campaign is still incomplete, the sponsoring organization runs the risk of construction ending with this campaign incomplete, which can spell disaster. Donations will come to a halt at opening, if not before. Until construction starts, however, the sponsoring organization has large leeway in deciding how long a capital campaign can last.

3. Available Real Estate (Even When Cheap or Free) Is Not in Itself a Reason to Build. From empty lots and abandoned department stores to old factories, real estate has a way of becoming available to arts organizations. Sometimes it is available at a discount or even for "free." What arts leaders need to constantly remind themselves is that real estate availability should not be the starting point for decision making about cultural building. Human nature being what it is and the power of bargains being strong, however, it is often hard to ignore or walk away from a real estate opportunity.[6]

The problem that arises when buildings or lots "become available" is that a real estate event often triggers a planning process, rather than a documented institutional need leading to a planning process designed to find a way to satisfy this need. The reason that real estate should not trigger a planning process is that it is always possible to find ways to use a bigger and better building. Why accept the reality that the existing facility represents an organization's capacity and support in the community, when it is much easier to see real estate as the thing that is actually holding a museum or performing arts group from achieving its full potential? It is much harder to decide that a new building is appropriate on the basis of a fair assessment of the stage of development of the institution and the breadth and depth of its support in the community, than it is to jump at the chance to acquire the parking lot next door. Real estate can and does excite the passions of board members, many of whom have experience in this domain. The dangling of property can set off a chain of fast and furious phone calls among board members, all of which are animated by a sense that the organization must act quickly or miss out on the chance at hand.

In assessing whether a real estate opportunity is significant enough to disrupt normal strategic planning processes, an organization needs to know that acquiring the property will be a net positive, regardless of whether the planning process that will follow indicates that building is the right move. Thus, when the Washington Opera accepted the gift of a large shuttered downtown department store, it knew that even if the venue proved unusable for its rehearsal or performing space needs, it would be a valuable asset to sell to a downtown developer. When the opera opted to stay at the Kennedy Center, it was able to convert the real estate it had acquired into a sizable endowment. Real estate is valuable if it has flexible uses and is a net positive for the organization regardless of its use.

4. Use Anchoring to Fight Design Creep. Like kids in a toy store, arts organizations that embark on the design of a new home can ask for everything they see. Design bloat will increase the cost of a cultural building project and can make it unaffordable. The organization will then either scuttle the project or, worse, pursue it despite the costs. This latter option is often chosen because of a cognitive bias toward the irrational escalation of commitment, which makes it seem as if we need to stick with our chosen course given how much we've already committed.

During decisions like these and all throughout the design process, reminders about the most important goals for the building projects are useful. Therefore, at the very beginning of planning, arts organizations should create anchoring documents and images for their leadership teams. These anchors can be used by individuals to stay mindful of why they pursued the project and what about it is most important to their arts organization. Then these anchors can help stave off design creep and overcome cognitive decision-making biases.

Community Relations

5. Don't Ask for Community Input Unless You Are Ready to Listen and Respond. One of the first and most difficult-to-resist impulses during a planning and building process is to reach out to the community and seek input. Not only do arts organizations want to speak to the interests of their audience, they also want to be accepted by the broader community. While there are some elite arts organizations that operate openly and contently above the fray of community politics, most arts organizations want to be accepted and appreciated by the local community. For this reason, open houses and town hall meetings are often held before a building plan is unveiled. The goal of these exercises should be to absorb new perspectives on the building, to learn how the artistic production of the organization is perceived by the community, and to listen to the aspirations of the community as they relate to the future building plan.

Sometimes the listening effort involves surveys and focus groups. In a few instances, a design charrette may actually be organized to drive toward a common vision of what the new facility should look like and accomplish. All this listening can be a powerful source of ideas and input, which can then be fed to the design team. But listening creates expectations among those who are sharing their views.

The one challenge when it comes to community input is that it needs to be received graciously and then actually taken seriously. One of the most significant ways an arts organization can get a project off on the wrong foot is to announce a public event and then systematically ignore what is said. Listening must be a function of wanting to hear, and the willingness to hear the views of others requires that they be responded to in one way or another. Just because activists passionately want a flexible-use space in the new building for public use does not mean that it will be built. If it is not built, however, an explanation needs to be given why this space was impossible or impractical, one that honors the desire and stated needs of the stakeholders.

6. Have a Plan B for Major Swings in the Local Economy and Changes in Local Politics. The world has a way of changing, especially over the sometimes long periods in which cultural building projects are planned and financed. Sometimes, in the middle of a capital campaign, the local economy may take a turn for the better or for the worse. Major changes in the local economy can and do have a profound effect on donor behavior and the course of cultural building efforts. When the economy turns and growth slows, donors become more skittish. While they may be very wealthy, donors will still gravitate toward penny pinching. Some will even say and feel that the decreases in their multimillion dollar assets have made them feel poor. However, when the economy improves noticeably, donors are subject to a countervailing pressure to "spread the wealth around" and fulfill their civic duty.

Smart fundraisers know that business cycles have psychological effects on donors and the timing of a request can turn out to be critical. At the same time, if a campaign is in midstream when the economic conditions in a region worsen, the fundraiser needs to know that community support for the project may well shift. It may mean not that there is now opposition where there was once was support, but only that the enthusiasm may have diminished along with the bank balances of key supporters. Economic downturns can sour grassroots support for elite arts building projects. What was once a symbol of civic capacity and pride can easily become an extravagance purchased at the expense of attending to more critical human needs.

While it is tempting to treat building projects as analytic exercises involving costs and benefits inherent to the project itself, in reality the broader political economy of the projects must be understood and hedging strategies for risk implemented. Shifts in business climate and government budget shortages can radically change the nature and strength of support and a good project leader will be on the lookout for the first signs of any such shift.

7. Wait to Announce the Building Budget Until You Are Certain You Have a Solid Number. There is nothing more painful than to have to report back to funders, government officials, the press, arts leaders, and the media that a building project is going to cost more than expected. In many cases, there is a temptation to float a budget number just to orient the community and give a sense of the size of the anticipated project. The problem with floating budget estimates is that they often bear little resemblance to final cost projections. For this reason, one of the best moves a leader can make in driving a cultural building project forward is to say nothing about cost and project budget until the numbers are based on detailed plans and increase in certainty.[7]

The alternative to patience in announcing project budgets is not attractive. By raising a building budget in midcampaign, two things are communicated. The first is that the project may not be well managed or even that it could be in trouble. The second is that the pronouncements of the organization are not to be trusted and have little reliability. Neither of these is good. For this reason, humility about early estimates is called for. Early estimates should be treated as what they are—guesses that are not developed enough to be shared with the public.

When then is the right time to announce the budget? The answer is that the announcement should come at two different times and with two different levels of precision. During the fundraising phase of the project, a cost range should be quietly shared with key donors and this range should guide the design team in their early design work. Once a preliminary design exists and the campaign is well along, a tentative budget number based on a careful estimate of construction costs can be advanced. The accuracy of cost estimates increases dramatically once blueprints are available and further still once contractor bids on the project come in. At this point, a final building budget announcement is ready to be released. In handling this delicate and political task, there is a need for cautious incrementalism, one guided by a slow movement toward greater and greater budgetary precision that is communicated externally.[8]

Capacity

8. Offer Your Trustees the Opportunity to Dissent. One arts leader joked that she knew of boards that operated by having the only acceptable votes be "Aye" or "I resign." Yet challenges and objections can be a useful test and a useful source of ideas, particularly when the arguments against a decision come from supporters of the organization whose motives and goodwill can be trusted. In fact, as we argued in the capacity chapter, too much agreement can be a sign that the leadership team is considering only obvious and stale ideas.

Another arts leader compared a building project to riding a luge down an Olympic track. Once the push off is over and the rider lies down on the luge, there is little that can be done to control the speed, and momentum carries the rider down the track. While terrifying, this image does capture the dynamics of some of the larger arts projects. Once the word gets out that a building is on the drawing board and that funds are being sought, the whole endeavor becomes difficult to delay for deliberations or to stop. Reputations get tied up in the project, visions of the city and its cultural landscape start to form in people's minds, and the drive to get to the finish line is strong. Yet during all stages, leaving room for dissent among decision makers is critical to project vitality.[9]

9. Hire Staff Early. Having good people is critical. Having good people at the time when they are needed most is even more critical. As arts organizations of all kinds build new homes for themselves, one of the most tempting ways to save money is to postpone hiring until it is absolutely necessary and to avoid having new people on the payroll when the building process is still unfolding. Because building budgets are often exceeded and because frugality is a common trait, particularly in smaller arts organizations, the impulse will be strong to hold off on hiring until the very last moment so as not to "inflate payroll" before new revenue rolls in and new activities are actually being carried out. This impulse needs to be resisted. Having staff who will run programs after project completion already embedded in the organization during the building process will in many cases result in better projects as well as make the early stages of opening the facility far less stressful. Leadership teams need someone with a thorough understanding of how the building will be used. Staffers need a chance to learn organizational patterns and rituals, and to get comfortable in their roles. Waiting to the last minute to hire staff precludes this learning cycle from occurring.

One element of strategic capacity building during a construction and expansion process involves accurately assessing when some skills are best acquired through consulting contracts and when others are best built into the permanent operational capacity of the institution through hiring. This is a complex calculation that comes down to the specificity of the skill set and the projected needs of the institution. In general, the more specialized the skill set and the more episodic its need is, the more it makes sense to contract with a vendor in the marketplace for services. Conversely, the more general the skill set and the more likely it is to be needed on a regular basis, the more it makes sense to bring this capacity within the boundaries of the organization by making a permanent hire. Getting this analysis right is not easy but the stakes can be high, both when permanent staff turn out to be essential or when the use of consultants can actually prove to be a far more efficient way of meeting a particular need.

10. Keep Board Decision-Making Group Small, Diverse, and Unified. Although bigger is often better, when it comes to the governance oversight of cultural building projects, small is beautiful. When nonprofit boards get too large, they become more prone to delay, indecision, and regression to the safe center when it comes to project oversight and stewardship. Large groups of people are also harder to assemble and drive toward consensus, with most groups of any real size including at least some outliers and contrarians. Governing boards are often assembled to bring to the table a range of skills as well as valuable connections within the community. Board members can and do add value by delivering these skills at opportune moments when the organization calls on them. A diversity of backgrounds and areas of expertise can result in less blindness to risk and a decision-making process that is more sound and less likely to overlook potential pitfalls and solutions. Still, boards can be heterogeneous and have real divisions within them.[10]

When it comes to managing a complex long-term project like constructing a new building or addition, it is wise to set up a subcommittee of the board to oversee and guide the building project, and not to leave the work to the whole board. Not only is there regular board business that goes on during the construction process, there is also the reality that too many hands on a project will only impede decision making. Of course, many board members will want to get involved, and picking some and not others for added responsibility may hurt some feelings. But good governance of cultural building projects ultimately needs to be streamlined, so that organizations are capable of making quick decisions based on the ever-changing conditions on the ground.

Small groups also tend to be more cohesive. A shared vision of the project and ability to work well together will prove essential in what may well be a seven-to-nine year process from ideation to ribbon cutting.[11]

11. Bringing In a Star Architect Will Increase Building Costs. At the start of many of the larger cultural building processes, someone on the board starts to float names of architects for the project. The words "Piano, Calatrava, Gehry, Meier" may be uttered in moments of sheer excitement as a blue sky of possibility opens up for a governing board. Having a star architect design a project can be a very powerful way to draw attention to the project and signal its "world-class" status. Because star architects reject many projects that are offered to them, signing one up is something of a coup that can kick off a project process with a bang.

However, there are some important factors to consider when selecting a project architect. Architects whose work already enjoys prestige charge a premium. The construction costs of the buildings they design tend to be high as well. The greater cost is linked to the complexity of the geometry, to their use of fine building materials, and to their capacity to hold off requests for scaling down and simplifying the building. Star architects cannot be pushed around by boards and there is a sense that an arts organization is lucky to have the chance to work with one of the small group of the anointed.

There are many cases when the additional costs of using one of the best architectural minds of the day has yielded very successful buildings that have stood the test of time. There are other instances where the results may have been spectacular but achieved at the cost of putting the organization in financial trouble. In the end, boards and project leaders need to consider carefully how much value prestige architecture will bring to the project.

Mission

12. Be Ready to Adjust Programming Mix to Incorporate More Commercially Viable Material as Operation Costs Increase. One of the most difficult rules to accept when considering a new building or major addition is that artistic content is linked to financial position, and that an organization's financial position is linked to the construction and operating costs of its new building. This means that in practical terms, anyone contemplating a major capital outlay must be ready to put almost everything the organization does on the table, including the artistic programming. It would be nice if a theater that moved into a great new space with higher occupancy and maintenance costs could simply go on doing what they always had done. But more often than not, a theater that takes on a project will need to rethink what it offers to the public. There may be more seats to fill or larger electric bills to pay in the foreseeable future, but there is also a sense that the organization must "grow" into its new space. This may mean advertising more, but often it comes down to taking on more commercially viable productions.

Far from selling out, organizations that change in light of new conditions are in fact making sensible choices.[12] They are reacting to pressures that if ignored could weaken the organization over time and possibly lead it into substantial stress. In the context of the arts where there is aspiration for purity in creative choices, accepting this hard reality can sometimes be difficult. The choices facing a theater are rarely as stark as going from Brecht to producing a stage version of the sitcom "Friends," though Broadway Across America and other commercial series have come to be perceived as panaceas for many of the financial ills that plague performing arts centers. For most arts organizations, the needed changes are more subtle and may involve the types of sets used and the way texts are interpreted. The bottom line is that cultural buildings bring with them new staff, new operating expenses, and often large seating capacity. Being realistic about these changes—and how they may well affect artistic programming—is a critical part of successful management of these projects.

13. Acoustics and Similar Aesthetic Qualities, like Gallery Proportions and Light, May Be Lost on the Audiences. During the design process, tough choices will need to be made by museums and performing arts organizations related to the aesthetic qualities of the spaces. For many museum directors, the architectural values as well as the proportions or the quality of light in galleries are of enormous consequence. The visual appearance of the space and the building can be seen as vital to the mission of a fine arts institution. For performing arts organizations, great acoustics are a similar gold standard when sorting out the great venues from all the rest. Acoustics affect the way music and the spoken word are heard by the audience and hence matter a great deal to symphonies, operas, and theaters.

The main question that the quest for these aesthetic qualities raises relates to cost. How much is quality really worth and can it ever generate a positive return? This crass formulation of the question of how to think about aspects like acoustics at least recognizes that these decisions will have effects on the cost side of the ledger. While the benefits of excellence will be apparent to experts, it is not clear that they will carry much weight with the lay audience. Of course, wretched quality will be apparent, but when it comes to true excellence, it is dangerous to assume that it will be appreciated or even noticed. In the end, given the price tag of demanding perfection in these aesthetic considerations, cultural leaders should ask who, if not the majority of the audiences, truly stands to benefit from this investment.

The sum that any particular institution should spend on these aspects of its new facility depends on a host of local conditions, including the ease of fundraising for the added expense, the stance of the board toward these issues, and the expectations of the local patrons. In most cases, the decision comes down to a cost-benefit analysis, in which the cost side is very clear and the benefit side is far harder to quantify. Civic pride and desire to claim "world class" status often prevail.

14. Supply Does Not Create Its Own Demand. When a new building goes up, dreams of great crowds and bulging cash registers dance in the heads of arts leaders. The logic is simple and grounded in a powerful image. If you build it, they will come, just like in Bilbao. The Guggenheim success in building its titanium Gehry outpost in Spain has emboldened many arts leaders to try to capture the same magic with their own spectacular buildings. The dream is, people will come to be part of the special space that has been created by the new building, and the crowds will in turn translate into gate receipts, taking the project to new heights.

The idea that demand can be led by supply is an old one. French philosopher Jean-Baptiste Say pronounced three hundred years ago that "supply creates its own demand"—or, in literal translation: "Inherent in supply is the wherewithal for its own consumption"—and in the process defined himself as an early supply-sider. The art world is full of people who cherish the same belief and are willing in some cases to bet huge amounts of money that large and striking facilities will generate big audiences.

The only problem with Say's Law is that it has not been demonstrated to be a good predictor of behavior in the cultural sector. While there have been some cases where museums and performing arts centers observed a bump in attendance following their opening, in most cases this increase did not last long. In thinking about the consequences of a new building, it is dangerous to project—and even depend—on anticipated revenue increases over the long run related to the construction project being undertaken.[13]

15. A Great Building Will Not Lead to Artistic Excellence, But a Powerful and Compelling Artistic Vision Can Lead to a New Building. When an arts organization asks why its work is not more appreciated and why its audiences are not growing, it is a lot easier to focus on resource and facilities constraints than on artistic vision and quality. Buildings can be seen in some cases as solutions to organizational problems—even when they may not be even remotely related. By displacing blame away from vision and artistic quality to facilities, some arts leaders engage in a willful form of denial. In part this can be understood because of the powerful belief many arts groups have in what they do. The quality of one's own artistic work is difficult to judge dispassionately, and poor facilities are an easier problem to resolve than a problem of vision. Of course, a building will not solve artistic problems on its own.

On the other hand, a building can truly help take a proven and talented organization to the next level. Some theater companies may be able to do great work with a small space. With better backstage facilities, the group can actually expand the range of material it can stage and boost the technical quality of the productions. A new building, a major renovation, a large new addition, or even an adaptive reuse of an existing facility should be attempted only when artistic quality is established and recognized. Buildings are lagging indicators of artistic excellence. Buildings are almost never leading indicators of quality.

* * *

Though we have attempted to simplify the main strategic questions of any building project by identifying the most essential ones, at this point the task of strategic planning may seem monumental. Moreover, the stories both within this book and outside of it all seem to include projects where things do not go according to plan. As we have said at multiple points, uncertainty about key events is par for the course. One might almost wonder whether the exhausting list of crucial considerations, balances, alignments, and risks is worth keeping in mind at all. After all, the work involved will be exhausting and in the end, the carefully derived strategy and tactics may need to be abandoned as the result of some unforeseen event. Yet a truly strategic plan will allow an organization to reach alignment and consensus on issues that will present themselves in any project—even one radically altered by unforeseen events. The value of the process is in preparing the organization to deal with such surprises. As Dwight Eisenhower once said about military strategy, "Plans are nothing. Planning is everything."

Notes

1. Robert Campbell, "In Milwaukee, a Theatrical Space," *Boston Globe*, May 12, 2002.
2. Large projects in the arts are disruptive in an already turbulent field. In her overview of the cultural policy and management world, Wyszomirski observes "the past decade has been one of considerable challenge and change for non-profit arts and culture. It has also been of significant experimentation and improvisation. Old paradigms—whether financial, administrative, or political—are noticeably in decline and new operating paradigms are still protean." Margaret J. Wyszomirski, "Arts and Culture," in *The State of Nonprofit America*, ed. Lester M. Salamon (Washington, DC: Brookings Institution Press, 2002), 187–218.
3. Emphasizing such social benefits has become increasingly popular, but may have unintended side effects. Excessive focus on economic development benefits of the arts may hamper future artistic efforts by prioritizing the delivery of economic benefits over artistic agendas. Hughes wrote, "It may be regretted that there has ever been a necessity to demonstrate the economic significance of the arts or to link the arts and tourism." Howard L. Hughes, "Tourism and the Arts: A Potentially Destructive Relationship?," *Tourism Management* 10, no. 2 (1989): 97–99.
4. Measures of audience experience have been proposed lately as a measure of artistic excellence that would replace or augment traditional measures like awards, reviews, and attendance. Jennifer Radbourne, Katya Johanson, Hilary

Glow, and Tabitha White, "The Audience Experience: Measuring Quality in the Performing Arts," *International Journal of Arts Management* 11, no. 3 (2009): 16–29.

5. For a comprehensive overview of the challenges of market definition and segmentation, see Alan R. Andreasen and Philip Kotler, *Strategic Marketing for Nonprofit Organizations* (New Delhi: Prentice-Hall of India, 2004). Andreasen and Kotler argue that all good marketing starts with six big questions: "What customers or clients do we wish to serve? Where will we get our resources? How do we attract volunteers? How do we position ourselves against similar or competitive organizations? What approaches will we use to reach target audiences? (Most important) where and how will 'marketing thinking' fit within our organization—especially at the top management level?" (64).

6. A discussion of the multiple stages of developing a comprehensive strategic plan can be found in John Moore Bryson, *Strategic Planning for Public and Nonprofit Organizations: A Guide to Strengthening and Sustaining Organizational Achievement*, revised ed. (San Francisco: Jossey-Bass, 1995). "To deliver the best results, strategic planning requires broad yet effective information gathering, developing and exploration of strategic alternatives, and an emphasis on future implications of present decisions. Strategic planning can help facilitate communication and participation, accommodate divergent interests and values, foster wise and reasonably analytic decision-making, and promote successful implementation" (5).

7. The idea of strategy as alignment or fit is expounded in Mark Harrison Moore, *Creating Public Value* (Cambridge, MA: Harvard University Press, 1995). Moore's analysis focuses on public sector organizations, but his core ideas are reflected in our mind.

8. Philanthropy has undergone a period of change in recent decades. Donors are increasingly demanding proof of impact or demonstrated results. This can raise substantial challenges to arts organizations. A discussion of the movement of philanthropy toward greater emphasis on performance measurement can be found in Thomas J. Tierney, "Toward Higher Impact Philanthropy," in *Taking Philanthropy Seriously*, ed. William V. B. Damon (Indiana University Press, 2006), 62–76.

9. Researchers have long observes that arts funding requires an integrated approach. For a discussion of changing patterns of cultural philanthropy and a broadening perspective of donors, see Margaret J. Wyszomirski, "Philanthropy and Culture: Patterns, Context, and Change," in *Philanthropy and the Nonprofit Sector in a Changing America*, ed. Charles T. Clotfelter and Thomas Ehrlich (Bloomington: Indiana University Press, 1999), 461–80. "Cultural philanthropists seem to be looking for the 'big picture,' which is leading them to rethink, undertake research, and design programs using a systems approach or an ecological perspective" (475).

10. Nonmarket benefits to communities from capital investments in arts facilities are the subject of C. D. Throsby, "Social and Economic Benefits from Regional

Investment in Arts Facilities: Theory and Application," *Journal of Cultural Economics* 6, no. 1 (1982): 1–14.

11. For examinations of the ways in which community sustainability is enhanced by vibrant arts organizations, see Yvan Allaire and Mihaela E. Firsirotu, "Theories of Organizational Culture," *Organization Studies* 5, no. 3 (July 1984): 193–226; Jennifer Radbourne, "Regional Development through the Enterprise of Arts Leadership," *Journal of Arts Management, Law, and Society* 33, no. 3 (2003): 211–27.

12. Complex projects require detailed planning. A useful workbook that guides the practitioner through the stages of the planning process is Michael J. Allison and Jude Kaye, *Strategic Planning for Nonprofit Organizations* (Wiley, 1997).

13. Roger Miller and Donald R. Lessard, "Evolving Strategy: Risk Management and the Shaping of Mega-projects," in *Decision-Making on Mega-projects Cost Benefit Analysis, Planning and Innovation*, ed. H. Priemus, B. Van Wee, and B. Flyvbjerg, Transport Economics, Management and Policy (Cheltenham: Edward Elgar, 2008), 145–72.

14. The concept of shaping episodes and temporary closures was also offered in a different context by Miller and Lessard in "Evolving Strategy."

15. The research was funded by the Mellon, MacArthur, and Kresge Foundations.

16. Joanna Woronkowicz, D. Carroll Joynes, Peter Frumkin, Anastasia Kolendo, Bruce Seaman, Robert Gertner, and Norman Bradburn, *Cultural Infrastructure in the United States: 1994–2008* (Chicago: NORC at the University of Chicago, 2011).

17. The other components of the overall research effort and their many findings will be the subject of a second book, which will offer a broad perspective on the building boom to complement the deep dive we present here.

CHAPTER TWO

1. For a useful overview of size and other essential considerations for design of performing arts spaces, see Richard Pilbrow, "An Auditorium and Stage Design Guide," in *Building Type Basics for Performing Arts Facilities* (Hoboken, NJ: Wiley, 2006).

2. Walter L. Crimm, Martha Morris, and L. Carole Wharton provide a good overview of design considerations for visual arts organizations in *Planning Successful Museum Building Projects* (Lanham, MD: AltaMira Press, 2009).

3. Studies have found that distinctiveness of location and venue do in fact contribute to the overall audience satisfaction with a given cultural event, along with other factors. For example, see D. E. Abfalter and P. J. Mirski, "Perceived Success in the Arts," in *8th International Conference on Arts & Cultural Management (AIMAC), Montréal*, 2005.

4. A study of intent to purchase future tickets among performing arts patrons found that audiences can be divided into two groups. The first is the most

familiar with the performing arts and repurchases tickets on the basis of the show's emotional resonance. The second is less involved with the arts and more influenced by peripheral elements like parking, navigability, and service rather than the performance in deciding to attend again. See M. Hume, G. S. Mort, and H. Winzar, "Exploring Repurchase Intention in a Performing Arts Context: Who Comes? and Why Do They Come Back?," *International Journal of Nonprofit and Voluntary Sector Marketing* 12, no. 2 (2007): 135–48. For further confirmation of the same results, see Margee Hume and Gillian Sullivan Mort, "The Consequence of Appraisal Emotion, Service Quality, Perceived Value and Customer Satisfaction on Repurchase Intent in the Performing Arts," *Journal of Services Marketing* 24, no. 2 (2010): 170–82.

5. Audience perceptions of the value of the performing arts venue is the subject of R. Mencarelli, "Conceptualizing and Measuring the Perceived Value of an Arts Venue as Applied to Live Performance," *International Journal of Arts Management* (2008): 42–59.

6. Simon Houpt, "Betting on the Bilbao Effect," *Globe and Mail*, July 29, 2003, R1.

7. D. Sudjic, *The Edifice Complex: How the Rich and Powerful—and Their Architects—Shape the World* (Penguin Books, 2006), 296–97.

8. An analysis of how taste functions in society can be found in P. Bourdieu, *Distinction: A Social Critique of the Judgement of Taste* (Cambridge, MA: Harvard University Press, 1984).

9. "Transcript of the John Tusa Interview with the Architect Frank Gehry," *BBC Radio 3*, n.d., http://www.bbc.co.uk/radio3/johntusainterview/gehry_transcript.shtml.

10. Research comparing individual evaluations and descriptions of concert hall acoustics finds significant variation among individuals' preferences for acoustics and ability to articulate and/or distinguish acoustical differences. See both the original research and the extensive literature review in A. Kuusinen, "Perception of Concert Hall Acoustics-Selection and Behaviour of Assessors in a Descriptive Analysis Experiment" (Master's thesis, Aalto University School of Electrical Engineering, 2011). Yet other studies suggest a convergence of opinion from lay assessors about concert hall acoustics is possible. See J. P. Migneron, J. G. Migneron, and J. F. Hardy, "Objective and Subjective Analysis of Acoustical Response in Newly Renovated Palais Moncalm, Quebec City, Canada," *Journal of the Acoustical Society of America* 123, no. 5 (2008): 3088.

11. Sudjic, *The Edifice Complex*, 286.

12. The Atlanta Opera, "The Atlanta Opera | Our History," 2009, http://www.atlantaopera.org/aboutus/ourhistory.aspx.

13. Tom Sabulis, "The Atlanta Opera Tries to Set a Clearer Tone in Management," *Atlanta Journal-Constitution*, May 9, 2004.

14. Pierre Ruhe, "This Group Has a Bent for the New," *Atlanta Journal-Constitution*, April 13, 2003; Pierre Ruhe, "Critic's Notebook: Opera Sees Pops as Budget Booster," *Atlanta Journal-Constitution*, July 27, 2003.

15. Tom Sabulis, "Scenery Shifts: Despite a Few Glitches, Atlanta Opera Fans Take to Troupe's Move to Civic Center," *Atlanta Journal-Constitution*, October 18, 2003.

16. Pierre Ruhe, "Opera Cancels Nov. 28 'Elixir of Love,'" *Atlanta Journal-Constitution*, November 14, 2003.

17. Tom Sabulis, "Longtime Opera Head 'Ready to Go': Executive Director Alfred Kennedy's Exit Clears Way for Changes in Atlanta Troupe," *Atlanta Journal-Constitution*, March 20, 2004.

18. Pierre Ruhe, "Hello, We've Got Problems: New Atlanta Chief Looks at Books and Makes Deep Cuts," *Atlanta Journal-Constitution*, August 22, 2004.

19. Sabulis, "Longtime Opera Head 'Ready to Go.'"

20. A version of this case study was published on the web. Ana Kolendo and Peter Frumkin, *Can Roanoke, Virginia, Become the Next Bilbao?*, Set in Stone: Building America's New Generation of Arts Facilities, 1994–2008 (University of Chicago Cultural Policy Center, 2012), http://culturalpolicy.uchicago.edu /setinstone/pdf/taubmanmuseum.pdf.

21. Kevin Kittredge, "From $250 to $66 Million," *Roanoke Times & World News*, September 30, 2001, http://rstories.com/artmuseum/.

22. "History," n.d., http://www.centerinthesquare.org/history.php.

23. "Cultivating Cultural Finds," *Roanoke Times & World News*, December 17, 1995, sec. Metro.

24. Kevin Kittredge and Megan Schnabel, "Center in the Square Accepts a 'Grand' Donation: Grand Home Furnishings Gives Its Campbell Avenue Site to Downtown Cultural Center," *Roanoke Times & World News*, August 5, 1998.

25. Kevin Kittredge, "Center in the Square a Cultural and Economic Dynamo? Or a Troubled Place Tainted by Fear and Distrust? Or Both?," *Roanoke Times & World News*, October 26, 1997, sec. Metro.

26. Ibid.

27. Kevin Kittredge, "Peggy's Gift," *Roanoke Times & World News*, January 27, 2002.

28. Ibid.

29. Ibid.

30. Kittredge, "From $250 to $66 Million."

31. Kevin Kittredge, "Shopping for Masterpieces," *Roanoke Times & World News*, June 13, 1999; Kevin Kittredge, "Art Museum Acquires Work of Winslow Homer; This Purchase, at $900,000, Was Not a Bargain like Wednesday's Million-Dollar Deal," *Roanoke Times & World News*, May 28, 1999; Kevin Kittredge, "Roanoke Gets Major Work; Steal of a Deal; $1 Million Bid, Much Less than Expected, Is a Winner," *Roanoke Times & World News*, May 27, 1999.

32. Kevin Kittredge, "Dreaming Big Art Museum's New Executive Director Is Still Getting to Know the Territory—but She's Ambitious about the Future," *Roanoke Times & World News*, March 14, 1995, sec. Metro; The Fralin Trust, "Forms 990 for FY2001, 2002, 2003, 2004, 2005, 2006, 2007, 2008," n.d.; Art Museum of Western Virginia, "Form 990 for Tax Year Beginning 7/01/2002

and Ending 6/30/2003," 2003; Kevin Kittredge, "Museums Not Panicking over Funds. Directors Say General Assembly Is Likely to Increase Amounts," *Roanoke Times & World News*, February 7, 2001; Kevin Daniels, "Art Museum Director Resigns; Appelhof Accepts Position in Minn.," *Roanoke Times & World News*, April 5, 1994, sec. Metro; Kevin Kittredge, "The Art of the Deal," *Roanoke Times & World News*, June 29, 2008, Metro edition, sec. Virginia; Wendi Gibson, "Museum Receives $237,800," *Roanoke Times & World News*, January 14, 1994.

33. Kevin Kittredge, "A Bold Vision: Roanoke Times Exclusive Report Series: Building for the Future," *Roanoke Times & World News*, March 20, 2005.

34. Kittredge and Schnabel, "Center in the Square Accepts a 'Grand' Donation."

35. Kevin Kittredge, "Seeking a Better Showcase: a Bigger Building Would Highlight a Growing Collection at the Art Museum of Western Virginia," *Roanoke Times & World News*, January 31, 1999.

36. Ibid.

37. Kevin Kittredge and Megan Schnabel, "Museum, Theater Merge. Roanoke Promises $4 Million and Site for Art Museum and IMAX Theater," *Roanoke Times & World News*, June 6, 2000.

38. Megan Schnabel, "Mayor Sees IMAX Theater in Financial Picture," *Roanoke Times & World News*, July 7, 1999, Metro edition, sec. Virginia; Schnabel, "IMAX Study Envisions Big Screen for Roanoke," *Roanoke Times & World News*, July 30, 1998, Metro edition, A1.

39. Duncan Adams, "His 'Deft Touch' Builds Partnerships, Buildings. Brian Wishneff—An Ambassador for Roanoke," *Roanoke Times & World News*, November 12, 2000.

40. Kevin Kittredge, "Search Yielded California Visionary with Southern Drawl; Roanoke Times Exclusive Report," *Roanoke Times & World News*, March 21, 2005.

41. Kittredge and Schnabel, "Museum, Theater Merge."

42. Kittredge, "Search Yielded California Visionary with Southern Drawl."

43. Kittredge and Schnabel, "Museum, Theater Merge."

44. Ibid.

45. Useful information for leaders developing building programs for both visual and performing arts organizations can be found in Catherine Brown, William B. Fleissig, and William R. Morrish, *Building for the Arts: A Guidebook for the Planning & Design of Cultural Facilities* (Santa Fe, NM: Western States Arts Foundation, 1984).

46. The Atlanta Opera, *Form 990*, filed June 30, 2009; June 30, 2008; June 30, 2010; and June 30, 2011, National Center for Charitable Statistics; Pierre Ruhe, "Atlanta Opera: $9 Million Bequest Offers 'Stability,'" *Atlanta Journal-Constitution*, April 3, 2011.

47. "Roanoke Valley Banking on Giving for Range of Causes," *Associated Press Newswires*, July 12, 2003.

48. Kevin Kittredge, "Plan for $10 Million IMAX Gift Receives Rave Reviews in Valley," *Roanoke Times & World News*, December 20, 2001.

49. Kittredge, "Search Yielded California Visionary with Southern Drawl."

50. Damon Littlefield, "Build up Western Virginia by Building a New Art Museum. All of the Region's Arts Organizations Would Benefit," *Roanoke Times & World News*, March 2, 2000.

51. Kittredge, "Search Yielded California Visionary with Southern Drawl."

52. Sue Lindsey, "Virginia Art Museum Gets Bold New Design," *Deseret Morning News*, May 11, 2008.

53. Kittredge, "Search Yielded California Visionary with Southern Drawl."

54. Art Museum of Western Virginia, "Art Museum of Western Virginia Unveils Design for New Building by Los Angeles Architect Randall Stout," March 21, 2005, http://web.archive.org/web/20070825010030/www.artmuseumroanoke.org/index.php?do=the_future:press_releases.

55. Kittredge, "Search Yielded California Visionary with Southern Drawl."

56. Kevin Kittredge, "Fancy Floor Stayed in Art Museum's Plans," *Roanoke Times & World News*, June 8, 2008; Art Museum of Western Virginia, "Construction Phase of New Art Museum Building Project to Begin," April 4, 2006, http://web.archive.org/web/20070825010030/www.artmuseumroanoke.org/index.php?do=the_future:press_releases.

57. Mike Allen, "Taubman Museum's Struggles," *Roanoke Times (MCT)*, July 25, 2010; Tom Angelberger, "Old Eyes Fail to See a Circus' Fleas," *Roanoke Times & World News*, September 9, 2005, Metro edition, sec. Virginia.

58. Kittredge, "The Art of the Deal"; Allen, "Taubman Museum's Struggles"; Kevin Kittredge, "Paying the Bills," *Roanoke Times & World News*, November 11, 2006.

59. Kittredge, "A Bold Vision."

60. Art Museum of Western Virginia, "Construction Phase of New Art Museum Building Project to Begin."

61. Allen, "Taubman Museum's Struggles."

62. Kittredge, "The Art of the Deal."

63. The estimate is based on the Fralin Trust and museum financial filings. The estimate assumes that the total Fralin Trust gifts minus the cost of the museum's major art acquisitions offers a rough estimate of the Fralin Trust donations toward the capital project.

64. Kevin Kittredge, "Art Unveiled," *Roanoke Times & World News*, February 27, 2007, sec. Metro; Kevin Kittredge, "Couple Give $15 Million to Museum," *Roanoke Times (MCT)*, January 1, 2008; Kevin Kittredge, "Ballet Theatre Boss Steps Down," *Roanoke Times & World News*, August 3, 2006, Metro edition, sec. Extra; Kimberly Templeton, "Taubman Museum of Art Will Open to the Public on November 8" (Taubman Museum of Art, n.d.).

65. Kevin Kittredge, "Namesakes Made Largest Gift," *Roanoke Times & World News*, October 30, 2008, Metro edition, sec. Taubman Museum.

66. Kevin Kittredge, "Corner Shots," *Roanoke Times & World News*, July 11, 2005, Metro edition, sec. Extra; Kevin Kittredge, "Disgust and Delight over Design," *Roanoke Times & World News*, September 6, 2005, Metro edition, sec. Virginia.

67. "'We Welcome Debate,'" *Roanoke Times & World News*, October 30, 2008, Metro edition, sec. Taubman Museum.

68. Dennis J. Kilper, "A Museum of Expensive Mimicry," *Roanoke Times & World News*, March 27, 2005, Metro edition, sec. Horizon Editorial; Fred A. Bernstein, "Hi, Gorgeous. Haven't I Seen You Somewhere?," *New York Times*, August 28, 2005, Late edition—Final edition, sec. Arts and Leisure Desk; SECT2.

69. Amanda Codispoti, "Funding Hardships Plague Nonprofits," *Roanoke Times & World News*, April 9, 2006; Rex Bowman, "Roanoke Museum Cost Rises Millions," *Richmond Times-Dispatch*, April 5, 2006.

70. Kevin Kittredge, "Mill Mountain's Second Stage to Encore as Offices," *Roanoke Times & World News*, February 8, 2009; Codispoti, "Funding Hardships Plague Nonprofits."

71. Judy Larson, "Art Boosts Both Culture, the Economy. Big Plans for Museum in Roanoke," *Roanoke Times & World News*, December 26, 1999; Herb Detweiler, "It Wasn't Smart to Build the Museum on a Flood Plain—Roanoke.com," *Roanoke Times & World News*, November 18, 2010, sec. Letters to the Editor., http://www.roanoke.com/editorials/letters/wb/267841 (site discontinued); Templeton, "Taubman Museum of Art Will Open to the Public on November 8"; "Museum Floor Plans | Taubman Museum of Art, Roanoke, Virginia: A Guide to the New Art Museum from The Roanoke Times and Roanoke.com," n.d., http://rtstories.com/artmuseum/museum_floor_plans.

72. In an exercise of revisionism, after the attendance proved disappointing, museum leaders began telling the *Roanoke Times* that their most conservative scenario projected 177,000 visitors a year.

73. Mike Allen, "Taubman Leaves Museum Board," *Roanoke Times (MCT)*, September 15, 2010; d/b/a Taubman Museum of Art, Art Museum of Western Virginia, "Form 990 for Tax Year Beginning 7/01/2008 and Ending 6/30/2009," 2009; Mike Allen, "Taubman Survives Tough First Year," *Roanoke Times & World News*, November 8, 2009, Metro edition, sec. Virginia; Mike Allen, "Taubman Officials Say No Takeover Is in Sight," *Roanoke Times & World News*, October 2, 2010, Metro edition, sec. Virginia; Allen, "Taubman Museum's Struggles"; Mike Allen, "Taubman Museum's Portrait Is Etched in Red Ink," *Roanoke Times*, January 8, 2012; Taubman Museum of Art, *Financial Statements: Years Ended June 30, 2010 and 2009*, n.d.; Kevin Kittredge, "Art Museum Director to Retire," *Roanoke Times & World News*, January 15, 2009; Rex Bowman, "Roanoke, Visitors Embrace New Star / 20,000 Visit Taubman in Its First Month—Officials Say Building Is Art, Too," *Richmond Times-Dispatch*, January 3, 2009, State edition, sec. Area/State.

74. Designing a new facility requires many tough choices about what to add to the project and what to take away. In his description of "pathways to excellence," Light observes that "the journey to high performance may not start with just

one step, but it does start with some level of self-awareness. Simply put, each nonprofit must map its own journey to high performance. . . . Each nonprofit must decide how it will winnow the list of possible destinations and strategies to fit its own aspirations, assets, and history" (117). Paul Charles Light, *Pathways to Nonprofit Excellence* (Washington, DC: Brookings Institution Press, 2002).

75. J. Scheff, "Factors Influencing Subscription and Single-ticket Purchases at Performing Arts Organizations," *International Journal of Arts Management* 1, no. 2 (1999): 16–27.

CHAPTER THREE

1. About the link between money and strategy, Drucker wrote: "Napoleon said that there were three things needed to fight a war. The first is money. The second is money. And the third is money. That may be true for war, but it's not true for the non-profit organization. There you need four things. You need a plan. You need marketing. You need people. And you need money." Peter Ferdinand Drucker, *Managing the Non-profit Organization* (Collins, 1992).

2. Some scholars argue that reliance on philanthropic money and earned income facilitates distortions and goal displacement in organizational missions within the arts, with programs altered for revenue maximization. K.V. Mulcahy, "Entrepreneurship or Cultural Darwinism? Privatization and American Cultural Patronage," *Journal of Arts Management, Law, and Society* 33, no. 3 (2003): 165–84.

3. Bent Flyvbjerg, "Public Planning of Mega-projects: Overestimation of Demand and Underestimation of Costs," in *Decision-Making on Mega-projects: Cost-Benefit Analysis, Planning and Innovation*, ed. Hugo Priemus, Bent Flyvbjerg, and Bert van Wee (Edward Elgar, 2008), 120–44.

4. Joanna Woronkowicz, D. Carroll Joynes, Peter Frumkin, Anastasia Kolendo, Bruce Seaman, Robert Gertner, and Norman Bradburn, *Cultural Infrastructure in the United States: 1994–2008* (Chicago: NORC at the University of Chicago, 2011).

5. Fundraising involves a simultaneous strategizing and interaction between givers and receivers. Susan A. Ostrander and Paul G. Schervish, "Giving and Getting: Philanthropy as a Social Relation," in *Critical Issues in American Philanthropy* (Jossey-Bass, 1990), 67–98.

6. Daniel Kahneman and Amos Tversky, *Intuitive Prediction: Biases and Corrective Procedures* (Office of Naval Research, Engineering Psychology Programs, 1977).

7. B. Flyvbjerg, "Curbing Optimism Bias and Strategic Misrepresentation in Planning: Reference Class Forecasting in Practice," *European Planning Studies* 16, no. 1 (2008): 3–21.

8. The reasons donors give are multiple. One attempt to develop a typology for funders is Karen Maru File and Russ Alan Prince, *The Seven Faces of Philan-*

thropy (Jossey-Bass, 2001). Here, the authors define seven types of donors: communitarian, devout, investor, socialite, altruist, re-payer, and dynast.

9. Fundraising is a difficult art. The multiple relationship and personality challenges that arise in capital campaigns are the subject of Ken Burnett, *Relationship Fundraising* (Jossey-Bass, 2002). Also of use to a fundraising practitioner is an understanding of how tax considerations guide the giving decision. See Eleanor Brown, "Patterns and Purposes of Philanthropic Giving," in *Philanthropy and the Nonprofit Sector in a Changing America*, ed. Charles T. Clotfelter and Thomas Ehrlich (Bloomington: Indiana University Press, 1999), 212–30.

10. For a review of literature on the consequences and trade-offs of reliance on various revenue streams like charitable giving, corporate giving, government grants, and business income, see Karen A. Froelich, "Diversification of Revenue Strategies: Evolving Resource Dependence in Nonprofit Organizations," *Nonprofit and Voluntary Sector Quarterly* 28, no. 3 (1999): 246–68.

11. "The time to reasonably think about the costs and benefits of debt is when there is no pressing cash need," writes Robert J. Yetman in his essay on key considerations in nonprofits' use of loans. The full extent of borrowing and its full costs need to be factored into a decision to proceed with any project that involves debt financing. Yetman, "Borrowing and Debt," in *Financing Nonprofits*, ed. Dennis R. Young (AltaMira Press, 2007), 243–68.

12. The challenge of developing a sustainable business model is immense. A discussion of the many possible forms that an arts organization's financial framework can take can be found in Jeanne Bell, Jan Masaoka, and Steve Zimmerman, *Nonprofit Sustainability* (Jossey-Bass, 2010).

13. The utility of endowments to both the public and the organization's beneficiaries has been challenged in recent years. Critics claim that the money invested in endowments for the sake of providing future income in perpetuity would be better spent on larger investments in programs that provide social returns today. Moreover, organizations insecure about their finances may be more innovative and less spendthrift. These objections pose a question about when the use of endowments is always appropriate. Yet in the case of building projects, an endowment is necessary, since it is one of the few financial vehicles that creates a fixed revenue stream to cover the new or increased fixed cost of maintaining a "privileged" asset that cannot be easily sold. See Woods Bowman, Elizabeth Keating, and Mark A. Hager, "Investment Income," in *Financing Nonprofits*, ed. Dennis R. Young (AltaMira Press, 2007), 157–81; Woods Bowman, "Managing Endowments and Other Assets," in *Financing Nonprofits*, ed. Dennis R. Young (AltaMira Press, 2007), 271–89.

14. Nonprofit leaders sometimes confuse the four types of funds that are used for sound financial management of a nonprofit: working cash, operating reserves, plant funds, and endowments. Working cash is used as a revolving fund for smoothing out cash flow over the course of the year, similar to a revolving line of credit. These are used by organizations with balanced budgets that

need to cover costs before cash flows come in. The money from the working cash fund is taken out and repaid over a short term. Meanwhile, an operating reserve is used to insulate an organization against economic fluctuations. An operating reserve is intended to cover deficits. A plant fund is intended to cover physical plant expenses, like construction and major maintenance. An endowment is not used for any of those three purposes. Instead, an endowment provides a steady, annual stream of income to support operations as well as improve the capital structure of a nonprofit organization. Working cash, operating reserves, plant funds, and endowments are frequently used together as investment cash to generate income. Yet each serves a separate purpose, and these four types of funds are not interchangeable. See Bowman, Keating, and Hager, "Investment Income"; Bowman, "Managing Endowments and Other Assets."

15. Different versions of both of these cases have been released online. Ana Kolendo and Peter Frumkin, *AT&T Performing Arts Center: Fundraising and Uncertainty*, Set in Stone: Building America's New Generation of Arts Facilities, 1994–2008 (University of Chicago Cultural Policy Center, 2012), http://culturalpolicy.uchicago.edu/setinstone/pdf/attpac.pdf; Ana Kolendo and Peter Frumkin, *The Art Institute of Chicago and the Decision to Start Building*, Set in Stone: Building America's New Generation of Arts Facilities, 1994–2008 (University of Chicago Cultural Policy Center, 2012), http://culturalpolicy.uchicago.edu/setinstone/pdf/aic.pdf.

16. James Cuno, Paul Goldberger, Joseph Rosa, and Judith Turner, *The Modern Wing: Renzo Piano and the Art Institute of Chicago* (Chicago: Art Institute of Chicago, 2009).

17. Ibid., 35.

18. Ibid., 30.

19. Ibid.

20. Ibid., 45.

21. Ibid., 47.

22. Ibid., 48.

23. Ibid., 46–47.

24. Much of fundraising involves building upon social ties and relationships. An empirical examination of New York's elite philanthropy scene and the way networks shape giving can be found in Francie Ostrower, *Why the Wealthy Give: The Culture of Elite Philanthropy* (Princeton, NJ: Princeton University Press, 1997).

25. For a discussion of the implications of donor rewards on donor motivations, see Jennifer Wiggins Johnson and Bret Ellis, "The Influence of Messages and Benefits on Donors' Attributed Motivations: Findings of a Study with 14 American Performing Arts Presenters," *International Journal of Arts Management* 13, no. 2 (2011): 4–15.

26. The dual nature of corporate philanthropy—the desire to both produce community impact and improve the profitability of the company—is explored in

Jerome L. Himmelstein, *Looking Good and Doing Good* (Indiana University Press, 1997). This tension often leads companies to avoid funding difficult and controversial projects. The arts are generally viewed as fairly safe, but controversy may imperil funding.

27. Andreasen provides a map of the different forms that corporate and nonprofit partnerships and alliances can take. Alan R. Andreasen, "Cross-Sector Marketing Alliances: Partnerships, Sponsorships, and Cause-Related Marketing," in *Nonprofits and Business*, ed. Joseph J. Cordes and C. Eugene Steuerle (Urban Institute Press, 2009), 155–91.

28. By not getting caught up in minutiae, Bill Lively demonstrated Royce Spence's insight that strong brands are anchored in purpose. "Purpose is a definitive statement about the difference you are trying to make in the world." Haley Rushing and Roy M. Spence Jr., *It's Not What You Sell, It's What You Stand For* (Portfolio, 2009), 10.

29. Philanthropy has undergone profound changes over the past two decades. On the move to transform philanthropy more into social investing, see Christine Letts, William P. Ryan, and Allen Grossman, "Virtuous Capital: Investing in Performance," in *High Performance Nonprofit Organizations: Managing Upstream for Greater Impact* (Wiley, 1999), 169–91. Here, the authors make the case that philanthropic funding can and should look more like venture capital investment. This implies a greater focus on measuring impact, a heightened level of engagement, and a longer time horizon. Also see Matthew Bishop and Michael F. Green, *Philanthrocapitalism* (Bloomsbury, 2008).

CHAPTER FOUR

1. Making decisions that affect entire communities requires skill and care. A discussion of the strategic importance of community consultation and involvement in decision making can be found in Suzanne Whitlock Morse, *Smart Communities* (Jossey-Bass, 2004).

2. R. Edward Freeman and John McVea, "A Stakeholder Approach to Strategic Management," *Social Science Research Network eLibrary* (2001), http://papers .ssrn.com/so13/papers.cfm?abstract_id=263511.

3. For a look at arguments for and against government funding for the arts in use globally, see Jennifer Craik, "Dilemmas in Policy Support for the Arts and Cultural Sector," *Australian Journal of Public Administration* 64, no. 4 (2005): 6–19.

4. Another theory for how artistic organizations decide which stakeholders to engage and how is proposed by Voss et al., who find that artistic organizations focus on partners whom they perceive to hold the same values. Glenn B. Voss, Daniel M. Cable, and Zannie Giraud Voss, "Linking Organizational Values to Relationships with External Constituents: A Study of Nonprofit Professional Theatres," *Organization Science* 11, no. 3 (2000): 330–47.

5. R. K. Mitchell, B. R. Agle, and D. J. Wood, "Toward a Theory of Stakeholder Identification and Salience: Defining the Principle of Who and What Really Counts," *Academy of Management Review* (1997): 853–86.
6. John King, "Fishers Give Up on Plan for Presidio Art Museum," *San Francisco Chronicle*, July 2, 2009.
7. John King, "New Salvos in Presidio Battle May Come Today," *San Francisco Chronicle*, June 1, 2009.
8. The role of civic entrepreneurs in driving complex, cross-sectoral projects to completion is discussed in Kimberly Walesh, Douglas C. Henton, and John Melville, *Grassroots Leaders for a New Economy* (Jossey-Bass, 1997). According to the authors, civic entrepreneurs have five common traits. They "see opportunity in the new economy," "possess an entrepreneurial personality," "provide collaborative leadership to connect the economy and the community," "are motivated by broad, enlightened, long-term interests," and "work in teams, playing complementary roles."
9. David Littlejohn, "Art: SFMOMA Fills In Some Blanks," *Wall Street Journal*, July 7, 2010; Carol Kino, "Private Collection Becomes Very Public," *New York Times*, June 6, 2010.
10. Jesse McKinley, "Founders of the Gap Now Plan a Museum," *New York Times*, August 8, 2007.
11. Ibid.
12. Joan Wildermuth, "Art Museum, History Site Vie for Space in Presidio; Some See Gap Founder's Plan as Too Modern for Main Post," *San Francisco Chronicle*, November 25, 2007; Loren Stein, "Congress Rides to the Presidio's Rescue," *Christian Science Monitor*, October 10, 1995.
13. Marisa Lagos, "Presidio Makeover Heads for Fight; Environmental Report Comes Out Today, but Critics Already Fuming," *San Francisco Chronicle*, June 9, 2008.
14. Nonprofit organizations of all kinds are surrounded by a sea of stakeholders. A useful and comprehensive examination of the challenges of nonprofit accountability can be found in Kevin P. Kearns, *Managing for Accountability* (Jossey-Bass, 1996). There he argues that a critical element of successful nonprofit management involves managing accountability to stakeholders. "Accountability, in essence, is the obligation of public and non-profit organizations to serve a higher authority—the public trust—which is the ultimate source of their mandate, their authority, and their legitimacy. . . . While the standards of accountability are formally codified in laws and regulations, they are also defined by implicit expectations of taxpayers, clients, donors, and other stakeholders. . . . The standards of accountability should be continuously monitored and incorporated into the organization's strategic management process" (11).
15. Wildermuth, "Art Museum, History Site Vie for Space in Presidio."
16. Ibid.; King, "New Salvos in Presidio Battle May Come Today"; King, "Fishers Give Up on Plan for Presidio Art Museum"; "Presidio," *Curbed San Francisco*,

n.d., http://sf.curbed.com/tags/presidio; Sarah Hromack, "Spotted: Don Fisher, Man of the People," *Curbed San Francisco*, August 15, 2008, http://sf.curbed .com/archives/2008/08/15/spotted_don_fisher_man_of_the_people.php.

17. While social capital and funding are often thought to be separate topics, Jon Pratt brings them together in a discussion of the connection between community and the financing of nonprofit organizations. Dwight Burlingame, *Critical Issues in Fund Raising* (Wiley, 1997).

18. The public's trust is a key component of all three of these stakeholder characteristics. A discussion of four key questions related to trust in nonprofits can be found in Regina E. Herzlinger, "Can Public Trust in Nonprofits and Governments Be Restored?" in *Harvard Business Review on Nonprofits* (Harvard Business Press, 1999), 1–29. In this article, Herzlinger poses four tests for nonprofit organizations seeking to hold public trust: "Are the organization's goals consistent with its financial resources? . . . Is the organization practicing intergenerational equity? . . . Are the sources and uses of funds appropriately matched? . . . Is the organization sustainable?" A broader discussion of trust can be found in Roderick Moreland Kramer and Tom R. Tyler, *Trust in Organizations* (Sage, 1996).

19. For a neo-Gramscian analysis of the propensity of wealthy individuals to use philanthropy to reinforce their interests, see Teresa Jean Odendahl, *Charity Begins at Home* (Basic Books, 1990).

20. Briggs argues that successful projects involve a conscious effort to build civic capacity and to engage community directly in the process of visioning and governing projects. Xavier de Souza Briggs, *Democracy as Problem Solving* (MIT Press, 2008).

21. Partnerships across sectors pose distinctive challenges owing to the contrasting cultures, aspirations, and management systems. One book that examines how these cross-sector conflicts are resolved as more and more work is accomplished through inter-sector collaboration is Martha Minow, *Partners, Not Rivals: Privatization and the Public Good* (Beacon Press, 2002).

22. Woronkowicz et al., *Cultural Infrastructure in the United States: 1994–2008*.

CHAPTER FIVE

1. In a study of musical performing arts organizations, Kushner concluded that organizational structure and organizational effectiveness are related in two important ways. First, failure to adopt or agree on a formal structure correlates with organizational failure. Second, for effective organizations, organizational structure and the distribution of influence is a reasoned choice, understood and supported by staff and volunteers. Roland J. Kushner and Peter P. Poole, "Exploring Structure-Effectiveness Relationships in Nonprofit Arts Organizations," *Nonprofit Management and Leadership* 7, no. 2 (1996): 119–36.

2. Paul Light argues that capacity evolves through a series of developmental stages, or what he refers to as five landings. These include an organic stage, an

enterprising stage, an intentional stage, a robust stage, and a reflective stage. Throughout this "spiral of sustainable excellence," attending to capacity in all its many dimensions is critical to success. Paul Charles Light, *Sustaining Nonprofit Performance* (Brookings Institution Press, 2004).

3. Abraham H. Maslow, *The Psychology of Science: A Reconnaissance*, 1st ed., Gateway ed. (Chicago: H. Regnery, 1966).

4. Particularly applicable to the leadership challenges inherent in building projects is Ronald A. Heifetz's work on leadership response to adaptive as opposed to technical problems. Adaptive problems are problems that cannot be solved "by the application of technical know-how or routine behavior." They cannot be resolved by a mere application of authority. Instead, Heifetz posits that leaders should use conflict and heterogeneity as the basis for adapting and learning. Leadership is not the exertion of authority, but the capacity to motivate and bring people together around this task of finding new solutions. Ronald Abadian Heifetz, *Leadership without Easy Answers* (Belknap Press, 1994).

5. Miller and Lessard, "Evolving Strategy."

6. For an overview of the challenges of managing an effective board meeting, see William G. Bowen, *Inside the Boardroom: Governance by Directors and Trustees* (Wiley, 1994), 43, where Bowen observes that big boards can be problematic and "14 or 15 seems to be a reasonable upper limit."

7. As conflicts arise in the management of complex projects, negotiation skills will often come in handy. For a definitive treatment of the process of negotiation, see Howard Raïffa, *The Art and Science of Negotiation* (Belknap Press, 1982).

8. Cray et al. outline four decision-making models among leaders in the arts: rational, political, incremental, and "garbage can," or one that is reactive to random events. In capital projects within the arts, we have observed all four decision-making models in operation over the course of the same project. D. Cray, L. Inglis, and S. Freeman, "Managing the Arts: Leadership and Decision Making under Dual Rationalities," *Journal of Arts Management, Law, and Society* 36, no. 4 (2007): 295–313.

9. James Charles Collins, *Good to Great: Why Some Companies Make the Leap . . . and Others Don't* (New York: HarperBusiness, 2001), 21.

10. Ibid., 30.

11. Heifetz, *Leadership without Easy Answers*.

12. Ibid., 15.

13. Ibid., 23.

14. Ibid., 26.

15. Ibid., 87.

16. The conflict over which objectives and capabilities should be primary to an arts organization has been previously observed. "Most cultural institutions have identities composed of contradictory elements because they contain actors (artisans and administrators) within the organization who come from different professions; as a result, different groups of actors cherish and promote

different aspects of the organization's identity." Mary Ann Glynn, "When Cymbals Become Symbols: Conflict over Organizational Identity within a Symphony Orchestra," *Organization Science* 11, no. 3 (2000): 285–98.

17. We are indebted to Duncan Webb of Webb Management for this crystallization of the main challenges in consultant-client relationships and how these relate to outcomes.

18. On the challenge and need for recruiting, motivating, retaining, and promoting top talent in nonprofit organizations, see Christine Letts, William P. Ryan, and Allen Grossman, "Human Resources: Developing Employees to Advance Organizational Goals," in *High Performance Nonprofit Organizations: Managing Upstream for Greater Impact* (Wiley, 1999), 107–29. "Non-profits already have the advantage of compelling missions. If they can match those with compelling jobs, they can dramatically improve the prospects for recruiting and developing the best people, not to mention the prospect for delivering on their missions" (125).

19. Volunteers can be valuable instruments that can be easily mobilized to get projects or initiatives off the ground. Musick and Wilson provide a comprehensive overview of all dimensions of volunteer management and motivation as well as a frank discussion of the challenges of relying on unpaid workers. Marc A. Musick and John Wilson, *Volunteers* (Indiana University Press, 2008). For a more applied approach to the day-to-day challenges of getting the most out of volunteers, see also Kathleen M. Cole and James C. Fisher, *Leadership and Management of Volunteer Programs* (Jossey-Bass, 1993).

20. For a discussion of the multiple challenges of creating a high-performing board, see Chait, Ryan, and Taylor, where the authors posit three modes of leadership: fiduciary, strategic, and generative. The argument is made that high-performing boards are able to operate at all three levels simultaneously. Richard Chait, William P. Ryan, and Barbara E. Taylor, *Governance as Leadership* (Wiley, 2005).

21. Attracting board members to a new organization can be challenging, given that trustees often desire to be affiliated with well-known and well-funded endeavors. On the motives and objectives of trustees in large arts organizations, see Francie Ostrower, *Trustees of Culture* (Chicago: University of Chicago Press, 2002).

22. Misha Berson, "Portland Theater Takes Center Stage," *Seattle Times*, October 15, 2006.

23. Gerding Theater at the Armory and Portland Center Stage, *Voices of the Armory: A Chronicle of the Transformation of a 19th Century Icon into a 21st Century Theater* (Friends of the Armory, 2006).

24. Marty Hughley, "Your Comments: What's Up with Paying Down Gerding Theatre Debt?," OregonLive website, October 6, 2010, http://www.oregonlive.com/performance/index.ssf/2010/10/your_comments_whats_up_with_pa.html; Marty Hughley, "US Bank Helps Portland Center Stage with $1.5 Million of Armory Fund Debt," OregonLive website, September 23, 2010, http://www

.oregonlive.com/performance/index.ssf/2010/10/your_comments_whats_up
_with_pa.html.

25. Evrard notes some of the same conflicts over which domains of knowledge, particularly the choice of management science versus artistic disciplines, should most influence the shaping of teaching and research within the fledgling new academic discipline of arts management. Y. Evrard and F. Colbert, "Arts Management: A New Discipline Entering the Millennium?" *International Journal of Arts Management* 2 (2000): 4–13.

26. On the subject of the relationship between business management and arts management, three schools of thought can be found within the academic literature. First is that general management skills and concepts are completely adequate to arts organizations. Second is that arts organizations differ so much from other organizations that an entirely different set of management principles and skills is necessary. Third is that the business sector is the sector that should be importing management strategies from the arts world rather than vice versa. A brief discussion of these three schools of thought can be found in I. Palmer, "Arts Managers and Managerialism: A Cross-Sector Analysis of CEOs' Orientations and Skills," *Public Productivity & Management Review* 21, no. 4 (1998): 433–52. The article goes on to examine which frame of reference on strategy decisions arts CEOs actually use in making decisions. For an article advancing the theory that business should borrow from the arts, see N. J. Adler, "The Arts & Leadership: Now That We Can Do Anything, What Will We Do?" *Academy of Management Learning and Education Archive* 5, no. 4 (2006): 486–99.

27. Toni Lacy, "New Crisis at Lorton: Foul Food; Angry Inmates Staged Protests, Judge Is Told," *Washington Post*, February 15, 1996.

28. Large complex building projects attract a range of personalities and styles. Dennis Young's typology of nonprofit entrepreneurs is helpful in sorting out how mission and leaders' personalities are intertwined. Susan Rose-Ackerman, ed., *The Economics of Nonprofit Institutions: Studies in Structure and Policy*, Yale Studies on Nonprofit Organizations (Oxford University Press, 1986).

29. Recruiting, retaining, and training board members is a central task in building capacity. Cyril Houle provides a discussion of how to maximize the "human potential" of the board in his early treatment of governing boards. Cyril Orvin Houle, *Governing Boards* (Jossey-Bass, 1989).

30. Getting the most out of volunteers can be much harder than it appears. Without the ability to use pay as an incentive, managers are left with a complex challenge of motivating and retaining the best talent. Much has been written on effective volunteer management, including Brian O'Connell and Ann Brown O'Connell, *Volunteers in Action* (Foundation Center, 1989); Tracy Daniel Connors, *The Volunteer Management Handbook* (Wiley, 1999); Paul J. Ilsley, *Enhancing the Volunteer Experience* (Jossey-Bass, 1990).

31. Houle discusses the challenges of getting the CEO and board relationship right and comments: "The normal day-to-day relationship between the board

and the executive is that of a responsible partnership. Neither of the two can mark out any one institutional activity as its central concern, nor can it permit itself to be denied authority over any such activity. . . . The value of the board-executive system of dual authority lies in the fact that it creates combinations of influences that in some sense run counter to one another but that are needed for effective results." Houle, *Governing Boards*, 86–87. Houle also points out that this relationship is dynamic and in constant need of nurturing.

32. Office of Financial & Program Audit, County of Fairfax, Virginia, *Quarterly Report*, June 2011.

CHAPTER SIX

1. On sources of internal resistance to change and ways of addressing them, see Jeffrey D. Ford and Laurie W. Ford, "Decoding Resistance to Change," *Harvard Business Review* (April 1, 2009).

2. The challenge of defining and pursuing a clear mission often falls to boards. A discussion of the way in which boards manage mission can be found in John Carver, *Boards That Make a Difference* (Jossey-Bass, 1997).

3. Michael O'Neill provides a framework for understanding the ethical trade-offs and challenges in the nonprofit sector when money must be raised. See also Duronio's essay, which provides an overview of the emergence and practices of the broader fundraising profession today. Margaret Duronio, "The Fund Raising Profession," in *Critical Issues in Fund Raising*, ed. Dwight Burlingame (Wiley, 1997), 37–57; Michael O'Neill, "The Ethical Dimensions of Fund Raising," in *Critical Issues in Fund Raising*, ed. Dwight Burlingame (Wiley, 1997), 58–64.

4. Collaboration is often critical in large complex projects. However, as Austin notes, collaboration requires careful structuring and oversight. "Effective collaboration ultimately involves jointly tailoring a garment that fits the unique characteristics and needs of the partners." To succeed at this tailoring task, partners in any collaboration must achieve the seven Cs: Connection with purpose and people, Clarity in all work, Congruency of mission, strategy, and values, joint value Creation, effective Communication, Continual learning, and enduring Commitment. James E. Austin, *The Collaboration Challenge* (Jossey-Bass, 2000), 173.

5. Market orientation in programming need not lead to artistic retrenchment. Sorjonen's work (2011) sketches out several models in use by artistic organizations, some of which support a proactive stance toward the market, or programming based on an understanding of latent rather than recognized needs of audience segments. Hilppa Sorjonen, "The Manifestation of Market Orientation and Its Antecedents in the Program Planning of Arts Organizations," *International Journal of Arts Management* 14, no. 1 (2011): 4–18.

6. Woronkowicz et al., *Cultural Infrastructure in the United States: 1994–2008*.

7. In the past, literature has used the word "hedonic" to refer to the pleasure people derive from the arts. Though we opt for the word "transcendent" in this context, work defining and tracing cultural perceptions of the concept is useful. For a discussion of the definition of hedonic products and consumptions, see E. C. Hirschman and M. B. Holbrook, "Hedonic Consumption: Emerging Concepts, Methods and Propositions," *Journal of Marketing* (1982): 92–101.

8. George Yúdice, *The Expediency of Culture: Uses of Culture in the Global Era*, Kindle edition, 173–74, 182–83.

9. Megan Rosenfeld, "Michael Kahn's Star Turn," *Washington Post*, April 21, 1991.

10. Arthur C. Brooks, "Toward a Demand-Side Cure for Cost Disease in the Performing Arts," *Journal of Economic Issues* 31, no. 1 (1997): 197–207.

11. Ira S. Youdovin, "'Imaginary Coordinates' or Community Coordinates?," *Jewish Daily Forward*, July 2, 2008, http://forward.com/articles/13696/imaginary -coordinates-or-community-coordinat-/#ixzz1NJ3nH9oI.

12. Thomas Mullaney, "Creative Visions, but for Many Millions Less," *New York Times*, March 12, 2008.

13. Spertus Institute of Jewish Studies, *Form 990, Fiscal Year 2005*, n.d.

14. City of Chicago Community Development Commission, Department of Planning and Development, *Summary Sheet: Spertus Institute of Jewish Studies, Near South Tax Increment Financing Redevelopment Project*, October 11, 2005.

15. Spertus Institute of Jewish Studies, *Form 990*, June 30, 2008, National Center for Charitable Statistics.

16. Mullaney, "Creative Visions, but for Many Millions Less."

17. Hedy Weiss, "Spertus' New Building to Open Nov. 30; $55 Million Project Includes Classrooms, Theater, Gallery, Sky Garden, Kosher Cafe," *Chicago Sun-Times*, April 25, 2007.

18. Tara Burghart, "Spertus Institute to Open New Building," *Associated Press Newswires*, November 26, 2007.

19. Ami Eden, "Imaginary Independence: Spertus Museum Shuts Down Exhibit in Face of Jewish Protests," Telegraph | JTA—Jewish & Israel News website, June 24, 2008, http://blogs.jta.org/telegraph/article/2008/06/24/1000060 /imaginary-independence-spertus-museum-shuts-down-exhibit-in-face-of -jewish-protests.

20. Deanna Isaacs, "Too Much Light: A Provocative Show about the Holy Land at the Spertus Is Shut Down, Then Tweaked," *Chicago Reader*, May 29, 2008, http:// www.chicagoreader.com/chicago/too-much-light/Content?oid=1109704.

21. Manya Brachear and Charles Storch, "Controversy Closes Show at Museum: Art, Map Display in Jewish Studies Institute Criticized as 'Anti-Israel,'" *Chicago Tribune*, June 21, 2008, http://www.chicagotribune.com/news/nationworld /chi-spertus_21jun21,0,3780707.story.

22. "The Untimely Closing of Imaginary Coordinates: Three Perspectives," *Exhibitionist*, Fall 2008.

23. The deficit figure is from Form 990s, which account for investment losses under operations.

24. Deanna Isaacs, "The Business: A Museum in Sleep Mode; Pending Better Financial Times, the Spertus Cuts Its Hours to Two and a Half Days a Month," *Chicago Reader*, July 2, 2009, http://www.chicagoreader.com/chicago/the-business-a-museum-in-sleep-mode/Content?oid=1138063; Shia Kapos, "The Battle for Spertus; Struggle for Soul and Financial Stability Plays Out in Jewish Institute's Flashy New Home," *Crain's Chicago Business*, June 29, 2009; James Adams, "Fright Night at the Museums; The Recession Has Hit Canada's Public Galleries Hard—Forcing Some to Rethink Major Exhibitions, Writes James Adams," *Globe and Mail*, July 25, 2009.

25. Knowing whether an organization is successful in achieving its objectives is after all critical to being able to devise a strategy. Moreover, financial objectives are frequently the easiest to quantify, and failing to measure attainment of mission, capacity, or community goals can give financial management too much centrality in the decision making, to the detriment of the organization. For studies of setting and monitoring achievement of a balanced set of goals by nonprofit organizations in the arts, see J. Turbide and C. Laurin, "Performance Measurement in the Arts Sector: The Case of the Performing Arts," *International Journal of Arts Management* 11, no. 2 (2009): 56–70; L. Weinstein and D. Bukovinsky, "Use of the Balanced Scorecard and Performance Metrics to Achieve Operational and Strategic Alignment in Arts and Culture Not-For-Profits," *International Journal of Arts Management* 11, no. 2 (2009): 42–55; I. Gilhespy, "Measuring the Performance of Cultural Organizations: A Model," *International Journal of Arts Management* 2, no. 1 (1999): 38–52; I. Gilhespy, "The Evaluation of Social Objectives in Cultural Organizations," *International Journal of Arts Management* 4 (2001): 48–57. For a case study of an implementation of a balanced scorecard within the context of a museum, see K. Krarup, "Balanced Scorecard at the Royal Library, Copenhagen," *Liber Quarterly* 14, no. 1 (2004): 37–57.

26. The problem of coming up with nonprofit performance measurement is never laid more bare than in Paul DiMaggio, "Measuring the Impact of the Nonprofit Sector on Society Is Probably Impossible but Possibly Useful: A Sociological Perspective," in *Measuring the Impact of the Nonprofit Sector*, 249–73 (Kluwer Academic/Plenum, 2001).

27. Justin Wescoat Sanders, "The Merchant of Venice," *Portland Mercury*, January 22, 2004, http://www.portlandmercury.com/portland/the-merchant-of-venice/Content?oid=30597.

28. Gerding Theater at the Armory and Portland Center Stage, *Voices of the Armory*.

29. Ibid.

30. Marty Hughley, "Portland Center Stage Artistic Director Chris Coleman: Dramatic Change in Theater, Community," *Oregonian*, May 21, 2011, http://www.oregonlive.com/performance/index.ssf/2011/05/portland_center_stage_artistic_1.html.

31. Portland Center Stage, *Form 990: Return of Organization Exempt from Income*

Tax, June 30, 2008; Portland Center Stage, *Form 990: Return of Organization Exempt from Income Tax*, June 30, 2009; Portland Center Stage, *Form 990: Return of Organization Exempt from Income Tax*, June 30, 2010; Portland Center Stage, *Form 990: Return of Organization Exempt from Income Tax*, June 30, 2011.

32. It is impossible to manage mission without knowing where an organization is heading. On the link between strategic planning and mission management, see Bryson, *Strategic Planning for Public and Nonprofit Organizations*. "Mission clarifies an organization's purpose, or why it should be doing what it does; vision clarifies what it should look like and how it should behave as it fulfills its mission" (96).

CHAPTER SEVEN

1. In his discussion of nonprofit strategy, Phills points to the necessity for continuous scanning of the internal and external environment around organizations. The goal of this increased awareness is the ability to make "purposeful and adaptive change" (172). James A. Phills Jr., *Integrating Mission and Strategy for Nonprofit Organizations* (Oxford University Press, 2005).

2. The AMOA experience is not unique. Organizations struggle for many different reasons, some of which are described in Helmut K. Anheier and Lynne Moulton, "Organizational Failures, Breakdowns, and Bankruptcies: An Introduction," in *When Things Go Wrong*, ed. Helmut K. Anheier (Sage Publications, 1999), 3–17, where Anheier and Moulton point to three master reasons—political, structural, and cognitive—that organizations fail, break down, disintegrate, decline, or go bankrupt.

3. Ann Holmes, "New Austin Museum Shown as Work in Progress," *Houston Chronicle*, April 20, 1985, sec. Houston; Patricia C. Johnson, "Exhibit Emphasizes Museum's Need for New Building," *Houston Chronicle*, January 31, 1987, sec. Houston; Tara Parker Pope, "Progress of Museum Mired // Downtown Laguna Gloria Stalled by Wary Backers, Bureaucracy," *Austin American-Statesman*, February 25, 1989, Final edition, sec. News.

4. Michael Barnes, "Be It Ever So Humble, Temporary Home Downtown Is a Good Start on Austin Museum of Art's Future," *Austin American-Statesman*, December 5, 1996; Holmes, "New Austin Museum Shown as Work in Progress."

5. Pope, "Progress of Museum Mired"; Tara Parker Pope, "Austin Art Devotees Split over Museum," *Austin American-Statesman*, February 12, 1989.

6. Tara Parker Pope, "City Cuts Ties with Museum Project," *Austin American-Statesman*, December 15, 1989, Final edition, sec. City/State.

7. Pete Szilagyi, "Laguna Gloria Director Resigns," *Austin American-Statesman*, April 28, 1990, Final edition, sec. City/State.

8. Sharon Edgar Greenhill, "US Architecture: One That Got Away," *New York Times*, January 27, 1991, sec. Letters to the Editor.

9. Michael Barnes, "Art Museum's Fate Back in City's Hands," *Austin American-Statesman*, December 13, 1995.

10. Pete Szilagyi, "Groups Resurrect Museum Project // Arts Organizations Join to Plan Facility," *Austin American-Statesman*, January 31, 1993, Final edition, sec. News.

11. Michael Barnes, "Art Museum at Crossroads: Leadership, Orientation Skewed After Resignation, Lease Announcement," *Austin American-Statesman*, March 15, 1996.

12. Shilpa Bakre, "Third Time's a Charm or Three Strikes?" (report for course with Peter Frumkin, 2009); Madeline Irvine, "Museum of Art Opens Downtown Gallery," *Austin American-Statesman*, November 17, 1996.

13. Jeanne Claire van Ryzin, "A First Look at the Future of Austin Art," *Austin American-Statesman*, October 30, 1999.

14. Michael Barnes, "Museum of Art to Forgo $13.4 Million in City Money," *Austin American-Statesman*, August 17, 2000; "Laura W. Bush Leads Drive for Austin Museum of Art's New Building," *BusinessWire*, March 2, 1999; Jerry Mahoney, "Museum Fans Launch Drive to Raise Money," *Austin American-Statesman*, March 3, 1999.

15. Barnes, "Museum of Art to Forgo $13.4 Million in City Money"; Jeanne Claire van Ryzin, "Director Leaving City Art Museum," *Austin American-Statesman*, July 14, 2001; Jeanne Claire van Ryzin, "Museum Gives Up on New Building," *Austin American-Statesman*, February 11, 2004.

16. Jeanne Claire van Ryzin, "Museum-Condo Project in the Works," *Austin American-Statesman*, August 1, 2006.

17. Jeanne Claire van Ryzin, "Designs for Museum, Office Tower Unveiled," *Austin American-Statesman*, February 20, 2008.

18. Jeanne Claire van Ryzin, "Plans for Office Tower, Museum Downtown Idled," *Austin American-Statesman*, January 1, 2009; Jeanne Claire van Ryzin, "Austin Museum Lot Sale Shifts Decades of Downtown Building Plans," *Austin American-Statesman*, December 16, 2010.

19. Jeanne Claire van Ryzin, "Museum Pulling Out of Downtown," *Austin American-Statesman*, February 25, 2011.

20. Jeanne Claire van Ryzin and Ricardo B. Brazziell, "Merging Downtown Museums Could Be Best for Both," *Austin American-Statesman*, November 6, 2011, Final edition; Jeanne Claire van Ryzin, "Arthouse, AMOA to Begin Merger Talks," *Austin American-Statesman*, May 27, 2011; "Project Arthouse at the Jones Center Location Austin, Texas Architect Lewis.Tsurumaki.Lewis Architects," *Architectural Record*, February 1, 2011, sec. BTS; "Arthouse at the Jones Center and Austin Museum of Art Merge to Create New Museum for Austin and Central Texas," *News Press*, January 24, 2012.

21. Mark Moore defines strategic alignment in *Creating Public Value* as the achievement of fit between value, capacity, and support. The job of the executive is to lead the organization toward alignment, even if this involves taking on great personal and organizational risk.

22. A different version of this case has been published online. Ana Kolendo and Peter Frumkin, *The Art Institute of Chicago and the Decision to Start Building, Set in Stone: Building America's New Generation of Arts Facilities, 1994–2008* (University of Chicago Cultural Policy Center, 2012), http://culturalpolicy.uchicago.edu/setinstone/pdf/aic.pdf.

23. The challenge in any arts project is to resist what Thomas Sowell calls "unconstrained vision." There is a fundamental cleavage in the way people view the world. People who hold to the unconstrained vision believe that anything can be planned and executed with the application of reason. People who do not hold to this view believe that flaws constrain the attainability of perfect visions. It is tempting in many projects to believe that if enough reason and technical capacity is brought to bear on the problem, it can be solved. However, experience shows that some problems are so deeply rooted in human nature that they cannot be addressed. Those with a balanced perspective are most likely to be able to adapt. Thomas Sowell, *A Conflict of Visions* (Morrow, 1987).

CHAPTER EIGHT

1. This structure for framing the discussion was first suggested to us by Rob Gertner.

2. Strategy building involves using information and experience to adjust and make wise choices. In Lorton, there was a need to reassess and adjust along the way as the reality on the ground shifted. To have actionable data, an organization must invest in assessment. A practical guide to the many ways in which evaluation data can be collected inexpensively to guide managerial decision making can be found in J. Rugh, M. Bamberger, and L. Mabry, *Real-World Evaluation: Working under Budget, Time, Data, and Political Constraints* (Sage Publications, 2006).

3. Many of the projects floundered because of poor decision making about basic financial matters. A straightforward guide for practitioners on developing and managing a sustainable financial model can be found in Thomas A. McLaughlin, *Streetsmart Financial Basics for Nonprofit Managers* (Wiley, 2009).

4. Arts leaders are often confronted with multiple and competing managerial imperatives. For managers seeking an overview of management challenges that arise in almost all arts organizations and nonprofit organizations more broadly, see Darian Rodriguez Heyman, *Nonprofit Management 101* (Jossey-Bass, 2011).

5. In raising money for capital and operating expenses, it is essential that managers keep these two budgets separate. A discussion of how and why to manage these separate budgets can be found in Woods Bowman, *Finance Fundamentals for Nonprofits* (Wiley, 2011).

6. Buildings also offer the allure of permanence, stability, and even perpetuity. Not all organizations are destined to live forever, however. Some projects end in disaster and closure. A broader examination of the issue of nonprofit ex-

pansion and collapse can be found in Joseph Galaskiewicz, Wolfgang Biele-
feld, Mark A. Hager, Yoshito Ishio, and Joel Pins, "Growth and Decline among
Nonprofit Organizations," in *Nonprofit Organizations in an Age of Uncertainty*
(Aldine De Gruyter, 1998), 83–125.

7. The drive to meet capital goals can test the ethics of any leader. Fischer points
to three basic value commitments that must anchor any fundraising appeal.
"One, organizational mission that directs the work. Two, our relationship to
the people with whom we interact. Three, our own sense of personal integrity. . . . The fundraiser acting with integrity has the task of creating and maintaining a supporting network of relationships in order to further the mission
of the organization. We bring ethical sensitivity to decision-making when we
place particular decisions in the context of the three basic value commitments"
(21). Marilyn Fischer, *Ethical Decision Making in Fund Raising* (Wiley, 2000).

8. A step-by-step workbook on developing a communications plan is presented
by Janel M. Radtke, *Strategic Communications for Nonprofit Organizations*
(Wiley, 1998).

9. The oversight of complex building projects cannot reasonably be accomplished by one person. The work of boards is essential to bringing multiple
perspectives and talents to the resolution of the many challenges that arise.
Chait, Ryan, and Taylor provide a nuanced discussion not just of strategic and
fiduciary roles, but also of the generative role, in *Governance as Leadership*.

10. Beyond a small board group, these projects benefit greatly from what Collins refers to as a Type 5 leader, "someone who builds enduring greatness
through paradoxical blend of personal humility and professional will," in *Good
to Great*, 20.

11. Building a strong board that can guide a project through the inevitable ups and
downs requires finding people with both the practical skills and strong, ethical
commitments. Two books that provide advice on each of these objectives for
nonprofit organizations seeking to build effective boards are Carver, *Boards
That Make a Difference*, and David H. Smith, *Entrusted: The Moral Responsibilities of Trusteeship* (Indiana University Press, 1995).

12. For a discussion of the tension between high-brow and low-brow culture and
their interaction with organizational funding, see Dick Netzer, "Arts and Culture," in *Who Benefits from the Nonprofit Sector?*, ed. Charles T. Clotfelter (Chicago: University of Chicago Press, 1995), 174–206.

13. Accurately calibrating supply to demand is a core component of strategy. La
Piana argues that strategy plays out at three different levels: low, medium, and
high intensity. By intensity of relationship, La Piana means "the frequency,
depth, and overall strategic importance of the interactions or competitive conflicts between and among organizations" (51). Successfully tailoring supply to
demand requires working across all three contexts. David La Piana and Michaela Hayes, *Play to Win* (Jossey-Bass, 2005).

Index

Bilbao effect and, 9, 16–17, 202–4, 238, 240–41, 243n3; building stages and, 20–21, 54–63, 79–88; community credibility and, 6–8, 21–22, 26–27, 37–38, 88–103, 128–30, 197–98, 212–15; debt financing and, 16–17, 58–61, 70, 122–23, 149–50, 159–60, 163, 212–15, 226–27; endowment funding and, 68, 78, 81, 83–84, 94–95, 222, 230–33; expert knowledge and, 132–33, 136, 138–39, 141–42, 145–50, 154–64, 200; flexibility and, 194–95, 204–5, 208–24; forecasting costs and, 64–67, 138, 168–72, 229–33; governmental and foundation sources of, 6, 16, 40–41, 43–44, 47, 53–54, 57, 72–73, 94–95, 104–5, 117, 122–23, 139–40, 148–49, 162, 170–71, 173, 195–202, 228–29; mission's connection to, 62–63, 76–96, 100–103, 175–84, 238–41, 244n8, 262n25; operating costs and, 68–71, 92, 99–103, 230–33; pro bono services and real estate gifts and, 43–49, 53–61, 142–52, 195–97, 210, 232–33; recession's effect on, 53–54, 58–59, 82, 95–96, 126–27, 174, 183, 202, 204, 212–15, 223, 226, 234–36

gallery spaces, 1, 12, 28–30, 44–45, 60, 78–88, 99, 194–207. *See also* architecture; arts organizations
Gehry, Frank, 31, 54–55, 58, 80, 85
Georgia Tech University, 41–43, 52
Gerding, Bob, 145–46, 186
Gerding Edlen (company), 146
Gerding Theater at the Armory, 148–49, 184–93, *192*, 229
Getty Trust, 100
Gluckman, Richard, 201–3
Golden, Arthur, 114
Gordon, Deanna, 54–55
Governor's School for the Arts, 121
Graves, Michael, 55

Guggenheim Museum, 3, 30–32. *See also* Bilbao effect
Gunsaulus Hall, 80, 97–98

Hadley, Mark, 75, 94
Hanthorn, Dennis, 38–41, 50–53
Harman, Sidney, 169, 184
Harman Center for the Arts, 168–72, *170*
Harrison Opera House, 118, 120
Hassam, Childe, 46
Hausler, Richard, 153–58
Hayes, Michaela, 266n13
Heifetz, Ronald, 135–36, 257n4
Henton, Douglas C., 255n8
Herzlinger, Regina E., 256n18
High Museum, 46
Hines Interests, 203–4
historical preservationists, 35, 105, 109–10, 151–52, 156, 189
Homer, Winslow, 46
Hughes, Howard L., 243n3

"Imaginary Coordinates" exhibit, 172–77
IMAX theaters, 48–49, 56–57, 60, 166
IMG (company), 123
intuitive forecasts (term), 65–66

Jaffee Holden Acoustics, 220, 222
Jefferson Center, 59
Jenkins, Annika, 125
Jennings, Chris, 171
Jewish Daily Forward, 172–73
Jewish Federation, 173
Johnson, Verner, 55
Jones, Tommy Lee, 92
Jones Center, 205–6, *206*
Joynes, Carroll, 24

Kahn, Michael, 168
Kahneman, Daniel, 65–66
Kalita Humphreys Theater, 75–76, 101
Katz, Vera, 146–47, 186
Kennedy, Alfred, 35, 38